The
Moosewood
Cookbook

MK 92

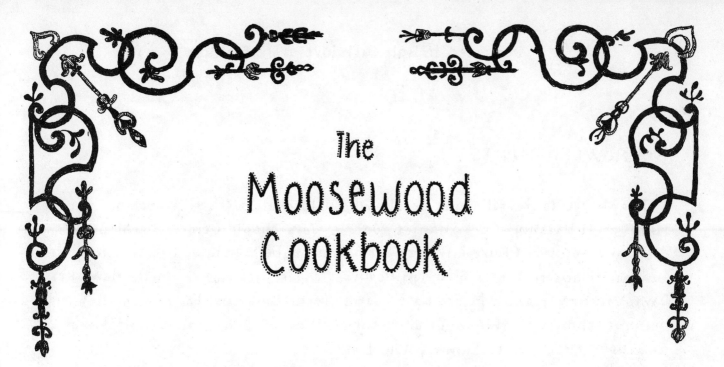

The Moosewood Cookbook

by Mollie Katzen

Ten Speed Press

Dedicated to Hal, with love and gratitude.

ACKNOWLEDGMENTS:

Thank you to the following people who helped me with this book in various ways: Hal Hershey, Carl Shames, Jackie Wan, Nicole Geiger, Brent Beck, Jo-Lynne Worley, Claire Rithner, Sal Glynn, Katie Meadow, George Young, Fuzzy Randall, Maureen Watts, Sharilyn Hovind, Joanie Shoemaker, Molly Hamaker, Dawn Van Hee, Frances Moore Lappé, and Anita Barrows. For reading list suggestions, thanks to Sharon Bloyd-Peshkin, Marilyn Borchardt, Dayna Macy, and Doug Moss. Hi to Sammy and Eve!

Cover design for the original edition: Meredith Barchat and Mollie Katzen
Revised cover design: Brent Beck, Mollie Katzen, and Hal Hershey
Frontispiece: "Still Life with Lilies" (conté crayon on paper), by Mollie Katzen
Author photo: Terrence McCarthy

10

Ten Speed Press
P.O. Box 7123
Berkeley, California 94707

Correspondence for the author can be sent to the above address.

LIBRARY OF CONGRESS CATALOGING-IN-PUBLICATION DATA

Moosewood cookbook / compiled, edited, illustrated, and hand-
    lettered by Mollie Katzen. — [Rev. and expanded ed.]
        p.   cm.

    Includes index.

    ISBN 0-89815-503-7   ISBN 0-89815-490-1 (pbk.)
    1. Vegetarian cookery 2. Cookery (Natural foods) I. Katzen,
Mollie. 1950-   .   II. Moosewood Restaurant.

TX837. M67 1992   92-24229
641.5'636--do 20   CIP

    2 3 4 5 6 7 8 9 10 — 96 95 94 93 92

Welcome to the Moosewood Cookbook!

As the fifteenth anniversary of the <u>Moosewood Cookbook</u> approached, I decided to revisit all the recipes. For some time now, readers have been requesting lighter versions of the same recipes they have come to know and love. At the same time, my own cooking has evolved, and I no longer use the same quantities of oil, butter, dairy products, or eggs. So without changing the character of the book or the nature of the recipes, I retested and rewrote them all. I trimmed a little butter here, a lot of oil there, intensified seasonings, deleted many eggs, presented new lowfat options, and added about 25 new recipes, including some for lowfat salad dressings, sauces, and desserts. I've worked to improve the organization of the book as well, and broadened the instructions. I hope the recipes will be optimally convenient ~ easy both to find and to follow.

Thank you very, very much to all the readers who have sent me letters of appreciation, feedback, and criticism over the years. You have contributed greatly to this book!

Mollie Katzen
Kensington, California
June 1992

✣ A Personal History of This Book ✣

Fifteen years after the Ten Speed Press publication of the <u>Moosewood Cookbook</u>, I remain amazed and gratified by the response this book has received. I still ponder the reasons. What has happened to shift the culture, so that it is no longer considered fringe behavior to cut down on one's meat intake or to eat vegetarian meals at least a few times a week? Greater awareness of our bodies and our health has played a major role. People want to eat meals that are easy to prepare, nutritious, and relatively inexpensive. Also, as the world has gotten smaller and we've been more exposed to diverse cultures, there has been a growing openness to — and fascination with — various ethnic styles of cooking, many of which place far less emphasis on meat, and more on creative preparation of simple ingredients. In addition, concern about the environment has led many people to become more aware of the impact our food choices have on the health of the earth. (For more discussion about this, see pp. 219-20.) This evolution toward reshaping and rethinking our eating habits has been gradual but steady. As meatless cooking is being welcomed more and more into the mainstream, and as the <u>Moosewood Cookbook</u> approaches its 15th birthday, I've been reflecting on my unexpected role in this movement, and have decided to share with you my personal story surrounding the creation of this book.

Although I always loved to cook, I never set out to write cookbooks, nor to be a food professional in any way. My earliest culinary exposure was to simple, largely processed foods. A child of the '50s and '60s, I was raised on Minute Rice, Campbell's soups, Velveeta cheese, and frozen vegetables — the miracle convenience foods of that era. We ate red meat about five nights a week; on the other two we ate chicken or fish. "Salad" meant iceberg lettuce, hothouse tomatoes, and mayonnaise. Cucumbers were sometimes included, but that was already edging toward the exotic. My biggest excitement came each Friday, when my mother would bake a challah (braided egg bread). I was enthralled, and would come in from wherever I was playing just in time to help her braid it. When she or my grandmother would bake desserts from scratch, I would be breathing down their necks with eagerness and fascination. My mother was tolerant and encouraging enough to allow me free run of the kitchen, and I learned early to prepare all the instant foods, but also to experiment and improvise. My focal point, at age 9 or 10, was chocolate desserts, and I invented several in earnest. I thank my mother for telling me she liked them.

My main interests, though, were art, music, and writing – I wanted to be an artist _and_ a musician _and_ a writer. I saw cooking as a trade that could be a source of income until my paintings were hanging in the Metropolitan Museum, my concerts sold out at Carnegie Hall, and my prize-winning novels and poetry published in many languages. I started cooking to earn money at age 16, flipping thin, grayish-colored hamburgers and deep-frying frozen potatoes in the coffee shop of a department store. Meanwhile, I drew, studied piano and oboe, and wrote umpteen tragic poems and humorous (at least, to me) stories in my room at night. It seemed a good strategy.

I continued to work at various food-related jobs, including bussing tables in my dorm at college. Yet I still didn't know very much about real food or cooking from scratch. I hadn't tasted a fresh green vegetable until the age of 12, when I was invited to dinner at the home of a friend whose mother had a vegetable garden. She picked fresh green beans for dinner, and served them lightly steamed in bowls, with a little warmed milk poured on top. I went wild! This was a radical new discovery for me! I kept thinking about those green beans long afterwards – until I had my second experience with fresh vegetables at age 18 in, of all places, the college cafeteria. The meat was uninviting, but the vegetables were fresh, wonderful, and abundant. After six months of ecstatically piling my plate high with freshly steamed broccoli, cauliflower, asparagus, etc., I realized I hadn't eaten any meat at all. I wondered if this made me a vegetarian, although at that time I didn't know anyone who was – and to be one was looked upon as a cross between an eccentricity and an affliction. Labels aside, my love of cooking and newfound infatuation with fresh vegetables led me to search for ways to cook interesting non-meat dishes. I found a job at a small macrobiotic restaurant, and there I discovered the beauty of simple legumes and grains. The year was 1970, and there were still no major vegetarian cookbooks in wide circulation yet, so this was largely uncharted territory. In addition to my personal journal of drawings and writing, I began an illustrated notebook filled with ideas for cooking with vegetables, grains, and legumes. I had no idea that this would ever coalesce into a cookbook, nor that I was in the thin of what would become the thick of a new lifestyle movement.

When I moved to San Francisco later that year to continue studying art, I discovered an exciting new restaurant that was serving fresh, creative, and sophisticated vegetarian food. The clientele was hip and fashionable, but I was drawn not by the "scene" but by the food. It was revelatory! Crêpes! Curries! Pesto! Stir-fries! Fresh fruit salads! This stuff was incredible! And the range of colors and textures of all the fresh fruits and vegetables added a visual component, providing a delightful bridge to my artistic impulses. I worked there for 1½ years and learned a great deal, not only about cooking but also about running a restaurant. My recipe notebook grew thick with ideas. During this time I received a visit from my brother and a friend, who were about to build a restaurant in Ithaca, New York, but didn't yet know what type of food they wanted to serve. When they dropped in on me at work and tasted the food, they knew this was what they were looking for. They invited me to join them in their project, and to bring this new cooking style with me. I hesitated, as I had planned to continue studying art. But the thought of starting a restaurant with unlimited creative freedom was too appealing to resist. After much thought, I decided to go for just three months, to help get things started. I did, and the result was the Moosewood Restaurant, opened by seven of us in January 1973.

Starting this restaurant was a labor of love. The kitchen was tiny, the storage facilities negligible. The wide variety of fresh produce, so readily available year-round in California, was a distant dream in upstate New York in January. The menu was minimal at first: simple soups, two regular salads (fresh fruit and raw vegetable, cut by hand), and two daily entrées (usually casseroles). Even though vegetarianism was gradually coming into its own — boosted tremendously by the publication in 1971 of Diet for a Small Planet, by Frances Moore Lappé, and The Vegetarian Epicure, by Anna Thomas, published in 1972 — we had no idea of how meatless cooking would be received. So we tried adding one meat entrée to the menu each night. Invariably it would be left over the next day, much to our surprise. The vegetarian dishes, on the other hand, were being ordered as fast as we could make them. Eventually, we dropped the meat, and with the exception of serving fish on weekends, the restaurant quietly and unofficially went vegetarian. The food, prepared with loving, sincere effort and served without dogma, must have spoken for itself. It seemed that our customers, whose numbers were swelling, and most of whom were neither vegetarians nor people we knew, just wanted some good homemade food.

We worked hard at the restaurant. I was there long hours every day, and pretty soon noticed I'd been there longer than three months. I didn't have a lot of time or energy left over to do ambitious art, music, or writing projects, but as I continued my illustrated recipe journals, the boundary between food and officially "creative" work began to blur. I loved being at the restaurant—it felt very challenging and fulfilling. The food was coming out better all the time. Some of the people who came to work there were innovative cooks, bringing with them their own ethnic backgrounds and personal styles. As most of us cooked by feel and not literally from recipes, I began to write down some version of what was being prepared, so we could standardize the cooking. At the same time, customers were asking for recipes, and I would often jot something down for them—on a napkin or whatever—after my shift. Eventually I put together a small, casual cookbook, for use both in the restaurant kitchen and in customers' homes. I handlettered the book because I intended it to be used by people I knew, or by acquaintances of acquaintances. It didn't occur to me that some day an expanded version, still in handlettered format, would be used by over a million strangers.

The first edition, funded by a small loan from a local bookstore, had 78 pages, spiral-bound. Eight hundred copies sold out in a week. Considering that Ithaca is a very small town, this was astonishing. No one was more astonished than I. I revamped it slightly, adding more drawings (a great excuse to do some art), and had it reprinted. Two thousand copies sold out in six months, followed by another printing the same size, which sold out just as quickly. Meanwhile, I had begun to receive mail orders—apparently from people who had passed through town, picked up a copy, and shared it with friends elsewhere. I couldn't handle the demand—I was still looking for time to paint, write, and practice music, and was spending too much time running to the post office to mail packages. People were encouraging me to seek national publication, but I was reluctant. It seemed too "commercial". Still, I approached a few publishers, and one major house was interested, but with a caveat: I would have to get rid of the whimsical drawings and the handlettering. Enter Ten Speed Press, a small, new outfit in Berkeley. I had no idea who they were, but was thrilled when they offered me complete artistic and editorial freedom. Their representative told me he thought this "natural-type" cooking was about to become a major trend, and that I could sell perhaps fifty thousand books over the next five years. (This was a huge number then.) Even though I didn't quite believe him, I decided to take the plunge. I signed on, spent most of the next year expanding and revising the book (still working shifts at the restaurant), and in the autumn of 1977 the Ten Speed edition was born. It caught on slowly. Meanwhile, I retired from the restaurant—the three months had become almost five years — and set out to find horizons beyond restaurant work. As of this writing, the Moosewood Restaurant is in its twentieth year and still going strong.

Now it is fifteen years later, and the Moosewood Cookbook's sales have exceeded the fifty thousand mark beyond anything I could ever have imagined. I live on the West Coast with my husband and children, and have a painting studio. I have published two more cookbooks, the most recent one illustrated with full-color still lifes. While the old fantasies of paintings hanging at the Met, recitals in major halls, and earth-shaking novels have faded, recently I spotted a familiar-looking marinated fresh vegetable salad at a food stand in the Pittsburgh airport. I remain overwhelmed by the enthusiasm with which my cookbooks have been received, and by the loving responses sent to me by readers. My ideas about what is important have changed. To be of use, to have the opportunity to impart information and skills that serve to enrich people's daily lives — this is what matters most to me. People have brought these books into their lives for the simple purpose of getting a few ideas for good things to cook and eat, and sometimes they have come out with more. I now realize that to have my work be broadly accessible and well embraced, and to have it contribute in any way to people's health and pleasure, has been the ultimate privilege.

❋ Contents ❋

❧ PANTRY NOTES ❧

In case you need a brief explanation of some of the ingredients used in this book:

BEANS & LEGUMES: Usually these recipes call for dry beans to be soaked and cooked. Occasionally, it's fine to substitute canned — individual recipes will indicate this. When you use dry beans or legumes, save money by buying in bulk.

BUTTER / MARGARINE: Butter is used in moderation, but in many cases, the recipe indicates that margarine can be substituted. There are some decent, good-tasting soy or safflower oil margarines available, if you prefer to avoid butter.

FOOD FROM CANS OR JARS: These recipes use very few canned (or jarred) foods, with the following exceptions: artichoke hearts or crowns, beans or chick peas (on occasion), water chestnuts, pineapple-in-juice, and tomato products (paste, purée, whole tomatoes, etc.)

DAIRY PRODUCTS: You can use lowfat (and often nonfat) everything: milk, cottage cheese, ricotta, sour cream, evaporated milk, yogurt, etc. Soy or rice milk can frequently be substituted.

EXTRACTS (VANILLA, ALMOND, ETC.): Use pure only.

FLOURS: Unless otherwise specified, use unbleached white flour.

FROZEN FOODS: I frequently tested these recipes with frozen unsweetened fruit (berries, cherries, etc.) with great success, when fresh were unavailable. You can also use frozen peas, corn, cooked squash, and if you're in a pinch, a 10-oz. package of frozen chopped spinach can substitute for 1 large bunch fresh in cooked dishes. Defrost and drain thoroughly before using.

GARLIC: Use fresh only and buy it frequently. The fresher, the better.

HERBS: If it's not specified, the recipe was tested with dried herbs, as these are more readily available year-round. However, if you have access to fresh herbs, by all means use them! Here's the exchange rate: 1 tsp. dried approximately equals 1 Tbs. minced fresh.

JUICES: Use fresh-squeezed lemon, lime, or orange juice in these recipes whenever possible.

OILS: For sautéing vegetables, use peanut, corn, or pure olive oil. For salads, use virgin or extra virgin olive oil, canola oil, or nut oils (walnut or hazelnut). Use virgin or extra virgin olive oil for drizzling on pasta. For seasoning certain soups, salads, and stir-fries, use Chinese sesame oil (available in Asian groceries). For information about oil sprays, see p. XVI.

NUTS, SEEDS, NUT BUTTERS: Use unprocessed, available (often in bulk) at natural foods stores and at many grocery stores. Tahini (raw sesame paste) is available in natural foods stores, in some specialty groceries, and in the imported foods section of many grocery stores.

PASTA: The recipes in this book were tested with dried egg pasta of various shapes, but you can also use fresh. More details are on p. 75.

RICE: Short- and long-grain brown rice are interchangeable in these recipes. There is no nutritional difference, and the cooking method is the same. Short-grain is chewier; long-grain is fluffier. Buy either kind in bulk at natural foods stores.

SOY SAUCE: Japanese soy sauces (tamari or shoyu) have a deeper, slightly sweeter flavor than Chinese, which are thinner and saltier (and sometimes contain additives, so read the label). Whichever kind you prefer, you can find good soy sauce in natural foods stores and in Asian markets.

SWEETENERS: To varying degrees, sugar, brown sugar, honey, and real maple syrup are used in the desserts. In some cases they are interchangeable. This is indicated on individual recipes.

TOFU: Tofu is soybean curd, available in many forms. It is high in protein, low in price, and has no cholesterol. Buy it by the pound, packed in water in little plastic tubs, by the piece — out of large buckets of water, or vacuum-packed — either in plastic wrapping or in small boxes (see p. 91). Tofu is available in natural foods stores, in Asian markets, or in the produce department of the grocery store.

☆☆☆☆☆☆☆☆☆☆☆☆☆☆☆☆☆☆☆☆☆☆☆☆☆☆
SOME USEFUL TOOLS (HIGHLY RECOMMENDED)
☆☆☆☆☆☆☆☆☆☆☆☆☆☆☆☆☆☆☆☆☆☆☆☆☆

☆FOOD PROCESSOR~ for puréeing, grating, mincing, and mashing. For pie crusts, too. This time- and skin-saving device might turn out to be one of the best kitchen investments you'll ever make!

☆BLENDER~ It still does some things better than a food processor—it makes smoother purées and is good for processing medium-sized amounts.

☆MINI-PROCESSOR~ finely minces garlic and fresh herbs in seconds flat. It has about a 1-cup capacity.

☆CITRUS SQUEEZER~ manual or electric.

☆CUTTING BOARDS~ one for fruit, one for vegetables, and one for onions and garlic.

☆MICROWAVE OVEN~ for reheating with little or no cleanup. With a microwave, you'll be encouraged to do more cooking in advance.

☆ELECTRIC MIXER~ hand-held or larger. This is a must for baking, especially when beaten egg whites are featured.

☆WIRE WHISKS~ of varying sizes.

☆BOWLS~ of varying sizes.

☆SEVERAL COLANDERS~ including one big enough for pasta.

☆A FEW KNIVES THAT YOU JUST LOVE~ straight-edged and serrated, of various sizes, all of them very sharp.

☆SEVERAL SPOONS THAT YOU JUST LOVE~ including a large slotted one.

☆A SOUP POT ~ (kettle or Dutch oven)

☆A LARGE PASTA-BOILING POT

☆A LARGE (10- to 12-inch) SKILLET ~ for sautéing. Nonstick = ideal.

☆A MEDIUM TO LARGE WOK ~ for stir-fries. Nonstick, if possible.

☆A 6- TO 8-INCH CRÊPE OR OMELETTE PAN ~ Again, nonstick, if possible.

☆SEVERAL SAUCEPANS WITH LIDS ~ various sizes.

☆A TIMER WITH A BELL ~ So you can think about other things in the meantime.

☆A GARLIC PRESS (optional) ~ I actually prefer to mince garlic in a mini-processor or on a cutting board with a sharp paring knife, but some people love to press their garlic.

☆BAKING PANS AND CASSEROLES ~ of various shapes and sizes.

☆TONGS ~ (useful for spaghetti); PASTA SCOOP ~ (useful for other shapes)

☆SPATULAS ~ metal and rubber.

☆ROLLING PIN

☆"WAFFLE" ~ heat absorber, to place under pots for very slow simmering.

☆VEGETABLE SCRUB BRUSH and /or PEELER

☆VEGETABLE STEAMER ~ a little metal basket to fit into a saucepan, letting you cook vegetables over water.

☆OVEN THERMOMETER ~ to help ensure the success of your baking.

❧ MODIFICATIONS ❧

A brief guideline to further reduce the fat, dairy, and egg content of these recipes:

LOWER-FAT COOKING:

Even though the oil content of these recipes has been pared down, you can reduce it still further by using <u>oil sprays</u>. These enable you to spray a mist of oil onto the food and/or the pan, instead of using oil by the tablespoon. Oil sprays are available commercially in many gourmet and natural foods stores. (The brands I know of are Pam, Bertolli, El Molino, and Trysons.) Used in combination with high-quality nonstick cookware, oil sprays can greatly reduce the fat content of your cooking without sacrificing flavor or texture.

You can prepare your own oil sprays by filling clean, dry spray bottles with the oil of your choice. Use the type of bottle that has a nozzle that permits you to adjust the intensity of the spray, and that has an "off" position, so it won't get clogged. Store in a cool, dark cupboard.

DAIRY REDUCTION OR SUBSTITUTION:

Milk can be substituted with soy milk or rice milk, both of which are nondairy and can be found in natural foods stores.

There are some lowfat, low sodium cheeses — as well as nondairy soy cheeses — available. Be sure to taste these before using them in your cooking. They might taste perfectly fine to you, but then again, they might not. Remember, you can always cut down on the amount of cheese prescribed in a recipe and in many cases, you can omit it altogether. Whipped tofu (puréed in a blender or food processor — or simply mashed) can sometimes substitute for cottage or ricotta cheese in casseroles. You might want to adjust the salt.

EGG OPTIONS:

Of the approximately 60 entrées, only 15 contain eggs, and of these, many are egg- or yolk-optional. If you need to reduce this further, experiment with egg substitutes. There are also desserts made without eggs, or with egg whites only.

FOR LISTS OF LOWFAT AND EGGLESS RECIPES, SEE APPENDIX, P. 221.

❧ A FEW NOTES ABOUT USING THIS BOOK: ❧

I've tried to address varying levels of cooking experience, so beginners won't get lost and more advanced cooks won't get bored. I hope I've found a middle ground, where enough but not too much is said.

Earlier editions of the <u>Moosewood Cookbook</u> have been rather loosely organized, which perhaps is being a bit generous. The original index, done in a casual style I made up myself, drove a lot of people crazy, and generated several enraged (and more than a few politely critical) letters from frustrated readers who had trouble finding recipes. One of the things I've learned from over 15 years of writing cookbooks is how to write a cookbook, and I've put my experience into organizing this one. (I've also learned to let professionals prepare the index.) At the beginning of each chapter is a detailed table of contents for that particular unit. In the back of the book, in addition to the (professionally prepared) index is an appendix (p. 221), so you can locate at a glance the lowfat, oil-free, and eggless recipes throughout the book. I hope you can easily find the recipes you want.

For the most part, I give precise measurements for most of the ingredients in most of the recipes. Occasionally I will say, "a medium-sized tomato" or "1 medium bunch of fresh spinach". In these cases, it is perfectly fine to use your own judgment; oftentimes these things are not rigid, and I want to encourage flexibility. Remember, cooking is not an exact science — it is more of an art. (Baking, on the other hand, is more of a science, and needs to be taken more literally.)

Here are three general tips for using these recipes:
1) Read through the recipes first, to get an overview of the procedures. Figure out what needs to be done ahead, what can be done while something else cooks, etc. This will help you feel more on top of things, and you'll enjoy cooking more.
2) There is an estimated preparation time and yield posted at the beginning of each recipe. When you are reading through the recipe, try to gauge your own pace. If you are a beginner or you like to work at a dreamy pace, the recipes will take longer to prepare than estimated.
3) "To taste" doesn't always mean literally tasting. Sometimes it means by sight or feel.

✳ TABLE OF CONVERSIONS ✳

✳ ✳ ✳ ✳ ✳ ✳ ✳ ✳

✳ DRY INGREDIENTS ✳

Beans (any type): ½ cup = 100 grams
Cornmeal, coarse (polenta): 1 cup = 170 grams
Cornmeal, fine: 1 cup = 150 grams
Herbs, dried = ¼ to ⅓ the amount of fresh herbs
Flour, white unbleached: 1 cup = 140 grams
Grains, dried (rice, bulgur, wheat berries, etc.): 1 cup = 200 grams
Sugar, brown: 1 cup (packed) = 200 grams
Sugar, powdered: 1 cup = 130 grams
Sugar, granulated: 1 cup = 200 grams

✳ BULK INGREDIENTS ✳

Cheese: 1 lb. = 4 to 5 cups (packed), grated
Nut butter (peanut, almond, etc. – or tahini): 1 cup = 250 grams
Nuts, chopped: ⅓ to ½ cup (2 oz.) = 50 grams
Onion: 1 small to medium-sized = approximately 1 cup, chopped
Raisins: ⅓ cup (2 oz.) = 50 grams
Sesame or sunflower seeds: ¾ cup = 100 grams

[1 lb. = 454 grams]

✳ LIQUIDS ✳

1 cup (8 oz.) = 250 ml.
1 Tbs. (½ fluid oz.) = 16 ml.
16 Tbs. = 1 cup

SOUPS

Many of these soups, which feature a variety of vegetables and legumes, can be the centerpiece of a meal, especially when served with rice or good bread and a light salad.

The hot soups can be made in advance and reheated gently on the stovetop or in a microwave. The cold soups that follow can be made up to several days in advance of serving. They keep very well if covered tightly and refrigerated.

Most of the soups from earlier editions of the Moosewood Cookbook are still here, many with only minor changes / improvements (most notably, the reduction of the butter or oil by as much as 1/2 to 2/3). You will find a few new recipes as well.

NOTE: Any soup containing milk can be converted to nondairy status by simply substituting soy milk. It will taste fine.

ABOUT STOCK:

I used water instead of stock in testing these recipes. But you can make your own stock and use it wherever water is indicated. Just be sure the stock is mildly flavored, so it won't dominate the soup.

To prepare a good, mild stock, add a variety of vegetables (or their parts) to a kettleful of boiling water, and simmer, partially covered, for about an hour. Let it cool, strain it, and give it a taste test before using, to be sure it's compatible with your intended soup.

Recommended for stock:

ONIONS	ZUCCHINI	MUSHROOMS	GREEN BEANS
GARLIC	POTATOES	APPLES	LETTUCE
CARROTS	SWEET POTATOES	TOMATOES	CORN
PARSNIPS	WINTER SQUASH		

TABLE OF CONTENTS: SOUPS

Cream of Asparagus

The original version called for 6 Tbs. butter. This new one has just 1½ Tbs.

Preparation time:
1 hour

Yield:
4 to 5 servings

2 lbs. fresh asparagus
1½ Tbs. butter
2 cups chopped onion
1½ tsp. salt
3 Tbs. flour

2 cups water
2 cups hot milk (lowfat ok)
2 tsp. dill
½ tsp. tarragon
white pepper, to taste

1) Break off and discard the tough asparagus bottoms. Slice off the tips and set them aside. Chop the remaining stalks into 1-inch pieces.

2) Melt the butter in a medium-sized skillet. Add onion, asparagus stalks, and salt. Sauté for about 10 minutes over medium heat. When the onions are clear and soft, sprinkle in 2 Tbs. flour, while constantly stirring. Continue to cook over the lowest possible heat, stirring frequently, another 5 to 8 minutes.

3) Add water, stirring constantly. Heat to a boil, then turn down to a simmer. After about 5 minutes, sprinkle in the remaining 1 Tbs. flour, mixing well. Cook another 8 to 10 minutes, stirring frequently.

4) Purée the soup with the milk, bit by bit, in a food processor or blender. Return the purée to a kettle or large saucepan, and season with dill, tarragon, and white pepper.

5) Cut the reserved asparagus tips into small pieces, and steam until just tender. Add these to the soup, heat very gently (don't cook or boil!), and serve immediately.

Spicy Tomato Soup

1 Tbs. olive oil
1 Tbs. butter (optional)
1½ cups minced onion
3 to 4 cloves garlic, minced or crushed
½ tsp. salt
1 tsp. dill (or more, to taste)
lots of freshly ground black pepper
1 1-lb.,12-oz. can "crushed concentrated tomatoes"
2 cups water
1 Tbs. honey (optional)
1 Tbs. mayonnaise or sour cream (lowfat OK)
2 medium-sized fresh tomatoes, diced

for the top {
  yogurt
  finely minced parsley and/or basil leaves
  finely minced scallions or chives
}

1) Heat olive oil (plus or minus optional butter) in a kettle or a Dutch oven. Add onion, garlic, salt, dill, and black pepper. Stir over medium heat for about 5 to 8 minutes, or until the onions are translucent.

2) Add canned crushed tomatoes, water, and optional honey. Cover and simmer over low heat for 20 to 30 minutes.

3) About 5 minutes before serving, whisk in mayonnaise or sour cream, and stir in diced fresh tomatoes. Serve hot, topped with yogurt and freshly minced herbs.

Gypsy Soup

About 45 minutes to prepare

NOTE: Chick peas need to be cooked in advance. (canned = ok)

...a delicately spiced Spanish-style vegetable soup...

Yield: 4 to 5 servings

The vegetables in this soup can be varied. Any orange vegetable can be combined with any green. For example, peas or green beans could replace– or augment– the peppers. Carrots, pumpkin, or squash could fill in for the sweet potatoes. Innovate!

�֍ ❨ ✦⁊✶ ❨✦⁊✶ ❨✦⁊✶ ❨ ✦⁊✶ ❨✦⁊✶ ❨ ✦ ⁊✶ ❨✦⁊

2 medium-sized ripe tomatoes
2 Tbs. olive oil
2 cups chopped onion
3 medium cloves garlic, crushed
1 stalk celery, minced
2 cups peeled, diced sweet potato
1 tsp. salt
2 tsp. mild paprika

1 tsp. turmeric
1 tsp. basil
a dash of cinnamon
a dash of cayenne
1 bay leaf
3 cups water
1 medium bell pepper, diced
1½ cups cooked chick peas

1) Heat a medium-sized saucepanful of water to boiling. Core the tomatoes, and plunge them into the boiling water for a slow count of 10. Remove the tomatoes, and peel them over a sink. Cut them open; squeeze out and discard the seeds. Chop the remaining pulp and set aside.

2) Heat the olive oil in a kettle or Dutch oven. Add onion, garlic, celery, and sweet potato, and sauté over medium heat for about 5 minutes. Add salt, and sauté 5 minutes more. Add seasonings and water, cover, and simmer about 15 minutes.

3) Add tomato pulp, bell pepper, and chick peas. Cover and simmer for about 10 more minutes, or until all the vegetables are as tender as you like them. Taste to adjust seasonings, and serve.

❨✦⁊✶❨ ✦⁊ ⁊✶❨✦⁊ ⁊ ✶❨✦ ⁊✶❨✦⁊✶❨ ✦⁊✶

Light Cream of Celery Soup

2 average person's fist-sized potatoes, peeled and diced
4 cups chopped celery (in 1-inch chunks) (you'll also need
       another cup a few ingredients from now)
3 cups water
1¼ tsp. salt (plus another ½ tsp. later)
1 to 2 Tbs. butter
a heaping cup finely minced onion
a heaping cup very finely minced celery (the innermost
       stalks work best for this)
1 tsp. celery seed
1 cup milk (can be lowfat), warmed
white pepper, to taste
4 to 5 Tbs. sour cream, half and half, or heavy cream
       (optional, for a richer tasting soup)
freshly minced chives and/or parsley for garnish (some-
       thing green to liven up the appearance)

1) Place potatoes, 4 cups of celery, water, and 1¼ tsp. salt in a medium-sized saucepan. Bring to a boil, turn the heat way down, and simmer, covered, for about 15 minutes ~ until everything is soft. Purée, and transfer to a larger saucepan or a kettle.

2) Melt butter in a small skillet. Add onion, finely minced celery, celery seed, plus ½ tsp. salt. Sauté about 8 to 10 minutes ~ until the vegetables are just tender. Add to purée.

3) Stir in remaining ingredients, except garnish. Heat gently (don't cook or boil), and serve topped with something minced and green.

Minestrone

For a minestrone that is more a stew than a soup, use the larger amounts of beans and pasta.

NOTE: These instructions assume the beans or chick peas are already cooked. You can soak and cook your own, or use canned (well rinsed and well drained).

2 Tbs. olive oil
2 cups chopped onion
5 medium cloves garlic, minced
1½ to 2 tsp. salt
1 stalk celery, minced
1 medium carrot, diced
1 small zucchini, diced and/or 1 cup diced eggplant
1 tsp. oregano
fresh black pepper, to taste
1 tsp. basil

1 medium bell pepper, diced
3 to 4 cups (or more) water
1 14½-oz. can tomato purée (approximately 2 cups)
1 to 1½ cups cooked pea beans, chick peas, or kidney beans
½ to 1 cup dry pasta (any shape)
1 or 2 medium-sized ripe tomatoes, diced (optional)
½ cup freshly minced parsley
parmesan cheese

1) Heat the olive oil in a kettle or Dutch oven. Add onion, garlic, and 1½ tsp. salt. Sauté over medium heat for about 5 minutes, then add celery, carrot, eggplant (if using zucchini, add it later, with the bell pepper), oregano, black pepper, and basil. Cover and cook over very low heat about 10 more minutes, stirring occasionally.

2) Add bell pepper, zucchini, water, and tomato purée. Cover and simmer about 15 minutes. Add beans and simmer another 5 minutes.

3) Bring the soup to a gentle boil. Add pasta, stir, and cook until the pasta is tender. Stir in the diced fresh tomatoes, and serve right away, topped with parsley and parmesan.

Hot & Sour Soup

1 oz. dried Chinese black mushrooms
8 cups water
3 Tbs. dry sherry or Chinese rice wine
¼ to ⅓ cup cider vinegar (to taste)
2 Tbs. soy sauce
1¾ tsp. salt
1 cake (¼ lb.) firm tofu, in thin strips
2 Tbs. cornstarch
2 beaten eggs (yolks may be omitted)
6 minced scallions (whites and greens)
¼ tsp. white pepper (to taste)
Chinese sesame oil (optional)

1) Place the dried mushrooms in a small bowl. Heat 2 (of the 8) cups of water to boiling; pour over the mushrooms. Cover with a plate, and let stand at least 30 minutes. (You can assemble the other ingredients in the meantime.) Drain the mushrooms, squeezing out and saving all the liquid. Slice the mushrooms, removing and discarding the stems.

2) In a kettle or Dutch oven, combine the remaining 6 cups of water, the reserved mushroom-soaking liquid, and the sliced mushrooms. Heat to a gentle boil.

3) Add sherry, vinegar, soy sauce, salt, and tofu. Lower the heat, and let simmer uncovered for about 10 minutes.

4) Place the cornstarch in a small bowl. Measure out about ¾ cup of the hot soup, and whisk it into the cornstarch. When the cornstarch is dissolved, stir this mixture back into the soup.

5) Drizzle the beaten eggs into the simmering soup, stirring constantly. Add scallions and white pepper. Cook only a few minutes more. Top each serving with a few drops of sesame oil, if desired.

MISO SOUP

~ almost instant soup! You can make an individual serving for your-self whenever the inspiration hits. Or you can multiply the amounts (simple math), do step 1 in advance, and divide it into serving bowls, adding step 2 just before serving.

Miso is a deep-flavored paste made from fermented soybeans and grains. There are several kinds available in the United States — usually in Japanese markets or in natural foods stores. The most common are red, white, Hatcho, and barley miso. Any one of them can be used to make this very simple and satisfying soup.

In traditional Japanese cooking, fish or vegetable stock (made from various kinds of seaweed) would be used to make Miso Soup. Water will also work very well, so you needn't do the extra work of making stock. But if you happen to have some good vegetable broth on hand, by all means use it.

NOTE: The optional wakame seaweed is available in Japanese markets and in some natural foods stores.

PER SERVING (easily multiplied):

1 Tbs. (more or less) miso
1 cup (more or less) boiling water
a few tiny cubes of soft tofu
a few delicate slices of scallion greens
optional additions:
- 1 to 2 Tbs. dried wakame seaweed, soaked in water for 10 to 15 minutes, then drained
- tiny carrot sticks (matchstick-like), lightly steamed
- finely shredded cabbage, lightly steamed
- a few leaves of spinach

1) Place the miso in the serving bowl. Add about ¼ cup of the boiling water and stir to make a uniform paste.
2) Stir in remaining water plus all remaining ingredients. Serve immediately.

✵ Summer Vegetable Soup ✵

Ultralight, this features the best offerings from a summer garden; it's like a salad in soup form. Use the freshest vegetables available, and make substitutions wherever necessary.

This recipe contains no oil or fat. If you choose not to add the optional buttermilk, it can also be completely dairy-free.

2 medium potatoes, peeled or not,
        and diced
4 cups water
3 to 4 large cloves garlic
1 to 1½ tsp. salt
black pepper, to taste
½ lb. green beans, trimmed & cut
1 cup small broccoli florets
1 cup chopped cauliflower

1 medium carrot, diced
½ lb. sugar snap or snow peas
2 small zucchini or yellow squash, diced
1 medium red bell pepper, in strips

OPTIONAL
{ 1 cup fresh corn
  a small bunch spinach, chopped
  1 cup buttermilk, room temperature
  freshly minced herbs, for the top }

1) Place potatoes and water in a medium-sized saucepan. Bring to a boil, lower heat, and simmer until the potatoes are tender. Add the garlic (whole cloves, peeled) during the last few minutes of simmering.

2) Purée the potatoes and garlic in their cooking water. Add salt and pepper to taste. Set aside until just before serving time.

3) Meanwhile, steam the vegetables until just tender in the following groupings: ⓐ green beans ⓑ broccoli, cauliflower, carrot ⓒ peas, zucchini, bell pepper, corn, spinach. (NOTE: A microwave does a good, fast job of steaming, with no added water.) Set the vegetables aside.

4) Heat the potato purée shortly before serving. Stir in the steamed vegetables and optional buttermilk at the last minute. Optional: a light sprinkling of freshly snipped herbs (ideally: basil, dill, parsley, and/or chives).

Succotash Chowder

Preparation time:
30 minutes, at most,
after beans are cooked

Yield: 6 servings,
possibly more

PRELIMINARY: Soak 1 to 1½ cups dry baby lima beans in water for at least 4 hours. Cook in plenty of simmering – NOT rapidly boiling – water for 35 to 40 minutes, or until perfectly tender. Try not to overcook the beans, or the soup will become gluey and lose its textural charm.

1 medium potato (average fist-sized), diced (peeling = optional)
1 Tbs. butter
2 cups chopped onion
3 to 4 medium cloves garlic, crushed or minced
3 stalks celery, minced
1½ tsp. salt
1 tsp. basil
½ tsp. thyme
3 cups corn (fresh OR a 1-lb. bag frozen, defrosted)
2 to 3 cups cooked baby lima beans
4 cups milk (can be lowfat)
a generous amount of fresh black pepper
finely minced parsley and/or chives (optional)

1) Cook the diced potato in boiling water until just tender. Drain well, and set aside.

2) Meanwhile, melt the butter in a kettle or Dutch oven. Add onion, garlic, celery, salt, and herbs. Sauté over medium heat for about 10 minutes, or until the onion and celery are tender. Stir in the corn, and sauté for about 10 minutes more. Add the cooked beans.

3) OPTIONAL: Purée some of the sauté in a food processor or blender. Return to the kettle. (This will make a thicker soup.)

4) Add potatoes and milk. Season to taste with black pepper; correct salt. Serve very hot, topped with minced fresh herbs, if available.

VEGETABLE CHOWDER

Instead of ¼ cup butter and ½ pint heavy cream, as in the original version, this new light one has only 1 Tbs. butter, no cream, and the option of lowfat milk. It still tastes luxurious.

Try not to shy away from the full amount of garlic. It gives the soup a rich flavor and is surprisingly smooth and subtle.

1 Tbs. butter	1 medium potato, diced
2 cups chopped onion	2 medium stalks celery, diced
6 cloves garlic, minced	2 medium carrots, diced
2 tsp. salt	2 cups chopped broccoli
½ tsp. thyme	2 cups chopped cauliflower
2 tsp. basil	½ lb. mushrooms, chopped

2 cups corn (frozen-defrosted is fine)
lots of fresh black pepper
1½ cups water
1 quart milk (lowfat ok), heated
optional: minced fresh herbs
　　　　(chives, basil, marjoram)

1) Melt the butter in a kettle or Dutch oven. Add onion, half the garlic, salt, thyme, and basil. Sauté over medium heat 5 minutes. Add potato, celery, carrots, broccoli, and cauliflower. Sauté another 5 to 8 minutes. Add mushrooms and corn, plus lots of black pepper. Sauté another 8 to 10 minutes.

2) Add water, cover, and simmer about 15 minutes, or until everything is tender. (Make sure the potatoes are done.)

3) Stir in hot milk and remaining garlic. Remove from heat until about 10 minutes before serving time, then heat gently. Serve topped with freshly minced herbs.

Chinese Vegetable Chowder

Simple and delicious ~ made with no dairy products, no eggs, no oil, no garlic, no onions!

The mushrooms need to soak for at least 30 to 40 minutes ahead of time, and this can be done a day or two in advance.

2 oz. dried Chinese black mushrooms
5 cups boiling water
a 1-lb. package frozen corn, defrosted
1 to 1½ tsp. salt
1 to 2 Tbs. soy sauce

black pepper, to taste
1 medium carrot, diced
1 stalk celery, minced
1 8-oz. can water chestnuts, minced

1) Place the mushrooms in a medium-large bowl, and pour in the boiling water. Cover with a plate and let stand for at least 30 to 40 minutes, or until the mushrooms are soaked through and very soft. Drain well, reserving both the mushrooms and the water, squeezing all the excess liquid from the mushrooms. Place the mushrooms on a cutting board and slice thinly, removing and discarding their tough stems.

2) Combine the mushroom water and the corn in a food processor or blender, and purée until as smooth as possible. (You will probably have to do this in more than one batch.) Transfer to a kettle or a large saucepan. (For a smoother soup, you can strain the purée on its way into the kettle.) Stir in salt, soy sauce, and black pepper to taste.

3) Lightly steam the carrot and the celery until just tender. (If you have one, a microwave oven will do this in 2 minutes.)

4) Add carrot, celery, and water chestnuts to the soup. Heat gently just before serving.

Cream of Broccoli

45 minutes
to prepare

2 Tbs. butter or margarine
1½ cups chopped onion
1 bay leaf
1 tsp. salt (more, to taste)
1 medium bell pepper, diced
4 cups chopped broccoli
2½ cups water
2 cups milk (lowfat ok)

½ cup sour cream (lowfat ok)
¼ tsp. allspice
black pepper } to taste
white pepper }
a dash of thyme
½ tsp. basil
1 cup broccoli florets, sliced thin
     and lightly steamed

1) Melt butter or margarine in a kettle or Dutch oven. Add onion, bay leaf, and salt. Sauté over medium heat until the onion is translucent.

2) Add green pepper, chopped broccoli, and water. Cover, and cook over medium heat for 10 minutes, or until the broccoli is very tender.

3) Remove the bay leaf, and purée the soup little by little with the milk in a blender or food processor.

4) Whisk in the sour cream and remaining seasonings. Heat gently. Serve hot, topped with lightly steamed broccoli florets.

Curried Squash & Mushroom Soup

Yield: 4 or 5 servings

Preparation time: 45 minutes. (Prepare other ingredients while squash bakes.)

NOTE: This soup can be made with no dairy products.

2 medium acorn or butternut squash
2 ½ cups water
1 cup orange juice
1 Tbs. butter or oil
1 cup chopped onion
2 medium cloves garlic, crushed
1 ¼ tsp. salt
½ tsp. ground cumin

½ tsp. coriander
½ tsp. cinnamon
1 tsp. ginger
¼ tsp. dry mustard
½ lb. mushrooms, sliced
a few dashes cayenne (to taste)
fresh lemon juice } optional
yogurt, for the top }

1) Preheat oven to 375°F. Split the squash lengthwise, remove seeds, and place face-down on a lightly oiled tray. Bake until soft (about 30 to 40 minutes). Cool, then scoop out the insides. Measure out 3 cups'-worth, place this in a food processor or blender with the water, and purée until smooth. (You may need to do this in batches.) Transfer to a kettle, and stir in the orange juice.

2) Heat the butter or oil in a skillet, and add onion, garlic, salt, and spices. Sauté over medium heat until the onion is very soft ~ about 8 minutes. (You may need to add a small amount of water to prevent sticking.) Add mushrooms, cover, and cook about 10 minutes over medium heat, stirring occasionally.

3) Add the sauté to the squash, scraping the skillet well to salvage all the good stuff. Add cayenne and heat gently. Once it is hot, taste it to correct the seasonings. This is a fairly sweet soup; you may choose to balance this by adding fresh lemon juice to taste and/or topping each bowlful with a small spoonful of yogurt.

Cauliflower~Cheese Soup

1 medium-large potato, peeled and diced
   (about 2 to 3 cups diced)
1 large cauliflower, cut or broken into
   florets (put aside 2 cups of florets)
1 medium carrot, peeled and chopped
3 medium cloves garlic, peeled
1½ cups chopped onion
1½ tsp. salt
4 cups water
2 cups (packed) grated cheddar (plus
   extra for garnishing each serving)
3/4 cup milk (lowfat OK)
1 tsp. dill
½ tsp. caraway seeds
black pepper, to taste

1) Place potato, cauliflower (except for the 2 cups reserved), carrot, garlic,
onion, salt, and water in a large saucepan. Bring to a boil, then
simmer until all the vegetables are very tender. Purée in a blender or
food processor, and transfer to a kettle or Dutch oven.

2) Steam the reserved cauliflower pieces until just tender. Add these to
the purée along with all remaining ingredients. Heat gently, and serve
topped with a little extra cheese.

Instead of sautéing the vegetables, you add them directly to the simmering soup. Thus, with the exception of the optional sesame oil garnish, this soup is fat-free.

◊ Split Pea Soup ◊

3 cups dry split peas
about 7 cups of water (more, as needed)
1 bay leaf
2 tsp. salt
½ to 1 tsp. dry mustard
2 cups minced onion
4 to 5 medium cloves garlic, crushed
3 stalks celery, minced
2 medium carrots, sliced or diced
1 small potato, thinly sliced
lots of freshly ground black pepper
3 to 4 Tbs. red wine vinegar (to taste)

TOPPINGS ⟨ Chinese sesame oil (optional)
a fresh, ripe tomato, diced
freshly minced parsley

1) Place split peas, water, bay leaf, salt, and dry mustard in a kettle or Dutch oven. Bring to a boil, lower heat as much as possible, and simmer, partially covered, for about 20 minutes.

2) Add onion, garlic, celery, carrots, and potato. Partially cover, and leave it to simmer gently for about 40 more minutes with occasional stirring. If necessary, add some water.

3) Add black pepper and vinegar to taste. Serve topped with a drizzle of sesame oil, diced tomato, and minced parsley.

Hungarian Mushroom Soup

1 hour
to prepare

2 Tbs. butter
2 cups chopped onion
1½ to 2 lbs. mushrooms, sliced
1 tsp. salt
2 to 3 tsp. dried dill (or 2 to 3 Tbs. freshly minced)
1 Tbs. mild paprika
2 tsp. fresh lemon juice
3 Tbs. flour
2 cups water
1 cup milk (can be lowfat) ~ at room temperature
black pepper, to taste
½ cup sour cream (can be reduced-fat variety)
finely minced fresh parsley, for the top

1) Melt the butter in a kettle or Dutch oven. Add onions, and sauté over medium heat for about 5 minutes. Add mushrooms, salt, dill, and paprika. Stir well and cover. Let cook for about 15 more minutes, stirring occasionally. Stir in lemon juice.

2) Gradually sprinkle in the flour, stirring constantly. Cook and stir another 5 minutes or so over medium-low heat. Add water, cover, and cook about 10 minutes, stirring often.

3) Stir in milk; add black pepper to taste. Check to see if it needs more salt. Whisk in the sour cream, and heat very gently. Don't boil or cook it after this point. Serve hot, topped with freshly minced parsley.

The original version of this recipe called for 6 Tbs. butter, 3 cups whole milk, plus ½ pint heavy cream. This new one has only 1½ Tbs. butter, a little milk, and no cream.

Mushroom Bisque

... and it tastes equally good, if not better.

1 hour to prepare

Yield: a good 8 servings

2 medium potatoes (the size of an average person's fist)
1½ cups water
1½ Tbs. butter or margarine
2 cups chopped onion
1 small stalk celery, minced
1½ lbs. mushrooms
1½ to 2 tsp. salt
1 to 2 small cloves garlic, minced
¼ tsp. thyme
3 Tbs. dry sherry
2 tsp. soy sauce
fresh black pepper, to taste
1 cup milk (can be lowfat)
croutons (recipe on p.20) ⎤
minced scallion greens or chives ⎦ optional toppings

1) Peel potatoes, chop into small pieces, and place in a small saucepan with the water. Cover, bring to a boil, and simmer until potatoes are tender.

2) Meanwhile, melt butter in a deep skillet or Dutch oven. Add onion and celery, and sauté over medium heat for about 5 minutes. Stir in mushrooms and salt, cover, and cook about 10 minutes, stirring occasionally. Somewhere in there, add garlic and thyme. (Adding garlic later keeps its flavor stronger.) Remove from heat; stir in sherry, soy sauce, and pepper.

3) Use a blender or food processor to purée both the potatoes in their cooking water and the mushroom sauté in its own liquid. (When you run out of the liquid, use the milk.) Combine the purées in a kettle or Dutch oven.

4) Stir, and heat gently; taste to adjust seasonings. Serve very hot, with optional but highly recommended toppings.

ONION SOUP

This soup is very, very simple and easy. Most of the preparation time, after the onions are sliced, is for simmering: slowly, thoroughly, deliciously. You can use this time to make the croutons and to prepare other components of the meal. The original recipe called for 6 Tbs. butter. I've reduced that amount to just 2 Tbs., yet the buttery flavor is still generously imparted.

2 Tbs. butter
4 large yellow onions, thinly sliced
1 tsp. salt
½ tsp. dry mustard
a dash or two of thyme
4 cups water
2 Tbs. soy sauce

2 to 3 Tbs. dry white wine (optional)
a few dashes of white pepper

TOPPINGS:
thin slices of Swiss cheese
croutons (recipe below)

1) Melt the butter in a kettle or Dutch oven. Add onions and salt, and cook over medium heat about 10 minutes, stirring occasionally.

2) Add mustard and thyme; stir and cover. Continue to cook very slowly for about 35 more minutes. The onions will be exquisitely soft and simmering in their own liquid.

3) Add water, soy sauce, optional wine, and white pepper. Simmer at least 10 minutes more. Taste to adjust seasonings. Serve topped with croutons and Swiss cheese. If you're serving the soup in ovenproof bowls, you can put them under the broiler briefly, to brown the cheese. Be careful handling the bowls!

HOMEMADE CROUTONS:

a) Sauté cubed bread in garlic butter for about 10 minutes, then transfer to a tray, and toast in a 300°F. oven until crisp. OR:

b) Brush thin slices of baguette on both sides with olive oil. (Optional: crush some garlic into the oil first.) Bake on a tray in a 350°F. oven until crisp (8 to 12 minutes, depending on thickness), but check on them frequently! They can look underdone one minute and burn the next.

Swiss Cheese & Onion Soup

2 Tbs. butter
2 medium onions, thinly sliced (about 4 cups)
1 to 2 medium cloves garlic, minced
1½ tsp. salt
2 tsp. dry mustard
1 to 3 Tbs. flour (depending on how thick you like your soup)
2 Tbs. dry sherry
2 cups water
1 tsp. prepared horseradish (the white kind)
1½ cups warmed milk (can be lowfat)
1½ cups (packed) grated Swiss cheese
white pepper
OPTIONAL TOPPINGS: croutons (see preceding page)
                       paprika~ or some minced pimientos

1) Melt the butter in a kettle or Dutch oven. Add onions, garlic, salt, and dry mustard, and cook over medium heat 8 to 10 minutes, or until the onions are very soft.

2) Gradually sprinkle in the flour, stirring constantly, then add the sherry and mix well. Add water and horseradish. Stir and cook for about 5 more minutes.

3) Add warm milk and cheese. After adding the cheese, stir assiduously with a wooden spoon for a good few minutes. Much to your delight, everything will become remarkably smooth and well blended.

4) Add white pepper to taste, and while you're at it, adjust the other seasonings as well. You might wish to increase the mustard, sherry, or horseradish (too late to decrease). Serve hot ~ plain, or topped with croutons and/or a light dusting of paprika and/or a small amount of finely minced pimiento.

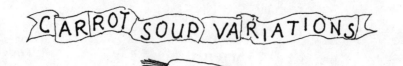

CARROT SOUP VARIATIONS

Each of the following Carrot Soup Variations is a thick, creamy purée that can be made with no dairy products. Each soup also keeps and freezes very well, and doesn't suffer from repeated reheatings.

❀➣ Gingered Carrot Soup ❀

Serve this as a thick sauce over rice for a simple supper. It also goes well with Samosas (p.170) and Raita (p. 99).

2 lbs. carrots
4 cups water
1 Tbs. butter or oil
1½ cups chopped onion
2 medium cloves garlic, minced
2 Tbs. freshly grated ginger
1½ tsp. salt

¼ tsp. each: cumin
ground fennel
cinnamon
allspice
dried mint

3 to 4 Tbs. fresh lemon juice
1 cup lightly toasted cashews
OPTIONAL: buttermilk, to
drizzle on top

1) Peel and trim carrots, and cut them into 1-inch chunks. Place in a medium-large saucepan with the water, cover, and bring to a boil. Lower the heat, and simmer until very tender (about 10 to 15 minutes, depending on the size of the carrot pieces).

2) Meanwhile heat the butter or oil in a small skillet. Add onions, and sauté over medium heat for about 5 minutes. Add garlic, ginger, salt, and spices. Turn heat to low, and continue to sauté for another 8 to 10 minutes, or until everything is well mingled and the onions are very soft. Stir in lemon juice.

3) Use a food processor or blender to purée everything together (including the toasted cashews). You will need to do this in several batches. Transfer the purée to a kettle, and heat gently just before serving. If desired, pass a small pitcher of buttermilk, for individual drizzlings.

Herbed Carrot Soup

You can make this with no oil. The onions and garlic can be cooked in the water with the carrots. Add the seasonings later, as the soup simmers.

2 lbs. carrots
1 medium potato (the size of a medium fist)
4 cups water
1 Tbs. butter or oil
1 cup chopped onion
1½ tsp. salt
2 medium cloves garlic, minced or crushed
½ tsp. thyme
½ tsp. marjoram or oregano
1 tsp. basil
1 to 2 Tbs. lemon juice (or, to taste)
optional: small amounts of finely minced
fresh mint,
chives,
and or
parsley,
for the top

1) Peel and chop the carrots and potato, and place them in a medium-large saucepan with the water. Bring to a boil, cover, and simmer until the vegetables are tender (10 to 15 minutes).

2) Meanwhile, heat oil in a small skillet. Add onions and salt, and sauté over medium heat for about 5 minutes. Add garlic and dried herbs, and sauté about 5 minutes more, or until the onions are soft. Stir in lemon juice.

3) Purée everything together in a blender or food processor, and transfer to a kettle or Dutch oven. Simmer gently 8 to 10 minutes. Serve hot, topped with a light sprinkling of fresh herbs.

White Bean & Black Olive Soup

NOTE: This recipe calls for 2 cups cooked white pea beans. Use 1 cup dry, and cook them, without prior soaking, in plenty of simmering (<u>not</u> rapidly boiling) water until tender (about 1¼ hours).

```
2 Tbs. olive oil
1 heaping cup chopped onion
1 stalk celery, diced
1 medium carrot, diced
1 to 1½ tsp. salt
1 tsp. oregano or marjoram
1½ tsp. basil
1 small (5 to 6 inches long) zucchini, diced
1 small bell pepper, chopped
3 to 4 medium cloves garlic, crushed
fresh black pepper
4 cups water
3 oz. (half a small can) tomato paste
¼ cup dry red wine (optional)
2 cups cooked white pea beans
1 cup sliced Kalamata (Greek) olives (or plain black ones)
1 Tbs. fresh lemon juice
finely minced fresh parsley  ⎫
a ripe tomato, diced         ⎬ TOPPINGS
```

1) Heat the olive oil in a kettle or Dutch oven. Add onion, celery, carrot, salt, and herbs. Sauté over medium heat 8 to 10 minutes, or until the vegetables are just tender.

2) Add zucchini, bell pepper, and garlic. Sauté 5 minutes more. Grind in some black pepper.

3) Combine water and tomato paste. Add to vegetables, along with the remaining ingredients, except toppings. Cover and simmer over low heat for about 15 minutes. Serve hot, topped with parsley and diced tomato.

Lentil Soup

...... gentle.

This is a very easy fat-free lentil soup that just about cooks itself. Only one pot is needed, so cleanup is easy.

Preparation time: about 1 hour

Yield: 6 to 8 servings

3 cups dry lentils
7 cups water
2 tsp. salt
6 to 8 medium cloves garlic, crushed
2 cups chopped onion
2 stalks celery, chopped
2 medium carrots, sliced or diced
optional: ½ to 1 tsp. basil
          ½ tsp. thyme
          ½ tsp. oregano
lots of freshly ground black pepper
2 to 3 medium-sized ripe tomatoes
red wine vinegar, to drizzle on top

1) Place lentils, water, and salt in a kettle. Bring to a boil, lower heat to the slowest possible simmer, and cook quietly, partially covered, for 20 to 30 minutes.

2) Add vegetables (except tomatoes), herbs, and black pepper. Partially cover, and let simmer peacefully another 20 to 30 minutes, stirring occasionally.

3) Heat a medium saucepanful of water to boiling. Drop in the tomatoes for 10 seconds, then take them out, peel off the skins, and squeeze out the seeds. Chop the remaining pulp and add to the soup. Let the soup cook for at least 5 minutes more.

4) Serve hot, with a drizzle of vinegar on top of each steaming bowlful.

Brazilian Black Bean Soup

New and Improved!
... and actually easier
than the original

PRELIMINARY: Soak 2 cups dry black beans in plenty of water for at least 4 hours (and preferably overnight.)

2 cups dry black beans, soaked
6 cups water
1 Tbs. olive oil
3 cups chopped onion
10 medium cloves garlic, crushed
2 tsp. cumin
2 to 2½ tsp. salt
1 medium carrot, diced

1 medium bell pepper, diced
1½ cups orange juice
black pepper, to taste
cayenne, to taste
2 medium tomatoes, diced (optional)

optional toppings: { sour cream
cilantro
salsa (recipe p. 96) }

1) Place the soaked beans in a kettle or Dutch oven with 4 cups water. Bring to a boil, cover, and simmer until tender (about 1¼ hours).

2) Heat olive oil in a medium-sized skillet. Add onion, half the garlic, cumin, salt, and carrot. Sauté over medium heat until the carrot is just tender. Add remaining garlic and the bell pepper. Sauté until everything is very tender (another 10 to 15 minutes). Add the sautéed mixture to the beans, scraping in every last morsel.

3) Stir in orange juice, black pepper, cayenne, and optional tomatoes. Pureé all or some of the soup in a blender or food processor, and return to kettle. Simmer over very low heat 10 to 15 minutes more. Serve topped with an artful arrangement of sour cream, cilantro, and salsa.

RUSSIAN CABBAGE BORSCHT

Preparation time: 1 hour

Yield: 4 to 6 servings

1½ cups thinly sliced potato
1 cup thinly sliced beets
4 cups water
1 to 2 Tbs. butter
1½ cups chopped onion
1 scant tsp. caraway seeds
1½ tsp. salt (or more, to taste)

1 stalk celery, chopped
1 medium-sized carrot, sliced
3 to 4 cups shredded cabbage
freshly ground black pepper
1 tsp. dill (plus extra, for garnish)
1 to 2 Tbs. cider vinegar
1 to 2 Tbs. brown sugar or honey
1 cup tomato purée

TOPPINGS { sour cream or yogurt
           extra dill

1) Place potatoes, beets, and water in a medium-sized saucepan.
   Cover, and cook over medium heat until tender (20 to 30 minutes).

2) Meanwhile, melt the butter in a kettle or Dutch oven. Add onion,
   caraway seeds, and salt. Cook over medium heat, stirring occasionally, until the onions are translucent (8 to 10 minutes).

3) Add celery, carrots, and cabbage, plus 2 cups of the cooking
   water from the potatoes and beets. Cover and cook over medium
   heat until the vegetables are tender (another 8 to 10 minutes).

4) Add the remaining ingredients (including all the potato and beet
   water), cover, and simmer for at least 15 more minutes. Taste to
   correct seasonings, and serve hot, topped with sour cream or
   yogurt and a light dusting of dill.

Mushroom-Barley Soup

Preparation time: 1¼ hours

Yield: 6 to 8 servings

½ cup uncooked pearl barley
6½ cups water
1 to 2 Tbs. butter
1 medium onion, chopped (about 1½ cups)
2 medium cloves garlic, minced
1 lb. mushrooms, sliced
½ to 1 tsp. salt
3 to 4 Tbs. soy sauce
3 to 4 Tbs. dry sherry
freshly ground black pepper

1) Place the barley and 1½ cups of the water in a large saucepan or a Dutch oven. Bring to a boil, cover, and simmer until the barley is tender (20 to 30 minutes).

2) Meanwhile, melt the butter in a skillet. Add the onions and sauté for about 5 minutes over medium heat. Add garlic, mushrooms, and ½ tsp. salt. Cover and cook, stirring occasionally, until everything is very tender ~ about 10 to 12 minutes. Stir in soy sauce and sherry.

3) Add the sauté with all its liquid to the cooked barley, along with the remaining 5 cups of water. Grind in a generous amount of black pepper, and simmer, partially covered, another 20 minutes over very low heat. Taste to correct seasonings, and serve.

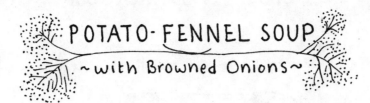

POTATO-FENNEL SOUP
~with Browned Onions~

This very simple and rich-tasting soup can be made with no dairy products.

Fennel is well known as a seasoning, particularly in seed form. It is less well known as a vegetable: a light green bulb that is crunchy, juicy, and deeply, though subtly, flavored.

1 Tbs. butter or oil
4 cups thinly sliced onions
2 tsp. salt
4 medium potatoes (average fist-size), not necessarily peeled,
   and sliced into thin pieces 1 to 2 inches long
1 cup freshly minced fennel bulb
½ tsp. caraway seeds
4 cups water
white pepper, to taste
OPTIONAL TOPPINGS:
 ~Sour cream, thinned (by beating with a little whisk in a little bowl)
 ~the feathery tops of the fennel, well minced

1) Melt the butter (or heat the oil) in a kettle or Dutch oven. Add the onions and 1 tsp. salt. Cook over medium-low heat, stirring occasionally, for about 15 to 20 minutes, or until the onions are very, very soft and lightly browned.

2) Add the potatoes, another ½ tsp. salt, the minced fennel bulb, and the caraway seeds. Sauté over medium heat for another 5 minutes, then add the water. Bring to a boil, then partially cover, and simmer until the potatoes are tender (10 to 15 minutes).

3) Taste to adjust salt; add white pepper. Serve hot, topped with a decorative swirl of thinned sour cream and/or minced feathery fennel tops.

Cream of Spinach Soup

For a lowfat version, simply skip Step 2.

1 large onion, chopped
2 medium potatoes, peeled and chopped
3 cups water
2 tsp. salt
1 lb. spinach, cleaned and stemmed
5 medium cloves garlic, peeled only
optional { 1½ to 2 Tbs. butter
3 Tbs. flour
1½ cups hot milk (may be lowfat)
white pepper and nutmeg, to taste

1) Place onion, potatoes, water, and salt in a large saucepan. Bring to a boil, cover, and simmer until the potatoes are tender. Remove from heat, add spinach and garlic cloves, and set aside.

2) Melt the butter over low heat in a small saucepan. Whisk in flour, and keep whisking over low heat 5 minutes. Drizzle in the milk. Continue to whisk and cook until smooth (about 5 to 8 minutes more).

3) Purée the vegetables in their cooking water; return the purée to the saucepan. Stir in the white sauce (or just the milk, if you're making the lowfat version). Adjust the salt, and add white pepper to taste. Serve hot, topped with a subtle sprinkling of nutmeg.

Gazpacho

20 to 30 minutes
to prepare,
plus time to chill.

Yield:
6 servings

4 cups tomato juice

½ cup finely minced onion

1 medium clove garlic, minced

1 medium bell pepper, minced

1 tsp. honey (optional)

1 medium cucumber,
  peeled, seeded, & minced

2 scallions, minced

juice of ½ lemon + 1 lime

2 Tbs. wine vinegar

1 tsp. each ⟨ tarragon / basil

¼ to ½ tsp. cumin

¼ cup freshly minced parsley

2 to 3 Tbs. olive oil

salt, black pepper, and
  cayenne — to taste

2 cups freshly diced tomatoes

Combine all ingredients.

(Optional: purée all or some)

Chill until very cold.

Chilled Cucumber- Yogurt Soup

Preparation time:
less than 10 minutes,
plus time to chill.

4 cups peeled, seeded, &
 grated cucumber
2 cups water
2 cups yogurt (nonfat OK)
½ to 1 tsp. salt
1 small clove garlic, minced
1 tsp. dried dill (or 1 Tbs. fresh)
1 Tbs. honey (optional)
minced fresh mint and chives

Yield:
4 to 6
servings

Combine grated cucumber, water, yogurt, salt, garlic, dill, and optional honey in a medium-sized bowl. Stir until well blended, and chill until very cold. Serve topped with finely minced fresh herbs, if available.

~chilled, creamy
potato-onion soup

Vichyssoise

Butter: reduced
Cream: optional
Recipe: flexible

Preparation time:
45 minutes,
plus time
to chill

Yield:
about 6 servings

2 Tbs. butter
3 cups chopped onions
1 to 1½ tsp. salt
4 medium potatoes (about 2 lbs.),
    peeled and diced
4 cups water

2 cups milk (lowfat ok)
OPTIONAL: up to ½ pint heavy cream
white pepper, to taste
freshly minced chives for the top

1) Melt the butter in a kettle or Dutch oven. Add onions and salt, and sauté about 15 minutes, or until the onions are very soft and beginning to brown.

2) Add potatoes and water, and bring to a boil. Lower heat, cover, and simmer until the potatoes are tender (about 10 to 15 minutes).

3) Purée until very smooth in a blender or food processor, and transfer to a medium-large container. Stir in the milk and optional cream; add white pepper.

4) Chill until very cold. Serve topped with finely minced fresh chives.

Green
Variation

Make Vichyssoise exactly as described above. When stirring in the milk, also add some combination (the more, the better) of puréed:

steamed spinach,
    steamed zucchini,
        steamed Boston (a.k.a. "butter") lettuce
            fresh watercress
                fresh herbs (basil, dill, parsley)

Top each serving with:

    peeled, seeded, and coarsely grated cucumber.

Cascadilla

Preparation time:
15 minutes,
plus time to chill

Yield:
4 to 6
servings

1 small cucumber~ peeled,
   seeded, and minced
1 scallion, finely minced
1 small clove garlic, crushed
½ tsp. dill
4 cups tomato juice

1 cup yogurt (nonfat OK)
1 small bell pepper, minced
3 to 4 raw mushrooms,
   thinly sliced
salt and pepper, to taste
OPTIONAL { croutons (p.20)
          { minced watercress

Combine
everything,
and
chill well.

Top with
croutons

and
watercress.

Chilled Beet Borscht

Preparation time:
about 40 minutes,
plus time to chill.

Yield: about
6 servings

4 large (3-inch diameter) beets
3 cups water
1 tsp. salt
1 to 2 Tbs. lemon juice, to taste
2 to 3 Tbs. sugar or honey, to taste
black pepper
1 to 2 Tbs. freshly minced dill (or 2 tsp. dried)
1 medium cucumber, peeled, seeded, and grated
2 to 3 finely minced scallions (whites and greens)
OPTIONAL: 1 medium-sized dill pickle, finely minced
2 cups buttermilk

OPTIONAL GARNISHES
{ a spoonful of sour cream or yogurt (nonfat OK)
{ slices of boiled potato
{ chopped hardboiled egg

1) Peel and trim the beets, and place them in a medium-sized saucepan with the water and salt. Bring to a boil, lower heat, partially cover, and simmer until the beets are tender (about 20 to 30 minutes). Remove the beets with a slotted spoon, and transfer the water to a medium-large bowl or container.

2) When the beets are cool enough to handle, grate them coarsely and return them to the water. Stir in remaining ingredients, except buttermilk and garnishes. Cover and chill until cold.

3) When the borscht is cold, stir in the buttermilk. Taste to adjust salt, pepper, lemon juice, sugar or honey. Serve topped with any combination of garnishes.

Chilled Berry Soup

Much more than just a soup, this refreshing tart-sweet preparation can be a summer beverage, a breakfast dish, or even a dessert.

Frozen berries work very well in here, so you don't need to wait for perfect fresh ones. Blue-, black-, rasp-, and strawberries can all be found in frozen, unsweetened form in the supermarket. You can also freeze your own during an abundant season. Frozen berries give off generous amounts of pure berry juice as they defrost, and you can include all of it in the soup. It creates an indescribably lovely color.

3 cups orange juice (preferably fresh-squeezed)
3 cups buttermilk or yogurt (nonfat OK)
1 to 2 Tbs. fresh lemon or lime juice
optional: 1 to 2 Tbs. sugar or honey
2 to 3 cups berries ~ any kind or any combination
    (Leave smaller berries whole. Larger ones
      should be sliced.)
optional: ⌐ a dash of cinnamon and/or nutmeg
      a few sprigs of fresh mint, for garnish

1) Whisk together orange juice and buttermilk or yogurt. Add lemon or lime juice and optional sugar or honey (or not), to taste. Cover and chill until serving time.

2) When you're ready to serve, place about ½ cup berries in each bowl. Ladle the soup on top. If desired, dust very lightly with cinnamon and/or nutmeg, and garnish with a few small sprigs of mint.

SALADS

Salads can be the opening act of a larger meal, or the backbone of a smaller one—especially when teamed up with soup and bread. Leftover salads can double as great sandwich fillings (see Salad Sandwiches, p. 119) and are also perfect for those times when you need more than a snack but less than a meal.

As an alternative to an entrée, try serving an assortment of salads, lavishly garnished, for a festive occasion. This is a great menu-planning strategy that allows you to make everything ahead of time, and then relax and really enjoy the company.

TABLE OF CONTENTS: SALADS

a good method for assembling
GREEN LEAFY SALADS

Assembling a green salad is a highly personalized endeavor, and of course there is no absolutely correct method. But the truth is, some salads are much better than others. Here are a few guidelines to help your salads be among the better ones:

1) Use a large enough bowl, so you'll have plenty of room to toss the salad thoroughly. Make it your special salad bowl — it will acquire more depth and soul with each use, and this will enhance something nameless (I don't know what) about the experience.

2) The basis for a green leafy salad is leafy greens: lettuces, spinach, and other tender green leaves that can be eaten raw. Use only the freshest greens! They should be immaculate and absolutely dry (use a salad spinner plus paper towels). Store in a crisper or in dry plastic bags in the refrigerator.

3) The optional extras = delicate clippings, shavings, and gratings of other vegetables, plus cherry or plum tomatoes, olives, nuts, slices of fruit (anything from apple or pear slices to citrus sections to fresh figs), crumbled pungent cheese, grated hardboiled egg, or homemade croutons (see p. 20). Have whatever you choose to add ready to be mixed in gently or laid on top just before serving.

4) If you want to make the dressing right in the bowl as you toss the salad, place a few tablespoons of olive oil, nut oil, or a combination in the bottom of the bowl with a clove or two of crushed garlic. Add crisp, dry greens a handful at a time, and toss after each addition, making sure everything gets evenly coated. Add small amounts of additional oil, if needed, plus small amounts of salt and vinegar (red wine, herb-infused, balsamic, fruit-flavored — experiment!) right before serving, and add optional extras. Bring a pepper mill to the table.

RULE OF THUMB: Be a benefactor with the oil,
a miser with the vinegar,
a poet with the salt, and
a demon with the pepper!

Warm Salad

... featuring an assortment of ultranutritious leafy greens, lightly cooked and delicately marinated. This can be a main dish unto itself, or a prelude or accompaniment to a simple pasta supper. However you serve it, be sure to include some fresh crusty bread to mop up the juices.

NOTE: Other types of greens can be substituted for the escarole, chard, and mustard. Try kale, collard, or dandelion greens.

3 Tbs. olive oil
1 small bunch escarole, chopped
1 medium bunch red or green chard, chopped
about 8 large leaves Napa or savoy cabbage, chopped
2 cups (packed) chopped mustard greens

1 to 2 tsp. salt	1 stalk celery, sliced
2 large cloves garlic, minced	½ small cauliflower, chopped
2 medium leeks, chopped	3 Tbs. balsamic or wine vinegar
2 cups chopped red onion	6 Tbs. (or more) parmesan
¾ lb. mushrooms, sliced	lots of fresh black pepper

1) Heat 1 Tbs. olive oil in a large wok or deep skillet. Add the escarole, chard, cabbage, and mustard greens, a little at a time, salting lightly after each addition, and adding more greens as soon as the ones in the pot cook down enough to make room. Use a fairly intense level of heat under the pot, and stir as you cook. When all the greens are wilted and tender, stir in the garlic. Cook and stir just a minute or two more, then transfer to a platter.

2) Add the remaining oil to the wok or skillet, and when it is hot, add leeks, onion, mushrooms, celery, and cauliflower. Salt lightly, and stir-fry quickly over medium-high heat until just tender (about 5 to 8 minutes). Add to the platter, mix gently to incorporate the greens, and sprinkle with vinegar and parmesan while still hot. Grind black pepper over the top, and serve hot, warm, or at room temperature, with thick slices of toasted bread to mop up the juices. (Sourdough bread is especially good for this.)

RAW VEGETABLE SALAD
. . . .

Most vegetables can be eaten raw if cut properly. In this salad, everything is minced very small or grated, so chewing is light and delightful and not a cumbersome chore. Visually, Raw Vegetable Salad can be beautiful, like edible confetti. Serve in glass bowls to maximize the aesthetic impact.

Use whatever is in season, and in any proportion. Sprouts, tomatoes, and/or mushroom slices can be used as toppings. Try pairing this salad with the Very Green Dressing, which follows.

carrots
celery
broccoli
cauliflower
cabbage (green and red)
bell peppers (all colors)
zucchini or summer squash
spinach

beets
cucumber
green beans
sugar snap or snow peas
red onion
scallions
radishes
fresh herbs

Peel wherever necessary; mince or grate everything and mix well.

VERY GREEN DRESSING
. . . .
Made with no oil!

a handful of parsley
a handful of fresh spinach
½ a small zucchini, cut in chunks
10 to 15 fresh basil leaves (2 tsp. dried)
1 medium clove garlic
1 cup buttermilk
¼ to ½ tsp. salt
1 tsp. lemon juice
OPTIONAL: a few pieces of ripe avocado;
    moderate amounts of other fresh
    herbs (chives, dill, cilantro)

Whip it up in a blender or food processor. Makes a generous cup.

SPECIAL SALAD DRESSINGS

BASIC VINAIGRETTE
~ the basic dressing for green salads. It keeps for weeks.

1 cup olive oil
4 to 5 Tbs. red wine vinegar
½ to 1 tsp. salt
1 to 2 medium cloves garlic, minced

Combine everything in a jar.
Cover tightly and shake well.

VINAIGRETTE VARIATIONS: (These are just a few suggestions. You can experiment even further with your own ideas.)
* add 3 to 4 Tbs. orange or apple juice, or
        2 Tbs. lemon juice plus a little grated lemon rind, plus
* very finely minced parsley and/or
* very finely minced other herbs (fresh or dried basil, dill, marjoram, chives, thyme)
* substitute some of the olive oil with a nut oil
* substitute different flavors of vinegar (fruit-infused, balsamic, champagne, etc.)
* add 1 to 2 tsp. good quality mustard
* for creamy vinaigrette: add 2 to 3 Tbs. mayonnaise, sour cream, or yogurt

SWEET & TART MUSTARD DRESSING
~ good on chilled cooked vegetables, especially Brussels sprouts, cauliflower, or broccoli

6 Tbs. olive oil
2 Tbs. Dijon mustard
4 Tbs. red wine vinegar
2 tsp. real maple syrup or honey
salt and pepper, to taste

Whisk everything together.
Cover and chill.

LOWFAT RANCH DRESSING
~ good on leafy salads made of sturdy greens, like romaine
or spinach.

1 cup buttermilk
optional: 2 to 3 Tbs. sour cream or mayonnaise (see p.44) OR
            ¼ cup lowfat cottage cheese
2 to 3 Tbs. dried onion flakes
¼ to ½ tsp. salt (to taste)
1 tsp. lemon juice
lots of black pepper

~ Whisk everything together. Keep in a tightly covered container in
the refrigerator.

LOWFAT CREAMY ROQUEFORT DRESSING
~ Make Lowfat Ranch Dressing, and add ½ cup crumbled Roquefort.

LOWFAT CREAMY GARLIC DRESSING
~ Make Lowfat Ranch Dressing, and add 1 to 2 cloves crushed garlic.

NONFAT GAZPACHO DRESSING
Oil-free and nondairy!

1 cup tomato juice
1 cup diced cucumber (peeled and seeded)
1 minced scallion
1 medium clove garlic
a few leaves fresh basil (or ½ tsp. dried)
1 to 2 Tbs. fresh (or 1 to 2 tsp. dried) dill
a small handful of fresh parsley
1 to 2 tsp. lemon or lime juice
salt and pepper, to taste

Purée everything together in a blender or food processor. Cover tightly and chill.

❧❧ HOMEMADE MAYONNAISE: ❧❧

For an oil-free version, see Plain Fake Mayo, p. 91.

❧ REGULAR (REAL) MAYONNAISE:

1 large egg
3 Tbs. cider vinegar
½ tsp. salt
½ tsp. dry mustard
1¼ cups oil (vegetable, olive, canola
~ or a combination)

1) Place the first 4 ingredients in a blender or food processor, along with 2 Tbs. of the oil. Process for a few seconds.

2) Keep the motor running as you drizzle in the remaining oil. As soon as all the oil is incorporated, turn off the machine. Scrape the mayonnaise into a container, cover, and refrigerate.

❧ TOFU (SOMEWHAT REAL) MAYONNAISE:

1 packed cup mashed tofu (firm or silken)
1 small clove garlic
1 tsp. good-quality prepared mustard
2 tsp. cider vinegar
¼ to ½ tsp. salt (to taste)
¼ cup olive or canola oil

1) Place everything except the oil in a blender or food processor. Process until very smooth.

2) Keep the machine running as you drizzle in the oil. When all the oil is incorporated, turn off the machine. Transfer to a container, cover, and refrigerate.

❧ VARIATIONS (use with either of the above):

❧ GREEN MAYO: Add a handful each of chopped parsley and chives to step 1.

❧ SESAME MAYO: Substitute a few tablespoons of the oil with Chinese sesame oil.

Macedonian Salad

...small cubes of roasted eggplant, marinated with fresh vegetables in a lemony, herby vinaigrette

1 large eggplant (about 9 inches long)-- or its approximate equivalent in medium or small eggplants-- peeled or not, and cut into 1-inch cubes, or even smaller

a little oil, for the baking tray

4 Tbs. olive oil	¼ cup (packed) finely minced parsley
2 Tbs. red wine vinegar	2 small scallions, very finely minced
1 medium clove garlic, minced	½ medium red bell pepper, minced
½ tsp. salt (more, to taste)	½ medium green bell pepper, minced
freshly ground black pepper	1 medium tomato, diced
½ tsp. basil	**OPTIONAL GARNISHES:**
¼ tsp. thyme	olives (Greek, oil-cured, or Niçoise)
¼ tsp. marjoram or oregano	yogurt
1 Tbs. fresh lemon juice	crumbled feta cheese

1) Preheat oven to 375°F. Spread the eggplant cubes onto a lightly oiled baking tray, and roast in the oven about 15 minutes, or until tender enough so a fork can slide in easily. Remove from oven.

2) Meanwhile, combine the olive oil, vinegar, garlic, salt, pepper, herbs, and lemon juice in a medium-sized bowl. Add the still-warm eggplant and stir. Cover, and let sit for at least 2 hours. (At this stage, it will keep in the refrigerator for several days.)

3) Add the remaining vegetables within an hour or two of serving. Serve garnished with olives and yogurt or crumbled feta cheese.

Tabouli

...the classic bulgur salad with garlic, parsley, lemon, mint, etc.

30 to 40 minutes to prepare

6·8 servings

You can prepare Steps 1 and 2 as much as a day or two in advance. The flavors get deeper as it sits around. A food processor does a perfect job of mincing scallions, parsley, and mint into a fine feathery state, which makes the salad much prettier and easier to eat.

1 cup dry bulgur wheat
1½ cups boiling water
1 to 1½ tsp. salt
¼ cup fresh lemon juice
¼ cup olive oil
2 medium cloves garlic, crushed
black pepper, to taste

4 scallions, finely minced (whites & greens)
1 packed cup minced parsley
10 to 15 fresh mint leaves, minced
   (or 1 to 2 Tbs. dried mint)
2 medium-sized ripe tomatoes, diced
OPTIONAL: • ½ cup cooked chick peas
         • 1 medium bell pepper, diced
         • 1 small cucumber, seeded & minced

1) Combine bulgur and boiling water in a medium-large bowl. Cover and let stand until the bulgur is tender (20 to 30 minutes, minimum).

2) Add salt, lemon juice, olive oil, garlic, and black pepper, and mix thoroughly. Cover tightly and refrigerate until about 30 minutes before serving.

3) About 30 minutes before serving, stir in remaining ingredients (including optional additions) and mix well. Serve cold with warm wedges of lightly toasted pita bread. (For more serving ideas, see Mezza, p.100.)

Lentil-Bulgur Salad

Similar to Tabouli, but more complex (although no more difficult to prepare), this salad is a perfectly balanced protein dish that can be served as a main course ~ especially for lunch on a hot summer day. All you need to complete the meal is toasted pita bread and some ripe fresh fruit for dessert. This is also a good dish to bring to potluck parties. You can easily double the amounts.

{ 1 cup dry lentils
{ 2 cups water

{ 1 cup dry bulgur wheat
{ 1 cup boiling water

¼ cup olive oil
¼ cup lemon juice
2 medium cloves garlic, crushed
1 tsp. salt
½ tsp. oregano
2 Tbs. freshly minced mint
  (or 2 tsp. dried mint)

2 to 3 Tbs. freshly minced dill
   (or 2 to 3 tsp. dried dill)
fresh black pepper, to taste
¼ cup (packed) freshly minced parsley
⅓ cup finely minced red onion
1 small bell pepper (any color), diced
½ stalk celery, finely minced
½ cup crumbled feta cheese
½ cup Niçoise olives (a scant ¼ lb.)
1 medium-sized tomato, diced
½ cup chopped toasted walnuts
squeezable wedges of lemon,
   for garnish

1) Place the lentils in a medium-sized saucepan, cover with water, and bring just to the boiling point. Turn the heat way down, partially cover, and allow to simmer without agitation for 20 to 25 minutes ~ or until tender but not mushy. Drain well, then transfer to a large bowl.

2) While the lentils are cooking, place the bulgur in a small bowl. Add boiling water, cover with a plate, and let stand 10 to 15 minutes while getting the other ingredients ready.

3) Add everything to the lentils, except tomato chunks, walnuts, and lemon wedges. Mix gently but thoroughly. Cover tightly and refrigerate.

4) Just before serving, top with tomatoes and walnuts. Garnish with lemon wedges.

White Rabbit Salad

3 cups cottage cheese (may be lowfat)

1 to 2 Tbs. honey (optional), to taste

2 to 3 Tbs. lemon juice, to taste

¼ cup (packed) raisins or currants

½ cup chopped, toasted nuts

1 Tbs. poppy seeds

2 medium-sized tart apples, diced

PLUS MANY OPTIONS:

fresh peach slices

fresh pear slices

seedless red or green grapes

orange sections

chunks of ripe honeydew or cantaloupe

Combine everything
and chill.

March Hare

HUNKY DORT!

Invented in
March 1973

15 minutes
to prepare

6 to 8
servings

COMBINE AND CHILL:

3 cups cottage cheese (may be lowfat)

2 Tbs. toasted sesame seeds

¼ cup lightly toasted sunflower seeds

1 medium carrot, diced very small

1 medium-sized ripe tomato, diced

1 scallion (whites and greens included), minced

1 small bell pepper ~ any color, minced

1 stalk celery, diced

1 small cucumber ~ peeled, seeded, and minced

½ cup (packed) finely minced parsley

a handful or two of alfalfa sprouts

2 to 3 Tbs. fresh lemon juice ⎫
⎬ to taste
salt (optional) & black pepper ⎭

1 to 2 hardboiled eggs, chopped (optional)

Thai Salad

Made entirely with ordinary and familiar supermarket items, this salad, with its tart-sweet-spicy-peanutty dressing, is surprisingly exotic. It's also very much fun to eat.

NOTE: Potatoes and eggs need to be cooked in advance. Ditto if you choose to fry the tofu. The dressing keeps for weeks, so make it any time.

THE DRESSING:

Place the peanut butter in a small bowl. Whisk in the water, and beat until well combined. Stir in remaining ingredients.

- 6 Tbs. good peanut butter
- 1 cup boiling water
- 4 Tbs. cider vinegar
- 1 Tbs. sugar or honey
- 1 to 1½ tsp. salt
- 3 to 4 medium cloves garlic, minced
- crushed red pepper or cayenne, to taste
- 2 tsp. lemon or lime juice

THE REST:

Pile up everything in a provocative yet compelling arrangement. Drizzle the dressing on top.

- 1 medium head crisp lettuce (Romaine is good.)
- 1 medium carrot, shredded or thinly sliced
- 1 small bell pepper, in thin strips
- 1 small cucumber ~ peeled, seeded, and sliced
- 2 medium-sized ripe tomatoes, in bite-sized chunks
- 2 medium (fist-sized) potatoes, boiled and sliced
- 4 to 6 hardboiled eggs, cut in wedges
- 3 cakes tofu ~ plain or fried, diced
- a small handful each (if available): minced fresh cilantro, mint, and basil
- optional: a handful or two of mung bean sprouts
- FUN OPTION: potato chips instead of, or in addition to, the boiled potato slices
- squeezable wedges of lemon or lime, for garnish

Sri Wasano's Infamous
Indonesian Rice Salad ☉

1) Place in a saucepan.
   Bring to a boil, lower
   heat, cover, and
   simmer until tender
   (35 to 45 minutes).

   { 2 cups brown rice
   { 3 cups water

2) While the rice cooks, combine in a large bowl:

   ⅓ cup peanut oil
   3 Tbs. Chinese sesame oil
   ½ cup orange juice
   1 to 2 medium cloves garlic, minced
   1 tsp. salt
   2 Tbs. soy sauce
   ½ tsp. crushed red pepper (to taste)
   2 Tbs. rice or cider vinegar
   1 cup chopped fresh pineapple (also ok
       to use canned-in-juice crushed pineapple)

3) Add the hot rice directly to the bowlful of dressing. Mix well. When it
   has cooled to room temperature, cover tightly and refrigerate until cold.
   Shortly before serving, stir in:

   3 scallions, finely minced (whites and greens)
   1 stalk celery, finely minced
   1 medium-sized red or green bell pepper, thinly sliced
   1 8-oz. can water chestnuts, drained & thinly sliced
   ½ lb. fresh mung bean sprouts
   ½ cup (packed) raisins or currants
   1 cup coarsely chopped peanuts and/or cashews,
       lightly toasted
   2 Tbs. sesame seeds
   OPTIONAL: fresh snow peas, for garnish

Preparation time:
45 minutes to an hour
(depends on how
much stuff you
choose to put in)

Kristina's Potato Salad

Yield:
6 main dish portions
(more, if serving
with other things)

This is a kitchen-sink-type of potato salad, brimming with fresh vegetables, and texturally enhanced by the addition of toasted nuts and seeds. Make it as simple or as chock-full as you have time, ingredients, and desire for. You can keep the fat content very low if you use homemade Tofu Mayonnaise (p.44 & 91) and yogurt. Serve this salad as a main dish for a summer lunch, especially if paired with a chilled soup from the previous chapter.

Boil until tender; drain and cool.

{ 6 medium potatoes (about 3 lbs.), scrubbed, and chopped into 1½-inch pieces (that's approximate, of course)

2 hardboiled eggs, chopped

1 medium bell pepper (any color), diced

3 to 4 finely minced scallions (whites and greens)

1 small cucumber (peel if waxed), seeded and minced

1 cup (packed) finely minced parsley

¼ cup (packed) minced fresh dill (about 1 Tbs. dried)

1 to 2 tsp. salt (to taste)

fresh black pepper

¼ to ⅓ cup cider vinegar (possibly more, to taste)

1 to 2 tsp. dry mustard

1 to 2 tsp. tarragon

1 to 2 Tbs. prepared horseradish

½ to 1 cup mayonnaise (see recipe for homemade, including Tofu Mayo, p.44 and Plain Fake Mayo, p.91)

½ to 1 cup yogurt or sour cream

OPTIONAL ADDITIONS:

a handful of alfalfa sprouts

1 medium carrot, diced

1 stalk celery, minced

thinly sliced radishes

fresh peas, raw or steamed

1 cup lightly toasted cashews

½ cup toasted sunflower seeds

2 to 3 Tbs. sesame seeds

fresh spinach leaves ⎫
cherry tomatoes   ⎬ for garnish
olives   ⎭

Combine well, season to taste, cover, and chill.

Preparation time: Soybeans
and grains cook for 1¼ hours.
Everything else takes about
15 minutes. (You can do the
cooking up to several days
in advance.)

Perfect Protein Salad

Crunchy cooked soybeans and chewy cooked wheat or rye berries are blended with minced fresh vegetables in a creamy lowfat dressing. A possibly interesting socio-historical note: I invented this recipe by default in 1973 while living in a house with about 10 other people. The ingredients of this salad— including a jar each of cooked soybeans and wheat berries—were the entire contents of our refrigerator. I just mixed them all together and behold, delicious!

The name was influenced by Frances Moore Lappe's first edition of <u>Diet for a Small Planet</u>, which I had just recently discovered at that time.

PRELIMINARILY: Soak the soybeans for at least 4 hours and the wheat or rye berries for at least 30 minutes. (Soaking them overnight is also fine.)

¾ cup dry soybeans, soaked

¾ cup dry wheat or rye berries, soaked

¼ to ⅓ cup cider vinegar (to taste)

1 tsp. salt

fresh black pepper, to taste

¼ cup minced fresh dill (or 2 tsp. dried)

¼ to ⅓ cup mayonnaise (see p. 44 and p. 91)

1 to 2 small cloves garlic, minced

½ cup finely minced parsley

1 cup cottage cheese or mashed tofu

3 scallions, finely minced

1 medium carrot, minced

1 small cucumber, peeled, seeded, & minced

a little bit of minced bell pepper

OPTIONAL: additional vegetables, such as minced red onion or celery, fresh alfalfa sprouts, sliced radish; fresh, ripe tomato slices, for garnish

1) Place the soaked soybeans in a medium-sized saucepan and cover with water. Place the soaked wheat or rye berries in another saucepan and add at least 2 cups of water. Bring each to a boil, partially cover, and simmer until tender. This will take between 1 and 1¼ hours. (You can also try just cooking them together in one large pot. Their cooking times are about the same.) When the soybeans are crunchy-but-tender, and the grains are chewy-but-tender, rinse them in a colander and drain well. Transfer to a medium-sized bowl.

2) Combine everything and mix well. Serve garnished with ripe tomato slices and behold, delicious!

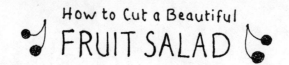

If you just want to eat a piece of ripe, fresh fruit ~ or cut up a little assortment to serve to a few people ~ instructions are probably unnecessary. But the prospect of preparing a giant bowlful of freshly cut fruit (to serve to unpredictable numbers or just to have around for unlimited high-level snacking) can be daunting. Here, to undaunt you, are some tips which I hope will be encouraging and useful. Then you can regularly and confidently serve wonderful fruit medleys to volumes of appreciative friends, and everyone will want to come over to your house all the time.

ORANGES AND GRAPEFRUIT:

Use a sharp serrated knife. Cut the skin first from the polar ends, and then from the sides. (If you simply pull off the peel with your hands, citrus fruit will retain the inelegant white matter under the skin, which you probably don't want in your fruit salad.) Hold the peeled fruit over the bowl, and cut with a gentle sawing motion in and out along each membrane, releasing segments of fruit. You will end up holding a fanlike piece of juicy refuse. Squeeze all the juice from this unit into the bowl, and discard the remains. You will have before you a bowlful of captivating citrus sections.

PEACHES AND PLUMS; APPLES AND PEARS:

Make sure they are not over- or under-ripe. Cut in half first, take out the pit or seeds, and cut into slices or chunks just before serving. (If you want to cut them in advance, drizzle with lemon juice, and cover tightly.) Stir in gently as you serve.

PINEAPPLE:

You can tell if it's ripe by smelling it. Use a stainless steel knife to cut off the top and the bottom, then carve off the skin from the sides. Be sure to cut far enough into the pineapple to get off all the traces of prickly skin. It's preferable to lose a little of the goods than to accidentally get a thorn in the mouth. (People shouldn't have to examine each mouthful before eating it.) Cut the pineapple in half, then in quarters lengthwise. Cut the center core strip from each quarter, then chop the remaining fruit into 1-inch pieces.

WATERMELON:

The seeds of a watermelon grow in line patterns. Take your chunk of fruit salad-to-be and examine it to discover the pattern of seeds. Then take a teaspoon handle and pull it through the pattern to evict the seeds. When the seeds are mostly gone, chop the watermelon into 2- to 3-inch pieces. Don't make them too small, or they'll disintegrate.

MELONS OTHER THAN WATERMELON:

Use a stainless steel straight-bladed knife or a cleaver. Cut off the skin from each end, then stand the melon on one end, and carve off the skin from the sides. After the skin is off, cut in half and remove the seeds. Chop the remaining melon into 1-inch pieces.

CHERRIES AND BERRIES:

Halve and pit cherries, and mix them in, OR leave them whole and use to garnish the top. Cut larger berries in half; leave smaller ones whole. Mix in gently or lay decoratively on top.

BANANAS, PAPAYAS, MANGOS, KIWIS:

Make sure they are ripe, but not too, too soft. Peel, slice, and lay on top just before serving. (They will mush into oblivion if mixed in.) If you must cut these fruits ahead of time, sprinkle generously with lemon or lime juice.

DEAD-OF-WINTER FRUIT SALAD:

If you want to have a fruit salad in the off-season, and you'd like it to be more interesting than just apples and bananas, try using frozen unsweetened fruit. Plastic bags of various berries, pitted cherries, and sliced peaches can usually be found in the frozen foods section of larger supermarkets. Frozen berries give off delicious and deeply-hued juice as they defrost (empty the bag into a bowl while the fruit is still frozen), and the resulting fruit salad will be very juicy and a wonderful dark reddish-purple color.

In addition to defrosted frozen fruit, a winter fruit salad can also contain: citrus sections, pineapple (fresh or canned-in-juice), apples, pears, and bananas.

TOFU SALAD

Unadulterated tofu is cloudlike and bland. Sometimes it's comforting, but sometimes it cries out for a little more action. This recipe calls for adulterating your tofu by marinating it in deep, strong flavors, which it readily absorbs. The crunchy vegetables provide a refreshing contrast.

This delicious salad gets more and more flavorful the longer it sits around, so go ahead and make it up to several days in advance.

The Marinade

4 Tbs. Chinese sesame oil

5 Tbs. rice or cider vinegar

1 Tbs. sugar

3 Tbs. soy sauce

optional: 1 to 2 Tbs. dry sherry or rice wine

2 to 3 medium cloves garlic, minced

½ tsp. salt (to taste)

crushed red pepper, to taste

optional: 1 tsp. minced fresh ginger

6 cakes (about 1 to 1½ lbs.) very firm tofu, well drained

8 to 10 medium-sized mushrooms

1 small carrot, shredded or cut into slender matchsticks

1 small bell pepper (preferably red), minced

optional: finely shredded cabbage

1 to 2 minced scallions

a handful or two of fresh mung bean sprouts

•optional toppings: •½ cup coarsely chopped peanuts
  •minced fresh cilantro
  •diced fresh, ripe tomato
  • a sprinkling of sesame seeds

1) Combine marinade ingredients in a large, shallow bowl or pan.

2) Cut the tofu into ½-inch cubes and add to the marinade, along with the vegetables. Stir gently.

3) Cover and let marinate at room temperature for at least 2 hours. Serve cold or at room temperature, topped with all or some of the garnishes.

SERVING IDEAS: ☆ as a sandwich in Pita Bread (p.113) with shredded cabbage and chopped tomatoes ☆ on hot rice, with Duck Sauce (p.97) or Chinese Mustard (p.120) ☆ in lettuce cups, with Chinese Green Onion Pancakes (p.115) and either of the above-mentioned sauces.

Alsatian Salad

Preparation time: 15 minutes   Yield: 4 to 6 servings

The original version of this dish was made with thinly cut cheese mixed with fresh vegetables in a creamy mustard dressing. Now that many people want to limit their cheese intake, I've added a Tofu Option, which is delicious! Use "savory baked" or "5-spice" tofu (a.k.a. "tofu kan"), both available in natural foods stores. Use either kind by itself, or in combination with very firm plain tofu.

Made with tofu or cheese, this is a wonderful lunch entrée.

1) Toss together very gently in a medium-sized bowl:

3 cups cut cheese ~ in thin strips or in ½-inch cubes
   (Try a combination of cheddar and Swiss, or
   something smoked), OR:

3 cups firm tofu strips
1 small cucumber ~ peeled, seeded, and cut in thin strips
1 bell pepper (any color), in small, thin strips
1 minced scallion (include greens)
OPTIONAL: ½ cup finely minced red onion

2) Combine well and add to cheese or tofu mixture:

½ cup yogurt	¼ to ½ tsp. each:
3 Tbs. mayonnaise (see recipes, p. 44 + p. 91)	paprika
1 small clove garlic, minced	basil
2 tsp. Dijon mustard	tarragon
½ tsp. prepared horseradish	dill
salt and pepper, to taste	a handful of minced parsley

GARNISHES:
fresh greens (small and leafy, like spinach or arugula)
cherry tomatoes (in the summer, look for yellow pear-shaped ones)
raw or steamed vegetables
pickles
olives
crusty bread

Four Waldorf Variations

A cross between a fruit and a vegetable salad, Waldorf Salad can be a first or second course for dinner. It also makes a good lunch entrée. Serve it on a bed of crispy lettuce, with thick slices of whole wheat toast.

♩♪ MAYONNAISE NOTES: Two of these variations have mayonnaise in the dressings. You can find recipes for homemade (regular or tofu-based) on p. 44 and p. 91 (the latter recipe is oil-free!).

I. BLUE MOON

2 medium-sized tart apples, in chunks
2 perfectly ripe pears (any kind), sliced
1 stalk celery, minced
¼ cup (packed) raisins
2 to 3 Tbs. lemon juice
¾ cup chopped toasted walnuts

Dressing:
1 cup yogurt
3 to 4 Tbs. mayonnaise
⅓ cup crumbled blue cheese
1 Tbs. honey (optional, to taste)

Combine all salad ingredients. Stir together dressing ingredients in a separate bowl, then pour over salad and gently mix.

II. CALIFORNIA

3 medium-sized tart and/or sweet apples
2 navel oranges, sectioned
1 stalk celery, minced
¼ cup (packed) raisins or currants
1 cup sliced ripe mango or papaya
   (optional, if available)   } for the top
1 cup toasted cashew pieces

Dressing:
1 cup yogurt
½ tsp. lemon rind
2 to 3 Tbs. lemon juice
1 ripe avocado, mashed
1 to 2 Tbs. honey (to taste)

Combine apples, oranges, celery, and raisins or currants. Purée together all dressing ingredients in a blender or food processor. Combine apple mixture with dressing and mix well. Serve topped with slices of ripe mango or papaya (if you're lucky enough to have some) and toasted cashews.

III. WALDORF DELUXE

3 medium-sized tart apples, in chunks
2 to 3 Tbs. lemon juice
1 stalk celery, minced
1 to 2 cups seedless grapes, whole or halved
      (optional)
1 cup diced cheddar
¼ cup (packed) minced dates
¾ cup chopped toasted pecans

Dressing:
1 cup yogurt
¼ cup mayonnaise
½ cup orange juice
½ tsp. grated orange rind

Combine salad ingredients. Whisk together dressing ingredients. Combine everything and mix well.

IV. FRUIT & VEGETABLE WALDORF

3 medium-sized tart apples, in chunks
1 cup freshly chopped pineapple
1 navel orange, sectioned
1 stalk celery, minced
1 small carrot, thinly sliced
1 red bell pepper, thinly sliced
¼ cup (packed) raisins or currants
½ to 1 cup chopped toasted almonds

Dressing:
1 cup yogurt
½ cup pineapple or orange juice
    (or a combination)
¼ tsp. cinnamon
a few dashes ground cardamom

Combine everything, and mix well.

Preparation time:
1½ hours (mostly
bean-cooking time),
plus time to chill

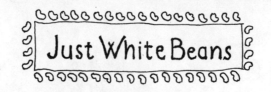

Just White Beans

Sometimes it's refreshing to have a bean salad that is a simple solo of lightly marinated beans, without a lot of little diced vegetables singing backup vocals. This is one such dish. It is delightful by itself, and downright smashing when topped with a mound of Pickled Red Onions (see below).

This salad keeps well for days if tightly covered and refrigerated. The beans can be cooked without prior soaking.

1½ cups dry white pea beans	freshly ground black pepper
3 Tbs. olive oil	½ tsp. basil
2 Tbs. red wine vinegar	¼ cup finely minced parsley
¾ to 1 tsp. salt	2 Tbs. fresh (2 tsp. dried) dill
1 to 2 medium cloves garlic, minced	Pickled Red Onions (below)

1) Place the beans in a medium-sized saucepan and cover with water. Bring to a boil, reduce heat, and cook, partially covered until tender but not mushy (1 to 1¼ hours). Drain well, and transfer to a medium-sized bowl.
2) Add remaining ingredients, mix gently, and taste to correct seasonings. Cover tightly and chill until cold. Serve topped with Pickled Red Onions.

Pickled Red Onions

Try these with any bean salad, in or with sandwiches, in countless other salads, as an antipasto dish, or even on top of homemade pizza. Pickled Red Onions are ridiculously easy to make, and keep practically indefinitely.

1 cup cider vinegar	1 tsp. salt
1 cup water	1 tsp. whole peppercorns
up to 3 Tbs. brown sugar	4 medium red onions, very thinly sliced

PRELIMINARY: Fill a teakettle with water and put it up to boil.
1) Combine vinegar, 1 cup water, sugar, salt, and peppercorns in a medium-sized bowl and stir until the sugar is dissolved.
2) Place the onion slices in a colander in the sink, and slowly pour all the boiling water over them. They will wilt slightly. Drain well, and transfer to the bowlful of marinade.
3) Cover and allow to marinate, refrigerated or at room temperature, for at least several hours. Store in the refrigerator, and use as needed.

MULTI-BEAN SALAD

Presoaked beans need up to 1¼ hours to cook. (Get everything else ready during this time.) Allow at least a few hours to marinate.

This festive and colorful salad is good with cornbread and any soup. Also, try serving it at room temperature over hot rice (you can melt some cheese into the rice) with steamed tortillas.

Try making this salad with a combination of 1 cup each: pinto, kidney, black, and garbanzo beans. Dry beans need to soak at least 4 hours – preferably overnight. Pinto, kidney, and black beans can be soaked, and then cooked, together. Garbanzos should be done separately.

4 cups dry beans, soaked
6 Tbs. olive oil
1 Tbs. minced garlic
3 to 4 Tbs. lemon juice
6 to 8 Tbs. red wine vinegar
1½ tsp. salt
lots of black pepper
¼ lb. fresh green beans

2 medium stalks celery, finely minced
⅓ cup very finely minced red onion
up to 1 cup (packed) finely minced parsley
1 small red or green bell pepper, minced
optional: a small amount of minced cucumber (peeled and seeded)
optional garnishes: cherry tomatoes
                        sieved hardboiled eggs

1) Cook presoaked beans in plenty of gently simmering water, partially covered, until just done. Keep the agitation to a minimum during the cooking, so the beans don't explode. Begin checking the beans for doneness at the 45-minute mark, just in case they are getting done early. The goal is: perfectly tender, distinct little morsels.
2) Combine oil, garlic, lemon juice, vinegar, salt, and pepper in a large bowl.
3) Trim the tips of the green beans, and steam until tender (5 to 8 minutes, or to your preference). Refresh under cold running water and drain well.
4) Drain the cooked beans and add them, still hot, to the bowlful of dressing. Add remaining ingredients and mix well. Let marinate for at least 2 or 3 hours (even longer is better).
5) Serve cold or at room temperature, garnished with cherry tomatoes, and, if desired, sieved hardboiled eggs.

Bermuda Salad

20 to 30 minutes
to prepare,
plus time to marinate

Yield: 4 to 6 servings,
depending on what goes
with it

~ marinated fresh whole green beans
and onion slices
with a touch of cheese ~

6 Tbs. olive oil
3 to 4 Tbs. red wine vinegar
1¼ tsp. salt
2 medium cloves garlic, minced
fresh black pepper, to taste
1½ cups thinly sliced red onion
3 cups boiling water
1½ lbs. fresh green beans, ends trimmed
1 to 2 cups (packed) mild or medium cheddar, grated
optional: about ½ cup finely minced parsley

1) Combine oil, vinegar, salt, garlic, and black pepper in a medium-sized bowl.

2) Place the sliced onion in a colander over the sink, and slowly douse it with 3 cups boiling water. Drain thoroughly, and transfer to the marinade, mixing well.

3) Steam the green beans until just tender, then immediately transfer to a colander and refresh them under cold running water. Drain well, and add to the marinade, along with the grated cheese (sprinkle it in as you mix gently). You can also throw in some finely minced parsley.

4) Marinate for at least several hours, either refrigerated or at room temperature, stirring occasionally. Serve cold or at room temperature.

About 45 minutes to prepare.
NOTE: You can do steps 1 + 2
a day or two in advance.

Marinated Vegetables

Delicately cooked vegetables, when marinated in a simple vinaigrette, make a festive and beautiful accompaniment to just about anything ~ or a light but filling main dish in their own right.

Steam the vegetables over water on the stove, or without water in the microwave. The following recipe is a sample method. Try substituting other vegetables ~ your favorites, or whatever is in season. Fresh or dry herbs can be used, depending on availability. Amounts are approximate and flexible.

1 medium cauliflower, in 1-inch pieces

1 medium bunch broccoli, cut in 2-inch stalks

2 medium carrots, sliced thin or in matchsticks

½ lb. mushrooms, sliced or quartered

1 small zucchini or yellow summer squash, in rounds

1 bell pepper (preferably red or yellow), thinly sliced

½ to ¾ cup olive oil

3 to 4 medium cloves garlic, minced

1 tsp. salt (maybe more later, to taste)

freshly ground black pepper

HERBS: (up to 1 tsp. if using dried; up to several Tbs. if using fresh):

> oregano or marjoram
> dill
> basil
> chives
> thyme

optional and flexible
~in other words, to taste

OPTIONAL ADDITIONS: red onion slices (very thin), cooked beans, marinated artichoke hearts, minced scallions, raw sugar snap or snow peas, small cubes of mild white cheese or firm tofu

⅓ cup balsamic and/or red wine vinegar

GARNISHES: olives, hardboiled egg slices, cherry tomatoes, feta cheese

1) Steam the vegetables until just tender in the following groupings: cauliflower + broccoli + carrots; mushrooms + zucchini; bell pepper.

2) Meanwhile, combine oil, garlic, salt, pepper, and herbs in a large bowl. Add the steamed vegetables (OK if still hot) and whatever optional additions you may opt to add. Mix well.

3) Stir in vinegar within 30 minutes of serving. (Minimizing exposure to vinegar helps the vegetables retain their bright colors.)

ANTIPASTO

"Antipasto" is a broad term referring to the first of several courses served in a traditional Italian meal. This can mean a simple dish or two of sliced tomatoes or marinated beans or vegetables, or an elaborate platter of cold sliced meats and cheeses.

In this section, I've put together a variety of vegetable preparations, all of which are very simple, and when served all (or partially) together with fresh bread or breadsticks, olives, a small platter of fruit and cheese, and a bottle of red wine can make a complete and elegant light meal.

All of the following can be made up to several days in advance, and are good served either cold or at room temperature. Leftovers go beautifully as toppings or garnishes for green salads, or as accompaniments to simple pasta dinners. "Antipasto servings" translates to "modest-sized side-dish-type servings."

Gingery Marinated Chick Peas

Preparation time: Presoaked chick peas need about 1½ hrs. to cook; everything else takes only about 10 minutes.

Yield: about 5 cups

This tastes best when made several days ahead (it gets better and better). Keep a batch around to put on top of green salads, or to serve mixed with hot rice, or by itself as an antipasto.

NOTE: You can use canned chick peas if you're in a pinch (rinse and drain them very well). Use 5 cups.

3 cups dry chick peas (soaked at least 4 hours) cooked until tender (1¼ to 1½ hours)

5 to 6 Tbs. olive oil
3 to 4 Tbs. lemon juice
1 to 2 large cloves garlic, minced
1 to 2 Tbs. finely minced ginger

2 to 3 Tbs. red wine vinegar
1 tsp. salt
½ cup finely minced red onion
freshly ground black pepper

1) Rinse and thoroughly drain the cooked chick peas.

2) Combine everything, mix well, cover tightly, and let marinate practically indefinitely. Stir from the bottom periodically during marination.

marinated small Artichokes

Sure, you could just open a jar, but these are a whole different animal, if you'll pardon the expression, and almost as easy. Really!

Use small artichokes (2-inch diameter or less). Unlike larger artichokes, in which the rough parts and the choke have had a chance to develop, little ones require only minimal trimming, and are otherwise completely edible.

1½ lbs. small artichokes
3 cups water
juice from 1 medium-sized lemon
⅓ cup red wine vinegar

⅓ cup olive oil
1½ tsp. salt
1 tsp. whole peppercorns
4 medium cloves garlic, peeled

1) Cut off the tips and stems of the artichokes. Shave off any extraneous outer leaves with scissors or a paring knife. You can leave the artichokes whole or cut them lengthwise into smaller chunks ~ whatever seems more appealing.

2) Combine everything in a saucepan. Bring to a boil, lower heat to medium, and gently boil, uncovered, until the liquid reduces to approximately 1 cup. This will take 30 to 40 minutes.

3) Remove from heat and cool to room temperature. This will keep for several weeks if stored in a tightly covered container in the refrigerator. Serve cold or at room temperature.

Bell Peppers

6 medium-sized bell peppers (try to get a mix of colors)
2 Tbs. olive oil
½ tsp. salt
½ to 1 tsp. basil
½ tsp. marjoram or oregano

fresh black pepper, to taste
2 medium cloves garlic, minced
1 to 2 Tbs. red wine vinegar

1) Stem and seed the peppers, then cut them into thin strips.

2) Heat olive oil in a heavy skillet. Add peppers, salt, herbs, and black pepper. Cook, stirring over medium heat for about 5 minutes. Then add garlic. Sauté another few minutes, or until the peppers are just tender.

3) Remove from heat, and immediately stir in the vinegar. Let marinate at room temperature for at least an hour. Store in the refrigerator, tightly covered. Serve at any temperature.

Cauliflower and Carrots

15 minutes to prepare

Yield: 6
antipasto servings

1 to 2 Tbs. olive oil
4 cups small (1-inch) cauliflowerets
3 medium carrots, in thin 1½-inch strips
½ tsp. salt (more, to taste)
2 large cloves garlic, minced

1 to 3 Tbs. balsamic vinegar
   (to taste)
fresh black pepper
OPTIONAL: a few leaves of
   fresh basil, cut in strips

1) Heat olive oil in a medium-sized skillet. Add cauliflower, carrots, and salt, and sauté over medium heat until tender (8 to 10 minutes). Stir in garlic during the last few minutes of cooking.

2) Transfer to a bowl; add vinegar, black pepper, and optional basil. Serve warm, cold, or at room temperature.

Preparation time:
   20 minutes

Swiss Chard

Yield: 4 to 6
antipasto servings

The following instructions are for preparing the chard in two batches, as it is quite bulky until it cooks down. If you have a very large wok or skillet, you might be able to fit it all into one effort.

1½ lbs. Swiss chard (ruby and/or green)
2 to 3 Tbs. olive oil
6 medium cloves garlic, minced
salt and pepper, to taste
2 Tbs. balsamic or red wine vinegar

1) Coarsely chop the chard (include as much of the stems as feasible.)

2) Heat a wok or a large heavy skillet. Add 1 Tbs. olive oil and half the chard. Turn up the heat, and stir-fry for several minutes. When the chard begins to be limp, add half the garlic, and stir-fry for just a few minutes more.

3) Transfer to a platter or bowl. Sprinkle lightly with salt, heavily with pepper, and toss with 1 Tbs. vinegar.

4) Repeat with the remaining half of the ingredients. Taste to adjust seasonings. (You may wish to add a little more olive oil.) Serve hot, cold, or at room temperature.

Marinated Mushrooms

Preparation time:
25 minutes

Yield: 4 to 6
antipasto servings

1 lb. small mushrooms (1-inch diameter)
3 Tbs. olive oil
1 to 2 Tbs. lemon juice
½ tsp. salt
¼ to ½ tsp. thyme
1 medium clove garlic, minced
fresh black pepper
a handful of finely minced parsley

1) Clean the mushrooms thoroughly, slicing off and discarding the stems. Place the mushroom caps in a saucepan with no added water, cover, and cook them over medium heat 10 to 15 minutes.

2) Meanwhile, prepare the marinade by combining all the remaining ingredients in a medium-small bowl.

3) Drain the mushrooms. (For a great soup stock, reserve the liquid.) Place the mushrooms in the marinade, stir gently, and let marinate, either refrigerated or at room temperature, for at least several hours. Stir occasionally during marination. Serve cold or at room temperature.

Roasted Green Beans
with garlic & pine nuts

Preparation time:
30 to 40 minutes,
including roasting

Yield: 6
antipasto servings

2 Tbs. olive oil
1 lb. fresh whole green beans, trimmed
1 cup thinly sliced onion
10 to 12 medium cloves garlic, peeled
salt and pepper
1 to 2 Tbs. balsamic or red wine vinegar
1 cup lightly toasted pine nuts

1) Preheat oven to 400°F. Brush a large baking tray with 2 Tbs. olive oil.
2) Spread the green beans, onions, and garlic cloves on the tray and sprinkle lightly with salt and pepper.
3) Bake for 20 minutes, intermittently stirring or shaking the tray. Taste a green bean to see if it's as tender as you like it. If not, put it back in for another 5 or 10 minutes.
4) Remove from oven; transfer to a bowl. Drizzle with vinegar, and possibly grind in some additional black pepper. Serve at any temperature, topped with lightly toasted pine nuts.

Odessa Beets

Preparation time: The beets
need 45 minutes to bake;
after that, about 10 minutes

Yield: 6 or more
servings

Except for its special guest ingredient, pineapple, this recipe is authentically Ukrainian. Traditional versions might have even more garlic and a little mayonnaise. You can try it that way if it sounds good to you. This version has no added oil.

Odessa Beets keep beautifully for at least a week. Serve them alongside just about anything, even as an accompaniment to other salads. Try using this recipe as a stuffing in baked acorn squash, or as a side dish with Solyanka (p.136). You can put it in a salad sandwich (p.119) or just eat it straight. Even if you think you hate beets, there's a good chance you will love this salad.

5 to 6 medium beets (2- to 2½-inch diameter)
2 to 3 Tbs. lemon juice
8 to 10 prunes, pitted and thinly sliced
2 to 3 medium cloves garlic, minced
½ tsp. salt
black pepper, to taste
½ cup finely chopped walnuts
1 cup finely chopped pineapple (fresh or
        canned-in-juice)

1) Preheat oven to 400°F. Wrap the beets in foil and bake until very tender (40 to 45 minutes). Rinse under cold running water as you rub off the skins. Trim the ends and coarsely grate. (A food processor fitted with the grating attachment does this in seconds.) Transfer to a medium-sized bowl.

2) Add all remaining ingredients and mix well. Chill until serving time.

Balkan Cucumber Salad

Preparation time:
10 to 15 minutes

a delicious, refreshing, very easy salad,
made without oil

Yield:
6 servings

½ cup very thinly sliced red onion
4 medium cucumbers (6 to 7 inches long)
1 tsp. salt
freshly ground black pepper
1½ cups yogurt
1 or 2 small cloves garlic, minced
1 to 2 tsp. honey (optional)
2 Tbs. freshly minced mint leaves (or 2 tsp. dried)
¼ cup (packed) finely minced parsley
2 scallions, finely minced (greens included)
1 to 2 Tbs. freshly minced dill (or 1 to 2 tsp. dried)
1 cup chopped walnuts, lightly toasted

1) Soak the onion in cold water for about 30 minutes while you get
everything else ready. Drain thoroughly and pat dry before adding
to the salad.

2) Peel (unless they're homegrown or unwaxed, in which case, don't)
the cucumbers, seed them, and cut them into thin rounds.
Place them in a medium-sized bowl.

3) Add remaining ingredients except walnuts, and mix well. Cover and
refrigerate until serving time.

4) Sprinkle the walnuts on top just before serving.

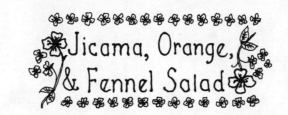

20 to 30
minutes
to prepare

Jicama, Orange, & Fennel Salad

Yield: 4 to 6
servings

❀ Jicama ("hee-ca-ma") is a Mexican tuber that looks like a light brown turnip. It is incomparably crisp and fresh-tasting as a snack, and goes beautifully with dips. If you can't find it, substitute sunchoke or radish.

❀ Serve this salad as a second course, in place of dessert. It is so satisfying and re-freshing, all yearnings for a sugary follow-up will instantly fade.

4 navel oranges
1 jicama (or a piece of one), about
   the size of a medium apple
1 small fennel bulb (2- to 3-inch diameter)
a few sprigs of arugula, if available
about 10 leaves of Belgian endive —OR—
   a handful of fresh spinach

DRESSING:
4 Tbs. olive oil
2 Tbs. orange juice
2 Tbs. balsamic or wine vinegar
2 tsp. raspberry vinegar (optional)
1 medium clove garlic, minced
½ tsp. salt
2 tsp. honey

optional garnish: Pickled Red Onions (p. 60)

1) Cut off the ends of the oranges with a sharp serrated knife, then slice the peel from the sides. With a gentle sawing motion, cut along each membrane to release the orange sections into a small bowl. Set aside.
2) Peel the jicama, and cut into very thin slices about 1½ inches long. Slice the fennel into very thin strips; include the feathery tops. Chop the arugula.
3) In a small bowl, whisk together the dressing ingredients until the honey is dissolved. Refrigerate everything until serving time.
4) Assemble the salad on a small platter shortly before serving. First, put down a layer of endive or spinach (a starburst pattern looks real nice), then a layer of jicama slices. Drizzle on some of the dressing, then sprinkle on fennel and arugula. Arrange orange sections on top, and spoon on a little more dressing. Garnish, if you are so inclined, with a few slices of Pickled Red Onion.

Marinated Sweet Potatoes & Broccoli

15 to 20 minutes to prepare;
at least 2 hours to marinate

3 medium-sized sweet potatoes or yams (1½ to 2 lbs.)

MARINADE:
½ cup walnut oil (if unavailable, use olive oil)
1 large clove garlic, minced
3 Tbs. lemon juice
2 Tbs. raspberry vinegar (if unavailable, use red wine vinegar)
1 to 1½ tsp. salt
1 Tbs. dry mustard
1 Tbs. honey
freshly ground black pepper

1 large bunch broccoli (1 to 1½ lbs.), cut into small spears

OPTIONAL GARNISHES: thin slices of green apple
                     chopped, toasted pecans

1) Peel the sweet potatoes, cut them in halves or quarters, then into thin slices. Put them up to cook, either in or over boiling water (in a steamer). Meanwhile, prepare the marinade.

2) Combine the marinade ingredients in a medium-large bowl. As soon as the sweet potato slices are tender, add them, still hot, to the marinade. Mix gently.

3) Steam the broccoli until bright green and just tender. Rinse under cold running water and drain completely. Lay the broccoli spears carefully on top of the salad. Cover tightly and marinate for several hours.

4) Within 15 minutes of serving, mix in the broccoli from on top. Serve garnished with thin slices of green apple and chopped, toasted pecans.

Carrot-Yogurt Salad

Preparation Time:
10 minutes (w/ food
processor); 20 minutes
(by hand)

Yield: 4 to 5 main-dish
servings for lunch. More,
if serving as a side dish.

1 lb. carrots, peeled and coarsely grated
2 medium-sized tart apples, grated
1 to 2 Tbs. lemon juice
1 to 2 Tbs. honey (optional)
pinch of celery seed
salt and pepper to taste
1 cup firm yogurt
OPTIONAL ADDITIONS:
1 Tbs. poppy seeds or toasted sesame seeds
¼ cup minced almonds or cashews, lightly toasted
½ cup very finely minced celery
a handful of raisins or currants
¼ cup shredded unsweetened coconut, lightly toasted
½ to 1 cup finely chopped pineapple (or crushed canned-in-juice)

Combine all ingredients and mix well. Chill. (This preparation goes
fast if you use a food processor with the grating attachment.)

COLESLAW VARIATION

Same as above, but with the following alterations:
1) Substitute 4 cups shredded cabbage plus 2 large carrots
   for the 1 lb. carrots.
2) Apples = optional.
3) Substitute cider vinegar for the lemon juice.
4) You can use half yogurt and half mayonnaise. (Recipes
   for homemade mayo are on p. 44 and p. 91)
5) Add ½ cup each: minced green pepper and red onion.
6) Same Optional Additions.

SAUCES AND DIPS

Even though they are often associated with complex and elusive cooking styles, sauces can actually be the key to simpler, not more complicated, menu planning. Those described in this chapter are accessible and nonmysterious, yet they have the impressive ability to transform plain cooked pasta, rice, beans, or vegetables into complete and interesting meals.

The sauce section begins with over a dozen ideas for pasta — some simpler, some a little more complex, and most showcasing vegetables and de-emphasizing oil or butter. Included are several variations on the theme of Italian Tomato Sauce, a traditional basil-and-oil pesto, plus two oil-free pesto ideas.

After the pasta sauces, you'll find a selection of ideas for dressing up plain cooked foods (vegetables, grains, etc.), including vegetable purées, which are the lightest of sauces, containing no fat or dairy. Also in the oil-free department is a series of tofu-based sauces, which are easy and delicious (and require no cooking). More traditional sauces are also included, plus sauces for stir-fried vegetables and a sample stir-fry recipe.

A few condiment recipes follow (including three versions of Salsa Fresca, two chutneys, and more), and then an assortment of dips, any of which could easily (and delightfully) be the focal point of a light meal. And if you love dips and appetizers so much that you would welcome an assortment of them — lavish or modest — as a complete meal, be sure to check out Mezza, p. 100.

TABLE OF CONTENTS: SAUCES AND DIPS

Pasta Sauces

This, plus the next 10 pages, contain ideas for pasta sauces, some traditional (Italian Tomato Sauce plus variations, Pesto, etc.), and some more unusual (Caramelized Onions, Stellar Mushroom Sauce, and more). I've tried to include some very easy and quick ideas, as well as a few more complex ones, so you can have a choice (and have lots of pasta in your life! There's nothing like a good plateful on a regular basis.)

These recipes assume you are using dried pasta. If you are using fresh, increase the amount of uncooked pasta by 50%. (So if the recipe calls for 1 lb. pasta, use 1½ lbs. fresh.) For a delicious and nutritious departure, try using cooked spaghetti squash sometimes, instead of pasta. Substitute 1 large (9- to 10-inch-long) squash, baked or boiled, for 1 lb. pasta.

TWO ULTRA-QUICK & EASY PASTA IDEAS

-For when you have no time to cook, and you need dinner Right Now.

1) <u>with Olive Oil, Garlic, Crushed Red Pepper, and Parmesan:</u>
- Cook pasta.
- Mince or crush some fresh garlic in the meantime.
- Drain the pasta, drizzle it with olive oil, stir in the garlic and some crushed red pepper, to taste.
- Sprinkle in some parmesan, and if you are slightly ambitious, top with a little minced parsley.

2) <u>with Marinated Artichoke Hearts from a Jar:</u>
For every 2 people:
    ½ lb. pasta (smallish shells, ziti, fusilli, or penne = best)
    1 6-oz. jar marinated artichoke crowns or hearts
    parmesan
    black pepper
- While the pasta cooks, drain the artichoke marinade into a serving bowl.
- Cut the hearts or crowns into bite-sized pieces, and add to the bowl.
- Add the drained pasta to the bowl, and toss. Serve immediately, passing the parmesan and a pepper mill.

Simplest Primavera

Pasta Primavera is a pasta-and-vegetable dish named in honor of the spring season. Ideally, it is full of the vegetable garden's earliest offerings. In keeping with that spirit, this simple version is made from the season's first greens: peas, scallions, herbs, and leafy greens.

....

1 lb. sugar snap or snow peas
5 or 6 scallions
4 Tbs. olive oil
OPTIONAL: 1 lb. leafy greens (kale, collard, or mustard),
    stemmed and coarsely chopped
½ tsp. salt
4 to 5 large cloves garlic, minced
a handful of fresh basil leaves, coarsely chopped (if
    unavailable, use parsley)
black pepper, to taste
1 lb. penne or fusilli (tube- or corkscrew-shaped pasta)
extra olive oil, for the pasta
parmesan

....

1) Trim the peas at both ends, remove the strings, and cut the pods in half across the middle (unless they're very small, in which case, leave them whole).
2) Cut the scallions in half lengthwise, then into 1½-inch pieces.
3) Put up the pasta water to boil. Cook the pasta while you sauté the vegetables.
4) Heat the olive oil in a large wok or skillet. If you are using the greens, add these first, along with the salt. Sauté for about 5 minutes over high heat, then turn heat down, and add peas, scallions, and garlic. Sauté for 5 minutes more. Stir in the basil (or parsley) and black pepper during the last minute or so. (If you are not using the greens, just begin the sauté with the peas, scallions, and garlic.)
5) When the pasta is done, drain it (or scoop it out of the hot water with a strainer or a slotted pasta scooper), and add it directly to the vegetables in the wok or skillet. Sauté the pasta with the vegetables for 2 or 3 minutes — until everything is fully mingled — and serve immediately. Pass a cruet of olive oil and some parmesan.

asparagus~mushroom sauce

Although designed for pasta, this sauce is also good in Crêpes (p. 142) or on rice or baked fish. If you have some left over, try filling an omelette with it. NOTE: The alcohol in the wine will evaporate during cooking.

1½ lbs. fresh asparagus — slender as possible, trimmed
    at the bottom and cut into 2-inch spears
2 Tbs. butter or margarine
1½ cups minced onion
1 tsp. salt
1 lb. mushrooms, sliced
½ tsp. tarragon
black pepper, to taste
1½ cups dry white wine
1 cup water
1 to 2 Tbs. flour (depending on how thick you like it)
6 to 8 cloves garlic, minced
1 lb. pasta (penne, ziti, or fusilli)
OPTIONAL: olive oil or extra butter for the pasta
parmesan
OPTIONAL: freshly minced dill, for the top

1) Steam the asparagus until just tender. Transfer to a colander over a sink and refresh under cold running water. Drain well and set aside.

2) Melt the butter or margarine in a large skillet. Add onion and salt, and sauté for about 5 minutes. Add mushrooms, tarragon, and pepper. Cover and cook over medium heat for 15 minutes, stirring occasionally.

3) Add wine and water. Turn up heat until the liquid boils. Sprinkle in the flour, whisking constantly until it completely dissolves. Lower heat, cover, and simmer about 10 minutes, stirring frequently. Add garlic, and cook about 5 minutes more. Set aside until serving time.

4) Gently reheat the sauce while you cook the pasta. Stir the steamed asparagus into the sauce at the last minute. Toss the drained pasta with a little olive oil or butter, if desired, and serve topped with sauce, parmesan, and possibly a little freshly minced dill.

Caramelized Onion Sauce

The proportions of ingredients in this delicious recipe are somewhat flexible. You can play with the amounts of onions and greens, and you can substitute other leafy greens (collard, escarole, mustard, etc.) for the arugula or spinach. Other soft pungent cheeses can be substituted for the feta or blue cheese.

NOTE: The alcoholic content of the wine will dissipate with cooking.

½ cup olive oil

4 to 6 large onions (however many you have the patience to slice), thinly sliced (about 6 to 8 cups)

½ tsp. salt

½ to 1 cup dry white wine

1 medium bunch arugula or spinach, stemmed and minced

1 cup crumbled feta or blue cheese

¾ to 1 lb. pasta (a short, shapely variety, like penne or fusilli)

1 cup chopped, toasted walnuts

parmesan

1) Heat olive oil in a large skillet or sauté pan. Add onions, and sauté over medium heat for about 15 minutes. Add salt, lower heat, and continue to cook for at least another 10 minutes (and up to an hour for really deliciously well-done onions.

2) Add white wine, turn heat back up to medium, and simmer uncovered for about 15 minutes. At this point the sauce can be set aside until you are ready to cook the pasta.

3) Turn the heat back on under the sauce when you are ready to cook the pasta. When the onions are hot, add the chopped greens, stir, and cook for about 5 minutes. Stir in the crumbled cheese, and turn heat to low while cooking the pasta.

4) After the cooked pasta is drained, add it to the sauce, and stir briefly in the pan before serving. Sprinkle with walnuts and parmesan, and serve.

Stellar Mushroom Sauce

Make this sauce with dried Chinese black mushrooms or with fresh shiitake mushrooms, if you are lucky enough to find them. (And if in the process you also happen to find fresh oyster or chanterelle mushrooms, use a combination!) These more exotic mushrooms impart a wonderful depth of flavor when used in combination with their more subtle domestic counterpart.

☆☆☆☆☆☆☆☆☆☆☆☆☆☆☆☆☆

2 oz. dried Chinese black mushrooms
   plus 3 cups boiling water
      -OR-
3/4 lb. fresh shiitake, oyster, and/or
   chanterelle mushrooms, chopped

2 Tbs. butter or margarine
1 lb. domestic mushrooms, chopped
1 cup minced onion
1 tsp. salt

6 Tbs. dry sherry
3 Tbs. flour
1 large clove garlic, minced
freshly ground black pepper
1/2 cup sour cream (lowfat OK),
   at room temperature
1 lb. fettucine
parmesan

PRELIMINARY, IF USING DRIED MUSHROOMS: Place the mushrooms in a small bowl. Add 3 cups boiling water, cover with a plate, and let stand 30 minutes. Drain the mushrooms, squeezing out and saving all the liquid. Remove and discard the stems; coarsely chop the mushrooms. Measure out 2/3 cup of the liquid for the sauce. (Save the remaining liquid for a delicious soup stock.)

(Put up the pasta water to boil.)
1) Melt butter or margarine in a deep skillet or Dutch oven. Add all mushrooms, onion, and salt. Cook uncovered over medium heat for about 10 minutes.
2) Stir in sherry. Turn heat to low, and have a whisk ready. Slowly sprinkle in the flour, whisking steadily. Keep whisking for a minute or two after all the flour is in.
3) Add garlic and black pepper, and continue to cook and stir over low heat another 5 to 10 minutes. (Meanwhile, you can cook the pasta.)
4) Stir the sour cream into the sauce, mixing well until it is completely incorporated.
5) Spoon a generous amount of sauce onto each individual plateful of hot pasta and top with parmesan.

☆☆☆☆☆☆☆☆☆☆ SOY GEVULT CASSEROLE ☆☆☆☆☆☆☆☆☆☆

A version of this sauce appeared in earlier editions of the Moosewood Cookbook in a casserole called SOY GEVULT. This dish can be made by combining 3 cups cooked soybeans with about 6 cups lightly steamed or sautéed vegetables (carrots, cabbage, zucchini, etc.). Stir in a batch of Stellar Mushroom Sauce, and bake in a 350°F. oven 35 to 40 minutes, or until heated through. Served with rice, this will feed 6 to 8.

🍅🍅 ITALIAN TOMATO SAUCE

Preparation time: 30 to 40 minutes

Yield: enough for 6 to 8 servings

🍅 The classic red sauce, without meat, and with 2 variations. Use any version of this in Lasagne (p. 132) or Eggplant Parmesan (p. 133), or on pasta of any size or shape.

Make a full batch even if you won't use it all in one meal. All of these variations keep well up to a week in the refrigerator, and much longer in the freezer.

2 to 3 Tbs. olive oil	1 1-lb., 13-oz. can tomatoes
2 cups chopped onion	1 6-oz. can tomato paste
1 medium-sized bell pepper, diced	1 Tbs. honey
2 tsp. basil	lots of black pepper
1 tsp. oregano	4 to 6 large cloves garlic, minced
1 tsp. thyme	
1½ tsp. salt	½ cup freshly minced parsley

1) Heat the olive oil in a Dutch oven or kettle. Add onion, bell pepper, herbs, and salt, and sauté over medium heat until the onion is very soft (8 to 10 minutes).

2) Add tomatoes, tomato paste, honey, and black pepper. Use a spoon to break up the tomatoes into bite-sized pieces. Bring to a boil, then lower heat and simmer, partially covered, for 20 to 30 minutes.

3) Add garlic, and cook about 10 minutes more. At this point, the sauce can sit for up to several hours, or be refrigerated for up to a week. Heat gently before serving, and add parsley at the last minute.

🍅 MARINARA VARIATION:

2 medium stalks celery, minced
1 lb. mushrooms, chopped
1 to 2 medium (6-inch) zucchini, diced
2 to 3 medium-sized ripe tomatoes, chopped
a handful of fresh basil leaves, chopped

} Add with step 1. Sauté until all vegetables are very tender.

🍅 CAVOLFIORE VARIATION:

1 large cauliflower, in 1-inch florets

} Steam until tender. Add to Step 2.

☙ SAUCE PUTTANESCA ☙

... intensely seasoned tomato sauce with a special guest star: the much-maligned but ever spunky anchovy. Of course, if you are a strict, not-even-fish vegetarian, this addition will be out of the question, and the sauce will still taste fine without it. But if you are a fish-eater, try the anchovies, even if you must overcome a degree of prejudice to do so. You will find that their flavor blends in surprisingly well.

This sauce is quick and easy — it doesn't require prolonged simmering—so you can whip it up after a busy day of work. Serve over any shape of pasta, accompanied by a green salad and some fresh crusty bread.

1 1-lb., 13-oz. can whole or crushed tomatoes
1 6-oz. can tomato paste
10 to 12 medium cloves garlic, thinly sliced
15 to 20 Kalamata (Greek) olives, carved off the pit and sliced
OPTIONAL: 3 to 4 anchovies, minced — OR— 1 to 2 Tbs.
          anchovy paste (can be increased, to taste)
black pepper   } to taste
crushed red pepper }
3/4 to 1 lb. pasta (any shape)
olive oil for the pasta
parmesan
freshly minced parsley
for PASTA MEDITERRANÉE: 1 cup crumbled feta cheese

PRELIMINARY: Put up pasta water to boil.
1) For a smoother sauce, purée the tomatoes in their liquid in a blender or food processor. For a chunkier sauce, cut the tomatoes into chunks with a knife, saving the liquid. (Skip this step if using crushed tomatoes.)
2) Combine tomatoes, their liquid, tomato paste, garlic, olives, and anchovies in a medium-sized saucepan, and gradually heat to a boil. Reduce heat, season to taste with black and crushed red pepper, and simmer about 10 minutes. (You can cook the pasta during this time.)
3) Drain the pasta, and toss with a little olive oil. Add the sauce, and serve immediately, topped with parmesan and parsley (and feta cheese, if desired).

Broccoli Sauce
for Pasta

During the height of the produce season, you can make this lovely dish particularly colorful by pairing a yellow bell pepper with red cherry tomatoes, or a red bell pepper with yellow cherry tomatoes. If you can't find Niçoise olives, use Kalamata (Greek), carved off the pit and sliced. If you use Niçoise olives, remind your guests to watch out for the pits.

2½ Tbs. olive oil
2 cups chopped onion
1 1½-lb. bunch broccoli, chopped
  into 1-inch pieces (shave and
  use as much of the stems as
  possible)
1 tsp. salt
1 large red or yellow bell pepper,
  cut into 1½-inch strips
2 cups water
2 Tbs. flour
2 cups cherry tomatoes
½ cup Niçoise olives
6 large cloves garlic, minced

¾ to 1 lb. fettucine
optional: extra olive oil, for
  the pasta
parmesan
freshly ground black pepper

OPTIONAL ADDITIONS:
• 5 to 6 sun-dried tomatoes,
  softened in hot water,
  and chopped
• 5 to 6 dried black mushrooms,
  softened in hot water,
  and sliced
• toasted pine nuts, for the top

1) Heat the olive oil in a large skillet. Add onion and sauté until very soft (10 to 15 minutes).
2) Add broccoli and salt, and sauté another 10 minutes or so — until the broccoli is just tender.
3) Add the bell pepper and sauté about 5 minutes more.
4) Turn up the heat, and add the water. Let it come to a boil, and sprinkle in the flour, whisking constantly until it is dissolved.
5) Turn the heat to very low, and gently stir in the tomatoes, olives, and optional sun-dried tomatoes and mushrooms. Stir in the garlic. Keep the sauce warm while you cook the pasta.
6) After the pasta has been cooked and drained, toss it with a little extra olive oil, if desired, and spoon the sauce on top. Sprinkle generously with parmesan and fresh black pepper, and, if available, a few toasted pine nuts.

Eggplant
Scallopini
Marsala

Preparation time:
45 minutes

Yield: about
6 servings

OPTIONAL PRELIMINARY: To peel and seed the tomatoes, heat a medium-sized saucepanful of water to boiling. Core the tomatoes, and drop them into the water for 10 seconds. Retrieve them, and pull off the skins. Cut them open; squeeze out and discard the seeds. Chop the remaining tomato pulp.

NOTE: The alcohol content of the wine will dissipate during cooking.

2 to 3 Tbs. olive oil
2 cups chopped onion
2 bay leaves
6 cups diced eggplant (about 1 large eggplant) (peeling optional)
2 medium-sized bell peppers, any color, diced
1 lb. mushrooms, chopped
2 tsp. salt
2 tsp. dried basil (or 2 Tbs. minced fresh)
1 cup marsala or dry sherry
3 to 4 medium-sized ripe tomatoes, chopped (Peeling and
    seeding = optional. See "optional preliminary" above.)
black pepper, to taste
8 to 10 medium cloves garlic, minced
1 lb. pasta—any shape
optional: additional olive oil, for the pasta
parmesan
finely minced parsley

1) Heat the olive oil in a deep skillet. Add onion and bay leaves, and sauté over medium heat until the onions are soft (5 to 8 minutes).
2) Add eggplant, peppers, mushrooms, salt, and basil. Cover and cook until the eggplant is tender (10 to 15 minutes), stirring occasionally.
3) Add wine, tomatoes, and black pepper. Simmer 10 to 15 minutes uncovered (the liquid will reduce). Stir in the garlic during the last 5 minutes. Meanwhile cook the pasta.
4) Drain the pasta, toss with a little additional olive oil, and ladle the eggplant on top. Sprinkle with parmesan and parsley, and serve.

Pesto

This most-famous potent, green version of pesto features basil, garlic, and olive oil. When tossed with hot pasta (especially long, thin varieties, like spaghetti or linguine), it adheres to each available surface, coating the pasta with intense flavor. This pesto keeps for weeks, or even months, if stored in a tightly lidded sterile jar in the refrigerator.

3 cups (packed) fresh basil leaves
3 to 4 large cloves garlic
optional: ⅓ cup pine nuts or
    chopped walnuts, lightly
        toasted

⅓ cup olive oil
⅓ cup parmesan
optional: salt and pepper,
    to taste

1) Place the basil leaves and garlic in a blender or food processor and mince well.

2) Add the nuts, if desired, and continue to blend until the nuts are ground.

3) Drizzle in the olive oil, as you keep the machine running. When you have a smooth paste, transfer to a bowl, and stir in the parmesan. Season to taste with salt and pepper. To serve, place room-temperature Pesto in a warmed serving bowl. Add hot pasta and toss thoroughly. Allow 2 to 3 Tbs. Pesto per serving.

MONDO BIZARRO SAUCE

Oil-free tomato-spinach pesto for pasta

You can choose to keep this fat-free or to add the optional nuts. This sauce is especially good on pasta with Ricotta Gnocchi (next recipe).

To peel and seed tomatoes: Drop them into simmering water for 10 seconds. Then retrieve them, and pull off the skins. Cut them open; squeeze out and discard the seeds.

4 or 5 large cloves garlic
⅓ cup fresh basil leaves
⅓ cup minced parsley
1 1-lb. bunch spinach, stemmed
2 to 3 medium-sized ripe tomatoes,
    peeled and seeded (see above)

½ cup parmesan, plus extra, for
    the top
½ tsp. salt
optional: ½ cup pine nuts or finely
    minced walnuts, lightly toasted
freshly ground black pepper
optional: olive oil for the pasta

Continued →

1) Place the garlic, basil, parsley, and spinach in a food processor or blender, and work into a uniform paste.

2) Add the tomatoes, and process just a few seconds more. Transfer to a bowl, and stir in parmesan, salt, and optional nuts (or save these for sprinkling on top).

3) Serve the room-temperature sauce with hot pasta (and possibly Ricotta Gnocchi) in a warmed serving bowl. Pass some extra parmesan, the pepper grinder, and if desired, a cruet of olive oil.

NOTE: See page 87 for another approach to oil-free pesto.

Ricotta Gnocchi

Preparation time:
30 minutes

Yield: about 2 dozen dumplings

Serve these savory cheese dumplings as an appetizer or on top of spaghetti – they taste great with any pesto (see above). You can make gnocchi up to several days ahead of time. They firm up as they refrigerate.

½ lb. mozzarella cheese
1 large handful parsley
2 large cloves garlic, minced
1 lb. ricotta (lowfat OK)
2 eggs

½ tsp. salt
¼ cup parmesan
black pepper, to taste
1¼ cups flour
optional: extra parmesan

1) Fill a large kettle with water and put it up to boil.

2) Meanwhile, grate the mozzarella (the grating attachment of a food processor does this fast) and transfer to a medium-sized bowl.

3) Mince the parsley and garlic – either by hand or in the food processor – and stir this into the grated cheese.

4) Beat together the ricotta and eggs (you can use the food processor). Add to the first mixture, along with salt, parmesan, black pepper, and flour. Mix well.

5) When the water boils, reduce heat to a simmer, and drop in small globs of batter by the tablespoon. Simmer for 15 minutes, then remove with a slotted spoon. They will be soft. Refrigerate until about 15 minutes before serving.

6) Shortly before serving, heat the broiler. Sprinkle the tops of the gnocchi with a little extra parmesan, if desired, and place them on an ovenproof plate or tray. Broil until golden and serve hot.

VEGETABLE PURÉES

These are the purest of sauces. Made almost entirely from a single cooked vegetable, each purée is a brilliant color and full-flavored. Use vegetable purées in any variety of ways (suggestions are included with each recipe). You'll be amazed at the enhancement such simplicity can offer. People will ask you for the recipes-and be shocked at the lack of complexity involved!

NOTES: ☆ There is no dairy or oil in any of these sauces! ☆ Guidelines are provided for seasoning to taste, so you can creatively tailor each recipe.

❀ RED PEPPER PURÉE ❀

2 large red bell peppers
a little salt

OPTIONAL: 1 small clove garlic, minced
black pepper, to taste

1) Core the peppers and cut them into large chunks.
2) Steam over boiling water for about 10 minutes, or until very soft.
3) Purée in a blender or food processor, and pass through a sieve into a bowl. Add a little salt, to taste (and optional garlic and black pepper). Spoon room-temperature sauce over Stuffed Eggplant (p.151) or Stuffed Zucchini (Zuccanoes, p. 154). Other uses: in or on omelettes, on baked potatoes or home fries (instead of sour cream), as a spread on toast.

❀ BEET PURÉE ❀

2 beets (2½-inch diameter)
½ cup apple or orange juice
2 Tbs. lemon juice
2 tsp. cider vinegar

2 tsp. honey
salt (about ½ tsp. or more)
black pepper, to taste

1) Place the beets in a small saucepan of water, and boil until tender (20 to 30 minutes). Cool until comfortable to handle.
2) Rub off the skins, and purée in a blender or food processor with the juices and vinegar.
3) Transfer to a small bowl. Stir in honey, salt, and pepper to taste. If necessary, thin to desired consistency with a little more fruit juice. Serve cold over sliced cucumbers for a very low-calorie salad, or at room temperature over hard boiled eggs; as a condiment to Kristina's Potato Salad (p. 52); as a topping for Zuccanoes (p. 154) or Stuffed Squash (p. 152).

❀ CARROT PURÉE ❀

3 medium carrots, peeled and
   cut into 1-inch chunks
¼ tsp. dill
½ to 1 cup water (possibly more)
3 to 4 Tbs. orange juice
¼ tsp. salt
(fresh-squeezed, if possible)

1) Place the carrot chunks in a small saucepan with ½ cup water. Bring to a boil, lower heat, and cover. Cook until very soft, adding small amounts of extra water, as needed. This will take about 15 to 20 minutes.

2) Purée until very smooth in a food processor or blender. You can go a step further by passing the purée through a sieve to get it silkier. Season to taste with salt, dill, and orange juice. Thin to desired consistency with extra water or orange juice, and correct seasonings one more time.

3) Serve on steamed asparagus or broccoli spears, on Crêpes (p. 142), on Zuccanoes (p. 154), on baked fish, and on whatever else you can think of.

❀ SPINACH PURÉE ❀

1 lb. fresh spinach, stemmed and cleaned

¼ to ½ cup water
1 medium clove garlic, minced
¼ to ½ tsp. salt
black pepper, to taste

1) Cook the spinach without added water in a covered pot for just a few minutes — until tender and very bright green.

2) Transfer to a blender or food processor, and add ¼ cup water. Purée until very smooth, and place in a small bowl. Thin to desired consistency with a little more water (or leave it thick). Season to taste with salt, garlic, and black pepper. Serve on cold steamed vegetables, on hot baked potatoes, on baked fish, on cold pasta...etc.

❀ PESTO IMPERSONATION ❀

Double the Spinach Purée recipe, and add <u>1 cup fresh basil leaves</u> to the spinach just before puréeing. <u>Increase garlic to 3 or 4 cloves</u>, and stir in <u>¼ cup parmesan.</u> Use as you would Pesto. This makes enough for 4 servings of pasta. NOTE: You may wish to toss the pasta with a little olive oil first, so it won't stick to itself.

Basic Stir-Fry Sauce

Designed to enhance Chinese-Style Stir-Fried Vegetables (recipe follows), this sauce is gingery, garlicky, and thickened just enough to give each vegetable a delicious, deeply flavored coating. You can also use this sauce (minus the cornstarch) for baked fish, or as a dipping sauce for Chinese Green Onion Pancakes (p. 115).

1/4 cup soy sauce	1 tsp. sesame oil
1 1/4 cups water	1 Tbs. sugar
1 Tbs. grated ginger	1 Tbs. plus 1 tsp. cider vinegar
2 large cloves garlic, minced	2 Tbs. dry sherry or Chinese rice wine

3 Tbs. cornstarch

1) Combine all ingredients except cornstarch in a small bowl or a 2-to 4-cup liquid measuring cup.

2) Place the cornstarch in a separate small bowl, and whisk in the mixture from Step 1.

Preparation time:
20 minutes for chopping;
15 minutes to stir-fry

Chinese-Style Stir-Fried Vegetables

There is no one correct method for stir-frying vegetables, and many of us already have our own individual (if not idiosyncratic) style. But just in case you are new to this, here is a basic method. (If you would like a more detailed description, including methods for cutting various vegetables, there is an 8-page section on sautéed vegetable dinners in the sequel to this book, The Enchanted Broccoli Forest.)

NOTE: Cook the rice or noodles first. Begin the rice at least 30 minutes before you start the stir-fry. (For 6 servings: 2 1/2 cups raw brown rice in 3 1/4 cups boiling water, covered, for about 40 minutes over lowest heat.) If you are using noodles, cook them just before you start the stir-fry. Use about 3/4 lb. (raw measure) vermicelli or flat egg noodles. Drain the cooked noodles, drizzle with a little sesame oil, and, if desired, keep them warm in a 200°F. oven.

Here is a sample assortment of vegetables that will feed 4 to 6 people. Remember, the amounts are approximate, and the vegetables themselves are flexible. Use whatever is in season. Harder, firmer vegetables (carrots, broccoli, etc.) take longer to cook and should go into the wok earlier. Medium-soft vegetables (mushrooms, zucchini, etc.) go in midway through the cooking. Very soft vegetables (leafy greens, etc.) go in last.

Have the sauce prepared and all the vegetables cut and at hand before beginning. The stir-fry goes quickly, and you don't want to overcook anything.

2 to 3 Tbs. peanut oil
1 medium-sized (3-inch diameter) onion, chopped
1/2 tsp. salt
a 1 1/2-lb. bunch broccoli, cut into 3-inch spears
1 medium (7-inch diameter) head cauliflower, broken or chopped into 1-inch florets
1 large carrot, in thin slices
4 cups coarsely chopped cabbage

1/2 lb. mushrooms, sliced
1 medium (7-inch) zucchini, quartered lengthwise and cut into 1-inch pieces
a few handfuls fresh spinach
1 batch Basic Stir-Fry Sauce (preceding page) or a double batch of Orange-Ginger Sauce (next page)

cooked rice or noodles

1) Heat a large (12-inch diameter or more) wok or a deep skillet for about 1 minute over medium heat.
2) Add oil, onion, and salt. Stir-fry for about a minute.
3) Add broccoli, cauliflower, carrot, and cabbage, and turn up the heat. Stir-fry for about 3 or 4 minutes, or until the vegetables begin to get tender.
4) Add mushrooms and zucchini. Stir-fry another 4 or 5 minutes, or until the zucchini begins to get soft. Add spinach.
5) Whisk the sauce from the bottom to reincorporate the cornstarch, and pour all of it in. Stir from the bottom of the wok or skillet, and keep the heat constantly high. Within about 3 minutes the sauce will thicken and turn all the vegetables shiny.
6) Remove from heat, spoon over rice or noodles, and serve right away.

Orange-Ginger Sauce

10 minutes to prepare   Yield: 1 cup

-No oil; nondairy.

Serve on stir-fried vegetables (see preceding pages), on vegetable-filled Crêpes (p.143), on plain cooked rice, on fish or chicken, or on Stuffed Squash (p.152-3).

2 Tbs. cornstarch
1 cup orange juice
2 to 3 medium cloves garlic, minced
1 Tbs. minced fresh ginger
¼ cup soy sauce

salt, pepper, and cayenne, to taste
OPTIONAL ADDITIONS:
½ tsp. grated orange rind
1 to 2 Tbs. honey
1 to 2 Tbs. dry sherry
1 scallion, finely minced

1) Place cornstarch in a small bowl (if you're using this for stir-fried vegetables) or in a small saucepan (if you're using this for anything else).
2) Add orange juice, and whisk until the cornstarch dissolves. Stir in all remaining ingredients (including optional additions).
3) If you are using the sauce for stir-fried vegetables, stir from the bottom, and add to the wok or skillet about midway through the cooking (see detailed instructions on the previous 2 pages). If you are using this for anything else, place the saucepan over medium heat, and gradually bring to a boil, whisking constantly. Lower heat to a simmer and cook, whisking frequently, until thick and glossy (3 to 5 minutes). Serve hot or warm.

Cashew-Ginger Sauce

10 minutes to prepare   Yield: 2½ cups

-Nondairy.

Use this quick & easy sauce on plain cooked rice, steamed broccoli, or baked eggplant slices. It's also a good accompaniment to curries (p.172-5) and Stuffed Cabbage (p.155).

2 cups toasted cashews
1 cup water
2 Tbs. minced fresh ginger
1 Tbs. soy sauce

1 Tbs. honey or sugar (white or brown)
2 Tbs. plus 1 tsp. cider vinegar
½ tsp. salt
cayenne, to taste

Purée everything together in a food processor or blender. When it is as smooth as you like it, transfer to a tightly lidded container and refrigerate. Heat gently before serving.

TOFU-BASED SAUCES

Preparation time:
5 minutes

Yield:
about 3/4 cup

♥ ♥

In my search for ways to make sauces without oil or dairy products, I was thrilled to discover something called silken tofu. It is the smoothest edible substance imaginable — and utterly neutral in flavor. Whether it is labeled "soft", "firm", or "extra firm", silken tofu has enough body to be whipped easily into a state resembling thick mayonnaise — and to hold this form, if stored properly, for days.

Here are 4 very simple sauces, made in less than 5 minutes each. They may put egg-and-oil-based mayonnaise out of a job in your home.

NOTE: Silken tofu comes in little vacuum-packed boxes, and is sold in most natural foods stores. Because of the ingenious way in which it is packaged, it has a long shelf life before it is opened.

♥ ♥

For each of the following, use 1 box (10 1/2 oz.) silken tofu, soft or firm. Place all ingredients in a blender, and whip until smooth. Store in a tightly covered container in the refrigerator. Serve cold or at room temperature. Each is good for sandwiches, baked potatoes, steamed vegetable topping, artichoke dipping, and anywhere you would use mayonnaise.

I. Plain Fake Mayo
   1 small clove garlic, minced
   2 to 3 tsp. cider vinegar
   1/2 tsp. salt

> > > >

II. Faux Aioli
   2 to 3 medium cloves garlic, minced
   1/2 tsp. salt
   1/2 tsp. dry mustard
   1/2 tsp. cider vinegar
   OPTIONAL: a small handful of freshly minced chives and /or parsley.

III. Greek Lemon Sauce
   (NOTE: In earlier editions, this was made with an egg plus an extra yolk. No more!)
   1 Tbs. fresh lemon juice
   1/2 tsp. salt
   a few dashes of white pepper

< < < <

IV. Horseradish Sauce
   (Formerly, this contained sour cream and egg yolks. Unnecessary!)
   2 tsp. fresh lemon juice
   1/2 tsp. salt
   2 tsp. prepared horseradish
   white pepper, to taste
   OPTIONAL: minced chives

♥ ♥ ♥ ♥ ♥ ♥ ♥ ♥ ♥ ♥ ♥

ZIPPY CHEESE SAUCE

Preparation time:
20 minutes

Yield: 4 to 5
servings

Here is your regular old-fashioned cheese sauce, spruced up a little. Whip this up whenever you need some comfort food in a hurry. Serve it in or over omelettes, over steamed vegetables (especially cauliflower, broccoli, or asparagus), or even over whole wheat toast with some sliced apples on top. And when you feel tugs of longing and nostalgia, you can mother yourself by mixing Zippy Cheese Sauce with cooked macaroni (use 3/4 lb. raw macaroni with a batch of this sauce for 3 to 4 servings) and some extra cheese. Bake it in a casserole with bread crumbs on top at 350°F. until heated through (about 30 minutes) for 1950s-style Macaroni and Cheese.

2 Tbs. butter or margarine
2 Tbs. flour
1 tsp. dry mustard
2 cups warm milk (lowfat OK)
1 cup (packed) grated cheese (a medium-sharp
        cheddar works well)
salt and white pepper, to taste
OPTIONAL ADDITIONS:
        1/2 tsp. prepared horseradish
        a few shakes Tabasco Sauce
        1 small clove garlic, minced

1) Melt the butter or margarine over low heat in a small saucepan.

2) Whisk in the flour and dry mustard; keep whisking for about a minute after it dissolves.

3) Add the milk. Cook over medium heat, whisking frequently, for about 5 minutes, or until thickened.

4) Add the cheese, and stir until it melts.

5) Season to taste with salt, white pepper, and optional hot stuff.

now very popular

Rarebit

... the old-fashioned Welsh cheese sauce, spiked with beer. Serve this over toast and/or steamed broccoli or asparagus. This also works beautifully as a sauce for baked or boiled potatoes.

NOTE: The alcohol content of the beer largely dissipates with cooking.

2 Tbs. butter or margarine
2 Tbs. flour
1 tsp. dry mustard
1½ cups beer or ale, at room temperature
   (OK if flat)
1 packed cup grated cheddar (about ½ lb.)
1 tsp. prepared horseradish
1 medium clove garlic, minced
salt, black pepper, and cayenne — to taste

UNDERNEATH THE SAUCE:
toast, and/or
steamed broccoli or asparagus, and/or
baked or boiled potatoes

NEXT TO, OR ON TOP OF, THE SAUCE:
chunks of ripe tomato
slices of tart apple
chopped, toasted walnuts

1) Melt the butter or margarine in a medium-sized saucepan. Sprinkle in the flour and dry mustard, whisking constantly.
2) Add the beer or ale, and keep whisking as you bring it to a boil. Lower the heat, and simmer for about 10 minutes, mixing frequently.
3) Add the remaining ingredients, and stir until the cheese melts. Serve hot over thick slices of toast (sourdough, rye, or pumpernickel are especially good) or over steamed vegetables and/or cooked potatoes. Garnish with tomatoes or apples, and if it appeals to you, a few toasted walnuts.

Nachos Sauce

Watch this sauce turn plain beans, rice, and tortillas into a special meal. Serve with a green salad topped with Guacamole (p. 108).

TO PEEL AND SEED THE TOMATOES: Cut out the cores, and immerse the tomatoes in simmering water for a slow count of 10. Retrieve the tomatoes, peel them, and cut them open. Squeeze out and discard the seeds; chop the remaining pulp.

2 Tbs. olive oil
1½ cups chopped onion
¾ tsp. salt
1 tsp. cumin
½ tsp. coriander
¼ tsp. cayenne
1 large bell pepper, diced

3 medium-sized ripe tomatoes, peeled, seeded, and chopped (see above)
2 Tbs. flour
12 oz. beer or ale (not too bitter)(OK if flat), at room temperature
3 medium cloves garlic, minced
1 to 2 tsp. sugar, if necessary (if the beer is still too bitter in spite of your best intentions)
2 cups (packed) mild white cheese (can be reduced or omitted)
optional: freshly minced cilantro, for the top

1) Heat olive oil in a medium-sized saucepan. Add onion and salt, and sauté for 5 minutes, or until the onion is soft.
2) Add cumin, coriander, cayenne, bell pepper, and tomatoes. Cover and cook over medium heat, stirring occasionally, for about 30 minutes. The peppers should be very tender.
3) Whisk in the flour, making sure all the lumps dissolve. Stir in the beer, bring to a boil, then lower heat to a simmer. Cook gently, uncovered for about 15 minutes. Stir in the garlic; cook 5 minutes more. Taste, and add sugar, if needed.
4) Add the cheese, stirring until it melts. Serve hot over beans and rice (or cooked vegetables or whatever) with freshly steamed tortillas. Sprinkle freshly minced cilantro over the top.

MEXICAN RED SAUCE

Preparation time:
about 30 minutes
mostly for simmering

Yield: enough for
6 servings of
Enchiladas (p. 167)
and 8 servings
of Tostadas (p. 168)

2 tsp. olive oil
1 cup minced onion
½ tsp. salt
1½ tsp. cumin
2 tsp. chili powder
3 cups chopped tomatoes (4 to 6 medium-sized ones) - peeling
   and seeding optional (see instructions on opposite page)
1 cup water or tomato juice
black pepper and cayenne, to taste
4 to 6 medium cloves garlic, minced
optional: freshly minced cilantro, for the top

1) Heat olive oil in a medium-sized saucepan. Add onion and salt,
and sauté over medium heat for about 5 minutes, or until the
onion is translucent. Add cumin and chili powder, and sauté
about 5 minutes more.

2) Add chopped tomatoes and water or juice. Bring to a boil,
partially cover, and lower heat. Simmer at least 30 minutes
(or even longer). Add the black pepper, cayenne, and garlic at
any time during the cooking. (The later you add the garlic, the
more distinct its presence.) Add the cilantro when you are finished cooking the sauce.

3) The sauce can be left in chunky form, or you can purée all
or part of it in a blender or food processor.

HOT SAUCE VARIATION:

Follow the recipe for Mexican Red Sauce. When you sauté the
onion, add 1 Tbs. or more crushed red pepper or 1 to 2 tsp.
finely minced serrano or jalapeño chilies. (Be very careful to
wash your hands thoroughly after handling any part of the
chilies, or even after thinking about them.)

SALSA FRESCA

Great as a dip for chips, with any bean dish, next to omelettes, with plain rice, on top of Tostadas (p.168-9), or in partnership with Zingy Bean Dip (p.106) or Guacamole (p.108). If you eat chicken or fish, try serving the Pineapple or Mango Salsa alongside—they make exquisite relishes.

Pineapple Salsa

2 cups minced fresh (or canned-in-juice) pineapple
2 medium cloves garlic, minced
2 to 3 Tbs. minced fresh mint
2 Tbs. fresh lime juice
¼ tsp. salt
¼ tsp. cumin
cayenne, to taste

15 minutes to prepare (w/ fresh pineapple) OR 5 minutes (w/ canned) —Yield: 2 cups

Combine everything, cover tightly, and refrigerate. This keeps a long time.
For an exotic taste sensation, try spooning a little of this onto a bowlful of Brazilian Black Bean Soup (p. 26).

Mango Salsa

2 Tbs. finely minced red onion
2 cups boiling water
1 average-sized (about 6 inches long) ripe mango (if you're lucky enough to find one) —about 1½ cups minced
2 Tbs. fresh lime juice
1 medium clove garlic, minced
½ tsp. salt
2 Tbs. minced fresh cilantro
optional: cayenne, to taste

10 minutes to prepare
Yield: 1½ cups

Place the minced onion in a small strainer over a bowl. Slowly pour the boiling water over the onion, then let it sit for 5 minutes. This will soften its bite, and turn it a striking shade of purple-pink.
Combine all ingredients and mix gently. Cover tightly and refrigerate.

Tomato Salsa

3 medium-sized ripe tomatoes
2 scallions, finely minced
2 medium cloves garlic, minced
a handful of parsley, finely minced
a handful of cilantro, finely minced
1 tsp. lightly toasted cumin seeds
¾ to 1 tsp. salt
1 Tbs. cider vinegar
1 Tbs. olive oil
1 Tbs. fresh lime juice
crushed red pepper, to taste

10 minutes to prepare
Yield: 1½ to 2 cups

Drop the tomatoes into a potful of simmering water for 10 seconds. Take them out, pull off the skins, and squeeze out the seeds. Dice the remaining pulp. Combine everything in a small bowl or container. Cover tightly and chill.

NOTE: To toast the cumin seeds, use a small skillet over a low flame or a toaster oven. With either method, watch them carefully so they won't scorch.

Preparation time:
10 minutes
to assemble;
30 minutes
to simmer

Yield:
about 2 cups

You can buy duck or plum sauce in most Asian groceries, but homemade is easy – and distinctly better. Keep this around to use as a condiment for many different things. You can mix Eastern metaphors by serving this alongside Thai Salad (p. 50) or Indonesian Rice Salad (p. 51), or with Samosas (p. 170). Duck Sauce is also good with squash casseroles (p. 140) or Stuffed Squash (p. 152).

This keeps very well for weeks if stored in a sterile airtight container in the refrigerator.

> 5 cups mixed peeled, chopped fruit (apples, pears, peaches, and/or plums
> 1 cup water
> ¼ cup cider vinegar
> ¼ cup (packed) light brown sugar
> ¼ tsp. salt
> 2 to 3 medium cloves garlic, minced
> ½ tsp. dry mustard
> optional: up to ½ tsp. crushed red pepper

1) Combine everything in a medium-sized saucepan and bring to a boil.

2) Turn the heat down, and simmer uncovered until all the fruit is very soft (about 30 minutes).

3) Cool thoroughly, then chill.

CHUTNEY

Serve chutney with any Indian dish (see pages 170 through 175), and with whatever else you can think of: sandwiches (see p. 117, and pages 120-21), soups, stews, and if you are not a vegetarian, with fish or chicken.

These 2 chutneys are easy to make. Just combine everything in a saucepan, bring it to a boil, and let it simmer. It's hard to go wrong. <u>Preparation time for each</u>: a few minutes to assemble, plus 45 minutes to cook. Then cool and chill. <u>Yield</u>: about 1½ cups each. Chutney keeps very well in the refrigerator if kept in a sterile, tightly lidded jar — and it goes a long way.

APPLE CHUTNEY

1½ lbs. tart apples
1 medium clove garlic, minced
1 Tbs. minced fresh ginger
1 tsp. cinnamon
1 tsp. cloves or allspice
½ tsp. salt
½ cup (packed) brown sugar
⅓ cup cider vinegar
cayenne, to taste

1) Coarsely chop the apples (peeling is optional). Place them in a medium-sized saucepan with all remaining ingredients. Bring to a boil, then lower heat to a simmer.
2) Simmer uncovered for about 45 minutes, or until everything is very soft. Cool, then transfer to a sterile jar with a lid. Chill.

TOMATO CHUTNEY

2 lbs. unripe tomatoes (about 6 medium-sized ones, the greener, the better)
2 Tbs. minced fresh ginger
1 tsp. mustard seeds
1 tsp. cumin seeds

1 tsp. coriander (optional)
¾ tsp. salt
¼ cup cider vinegar
¼ cup (packed) brown sugar
¼ cup white sugar
cayenne, to taste
2 Tbs. minced garlic

1) Dice the tomatoes, and place them in a medium-sized saucepan with all remaining ingredients, except the garlic.
2) Bring to a boil, lower the heat, and simmer uncovered for 45 minutes or until everything is well mingled and very soft. Add the garlic during the last 5 or 10 minutes of cooking. Cool, then transfer to a sterile jar with a lid, and chill.

One of the many condiments served in a traditional Indian meal, Raita is a yogurt preparation with small amounts of seasoning and a hint of minced or grated fresh vegetables. It is designed to cool and relax the palate between bites of heavier, more intensely seasoned dishes. Serve Raita with any curry (see pages 172 through 175) or with Samosas (p.170) or with Gingered Carrot Soup (p.22) or Curried Squash and Mushroom Soup (p.15). This can be put together in just minutes.

NOTE: For a deeper flavor, the cumin and optional fennel seeds can be lightly toasted first. Cook them without oil in a small, heavy skillet over medium heat, stirring frequently, for about a minute — or until they give off a toasty aroma.

2 cups yogurt

1 tsp. cumin seeds

salt and cayenne, to taste

OPTIONAL ADDITIONS (add some or all):

1 small cucumber (about 5 inches long), peeled, seeded, and minced or grated

1 small ripe tomato, diced

¼ cup finely minced onion

½ cup finely minced bell pepper (any color)

½ tsp. fennel seeds

Combine everything in a small bowl and mix gently. Cover tightly, and refrigerate until serving time.

10 minutes to prepare
(after chick peas are
cooked)

HUMMUS

A tangy and delicious chick pea purée from the Middle East, Hummus is a perfect dip or sandwich spread, and an ideal component for a Mezza (see below). Preparation is super-quick if you use a food processor.

NOTE: This recipe calls for 3 cups cooked chick peas. You can soak and cook dry ones, but canned work just as well.

2 to 3 medium cloves garlic, sliced
a large handful of parsley
2 healthy scallions, in 1-inch pieces
3 cups cooked chick peas (2 15½-oz. cans, rinsed and well drained)

6 Tbs. tahini
6 Tbs. fresh lemon juice
¾ to 1 tsp. salt (to taste)
optional: cayenne and a little cumin, to taste

1) Place garlic, parsley, and scallions in a food processor or blender, and mince.
2) Add chick peas, tahini, lemon juice, and salt, and purée to a thick paste. (You can also do the mincing and mashing by hand. The Hummus will have a coarser texture, but that can be nice, too.)
3) Season to taste, if desired, with cayenne and cumin (and correct the salt, if necessary). Transfer to a tightly lidded container and chill.

MEZZA

In Middle Eastern and some Balkan cuisines, it is common to serve a variety of appetizers, dips, salads, and garnishes on a platter (or several platters) at the beginning of a festive meal—or as the meal itself. Here is a list of the dishes in this book that could be used in any combination to make a Mezza at home for your family and friends. Don't forget to garnish lavishly—make it beautiful! Serve with Pita Bread (p. 113) and/or sesame crackers.

Tabouli (p. 46)
Lentil-Bulgur Salad (p. 47)
Eggplant Dips (p. 104-5)
Hummus (above)

Tahini-Lemon Sauce (p. 103)
Yogurt Cheese (p. 102)
Wicked Garlic Dip (p. 102)
Walnut Pâtés (opposite page)

Felafel (p. 116)
Balkan Cucumber
Salad (p. 69)
Stuffed Grape Leaves
(p. 149)

Garnishes: ☆ small sprigs of fresh herbs (parsley, mint, thyme, marjoram, dill, cilantro) ☆ pepperoncini ☆ Kalamata olives ☆ radishes, plus small, artful cuts of other vegetables ☆ feta cheese ☆ cherry tomatoes ☆ beautiful red pomegranate seeds sprinkled over the top of everything

Two Exotic Walnut Pâtés

Feta-Walnut Dip

10 minutes to prepare
Yield: about 6 servings

1 cup chopped walnuts
a handful of fresh parsley
1 cup crumbled feta cheese
½ cup water or milk
optional: 1 small clove of garlic

1 tsp. paprika
cayenne, to taste
a little olive oil
a little oregano (dried, or even
  better: a few fresh sprigs)

1) Place the walnuts and parsley in a blender or food processor, and blend with a series of quick spurts.
2) When the nuts are ground, add remaining ingredients except olive oil and oregano, and purée until smooth.
3) Transfer to a small serving bowl, cover tightly, and chill. Just before serving, drizzle the top with a little olive oil, and garnish with small sprigs of fresh (or a light sprinkling of dried) oregano. Serve on sesame crackers or toasted pita wedges, or as a dip for raw vegetables.

Vegetable-Walnut Pâté

30 minutes to prepare
Yield: about 6 servings

It really does taste like chopped liver.

1 Tbs. vegetable oil
½ cup minced onion
½ tsp. salt
1½ cups chopped fresh green beans
2 hardboiled eggs (yolks may
    be omitted)

¼ cup chopped walnuts
1 to 2 Tbs. white wine — or
    2 tsp. fresh lemon juice
1 to 2 Tbs. Mayonnaise (p. 44)
black pepper, to taste
a handful of parsley

1) Heat oil in a small skillet. Add onion and salt, and sauté over medium heat for about 10 minutes — until the onion begins to brown. Add the green beans, and sauté until they are tender (another 8 to 10 minutes).
2) Combine everything in a blender or food processor and grind into a uniform paste. (You can also chop or mash it by hand, à la countless grandmothers.) Serve as an appetizer with crackers and raw vegetables, or as a great sandwich spread.

✳ Yogurt Cheese ✳

Yogurt can be made into a lovely soft cheese by simply pressing out much of its water. You can use lowfat or even nonfat yogurt, and still, the resulting cheese will be thick and rich tasting.

The procedure:

1) Start with double the amount you want to end up with. So, in order to get 1 cup of yogurt cheese, use 2 cups of yogurt. Place a colander in the sink, and line it with about 6 layers of cheesecloth, cut to about 10 inches.

2) Place the yogurt in the cheesecloth, wrap the cloth around it, and secure it tightly with a clip or a bag tie.

3) Place a 2- to 3-lb. bag of beans on top, and let it sit there for at least 6 to 8 hours. The water from the yogurt will slowly drip out the bottom, and the creamy solids will remain. (NOTE: The longer it sits, weighted and dripping, the thicker the cheese will be.)

4) Remove the cheesecloth, wrap the cheese well, and refrigerate. To serve, top with a drizzle of olive oil and small amounts of freshly minced herbs (marjoram, dill, parsley, chives), or just a little salt and some freshly ground pepper. Serve as an appetizer (see Mezza, p. 100) or keep on hand for sandwiches.

Preparation time:
20 minutes

Wicked Garlic Dip

Yield: about 2 cups (a little goes a long way)

3 medium (average fist-sized) potatoes, peeled and diced
3 medium cloves garlic, peeled
up to ⅓ cup mayonnaise (see p. 44 and p. 91)
½ tsp. salt

1) Boil the potatoes until very soft, and drain well. Transfer to a food processor fitted with the steel blade, or to a mixing bowl.

2) Without waiting for the potatoes to cool, add the remaining ingredients. Whip until very smooth, using either the food processor or an electric mixer.

3) Cover tightly and chill. Serve as an appetizer (see Mezza, p. 100) or by itself, garnished with raw vegetables, or as a spread (great on sesame crackers or toasted pita wedges).

Tahini-Lemon Sauce

Make a batch of this on a regular basis — it's remarkably quick and easy. It can be thinned down to the consistency of a salad dressing (try it on romaine lettuce with chunks of ripe tomato and Kalamata olives) or left thick enough to be either a spread or a dip for raw vegetables and crackers. Find a consistency somewhere between thick and thin, and use it as a sauce for steamed greens, carrots, and cauliflower. Serve it with Felafel (p. 116), or drizzled over Hummus (p.100) in a pita bread (p. 113) sandwich. Tahini-Lemon Sauce is as indispensable as it is hard to categorize.   By the way, another attribute: it keeps for weeks if stored in the refrigerator in an airtight container.

NOTE: Earlier versions of this recipe contained yogurt or buttermilk. This one is dairy-free.

3/4 cup sesame tahini
5 Tbs. fresh lemon juice
1 small to medium clove garlic, minced
3/4 to 1 1/2 cups water (depending on desired thickness)
1/2 to 1 tsp. salt, to taste (will vary with amount of water used)
a handful of very finely minced fresh parsley
optional: cayenne, to taste

1) Place tahini, lemon juice, and garlic in a food processor fitted with the steel blade. (You can also use a blender.) Begin to process.

2) Keeping the motor running, slowly drizzle in the water, checking every now and then to monitor the consistency. When it is as thick/thin as you want it, turn off the machine.

3) Transfer to a small bowl or container, and season to taste with salt, parsley, and, if desired, cayenne. Cover tightly and refrigerate until ready for use.

EGGPLANT DIPS

Baba Ganouj ("Ga-NOOSH")

The classic Middle Eastern eggplant appetizer, plus a few variations on the theme. The instructions call for baking the eggplant, but if you have the opportunity to grill it over hot coals or to roast it over a direct flame, the Baba Ganouj will taste even better.

> 40 minutes to prepare

> Yield: 4 to 6 servings

a little oil, for the baking sheet
1 medium (7-inch) eggplant
2 medium cloves garlic, minced
1/4 cup fresh lemon juice
1/4 cup sesame tahini
1/2 tsp. salt
black pepper and cayenne, to taste
olive oil ⎫
freshly minced parsley ⎬ for the top

1) Preheat oven to 350°F. Lightly oil a baking sheet.
2) Slice the eggplant in half lengthwise, and place face-down on the baking sheet. Bake for 30 minutes or until very tender. Cool until it's comfortable to handle.
3) Scoop out the eggplant pulp, and discard the skin. Place the pulp in a food processor or blender, and add the garlic, lemon juice, tahini, and salt. Purée until smooth. (Another alternative is to mash by hand, leaving the eggplant a little chunky.)
4) Transfer to an attractive serving dish, cover tightly, and chill. Drizzle the top with a little olive oil and sprinkle with minced parsley just before serving. Serve with crackers. (Also, see Mezza, p.100.)

VARIATIONS:

I. 1 Tbs. olive oil ⎫
    1 cup finely minced onion ⎪ Heat olive oil in a small skillet. Add every-
    1/2 lb. mushrooms, minced ⎬ thing else and sauté 10 to 15 minutes,
    1/2 tsp. salt ⎪ or until tender. Stir into puréed eggplant
    1 tsp. dill ⎭ mixture.

II. 1/2 cup firm yogurt or Greek Lemon Sauce (p. 91) ⎫ Add to purée;
     1/2 tsp. cumin ⎭ mix well.

Spicy Eggplant Relish

45 minutes to prepare / Yield: 4 to 6 servings

Serve this as an accompaniment to any curry (p.172-75), with Samosas (p.170), Hummus (p.100), Felafel (p.116), or Tabouli (p.46). It is also good on plain crackers or as a dip for raw vegetables.

2 Tbs. olive oil
1 cup minced onion
1 medium eggplant (7 to 8 inches long), diced
½ tsp. salt
½ tsp cumin
1 medium-sized bell pepper, minced
1 medium clove garlic, minced
1 Tbs. lemon juice
cayenne, to taste

1) Heat olive oil in a medium-sized skillet. Add onion, eggplant, salt, and cumin, and sauté over medium heat for 15 to 20 minutes — until the eggplant is tender.

2) Add bell pepper, and sauté for about 10 minutes more.

3) Stir in garlic and lemon juice. Cook for about 5 more minutes. Add cayenne to taste, and adjust the salt, if necessary. You can leave it chunky, or mash a little bit by hand. Serve warm, at room temperature, or cold.

Zingy Bean Dip

Preparation time: less than 10 minutes

Yield: about 2 cups

It's hard to find anything new to say in the Bean Dip Department, but this one gets a few words in.

Canned pinto beans work so well in here that I encourage you to use them. Be sure to rinse and drain them well. If you also use a food processor, this recipe will be very quick.

Serve it with chips, vegetables, crackers, or warmed flour tortillas. Pair it with any Salsa Fresca (p. 96) for some serious appetizer activity.

To peel and seed a tomato: Drop it into a pan of boiling water for 10 seconds. Remove it, and peel off the skin. Cut the tomato open; squeeze out and discard the seeds. Chop the remaining pulp.

2 cups cooked pinto beans (1 15-oz. can),
     rinsed and well drained
2 Tbs. fresh lime juice
1 medium-sized tomato, peeled and seeded (see above)
1 to 2 medium cloves garlic, minced
a handful of parsley
a handful of cilantro
3/4 tsp. cumin
optional: 1 scallion, minced
1/4 to 1/2 tsp. salt
black pepper and cayenne, to taste

Whip it all up together in a food processor or a blender.

CHINESE PEANUT SAUCE

10 minutes to prepare

Yield: 1 potent cup

This sauce is verrrry intense! Try it as a dip for raw and/or lightly steamed vegetables, or as a dressing for cold cooked noodles (you can thin it with a little water for this). You can also use it for Eggplant and Peppers in Spicy Peanut Sauce (below), and serve it as an appetizer.

½ cup good peanut butter
½ cup water
2 Tbs. soy sauce
2 Tbs. sugar
3 medium cloves garlic, minced
1 tsp. cider vinegar
1 to 2 Tbs. minced fresh cilantro
cayenne, to taste
salt, to taste (if peanut butter is unsalted)

1) Place peanut butter in a small bowl. Add the hot water, and stir patiently with a spoon or a small whisk until uniformly mixed.
2) Stir in remaining ingredients and mix well. Cover tightly and refrigerate. Let come to room temperature before serving.

Eggplant & Peppers in Spicy Peanut Sauce

30 minutes to prepare

Yield: 6 servings

a little oil, for the baking tray
1 medium (7-inch) eggplant, unpeeled, and cut into inch-thick strips, then into 2-inch pieces
salt
1 large bell pepper ~ any color, cut into 1-inch pieces
1 recipe Chinese Peanut Sauce (above)

1) Preheat oven to 375°F. Lightly oil a baking tray.
2) Spread the eggplant pieces on the tray and salt lightly. Let stand 10 minutes.
3) Bake the eggplant until tender (about 15 minutes). (Prepare the sauce during this time.) During the last 5 minutes of baking, add the pepper pieces to the tray.
4) Cool the vegetables to room temperature, then transfer to a bowl or container. Add the Chinese Peanut Sauce and mix gently. Serve at room temperature or cold.

Guacamole

For chips and raw vegetables
AND
For Tostadas (p. 168-9)
AND
For Sandwiches
AND
On top of Salads
AND
Wherever else you wish to invite it along

BASIC GUACAMOLE:
2 Tbs. fresh lemon or lime juice
2 medium-sized ripe avocadoes
1 to 2 medium cloves garlic, minced
½ tsp. salt (possibly more, to taste)

OPTIONAL AUGMENTATIONS:
½ tsp. cumin (possibly more, to taste)
½ tsp. chili powder
black pepper and cayenne, to taste
tiny amounts of: minced green or red bell pepper
                 peeled, seeded, and finely minced cucumber
                 diced ripe tomato
2 to 3 Tbs. mayonnaise (see p. 44 and p. 91)

1) Place the lemon or lime juice in a medium-sized shallow bowl.

2) Add the avocado (you can just cut it open and spoon it out of its skin), and mash with a fork to whatever consistency you like.

3) Stir in remaining ingredients. Cover tightly and chill. NOTE: To help the Guacamole retain its color, add the avocado pits. Remove them just before serving.

A FEW BAKED THINGS
AND
SANDWICHES

Without expanding into a comprehensive thesis on bread baking (which can be found in the sequel to this book, <u>The Enchanted Broccoli Forest</u>), this chapter presents just a few choice recipes for simple breads. The popovers, corn breads, and flatbreads are all quick and unyeasted. Focaccia and Pita Bread are yeasted, but still quite easy and very rewarding.

Except for Felafel, the sandwich fillings that follow the breads are more suggestions than actual recipes. Perhaps you just need a few ideas for fitting a decent little hand-held meal into the middle of your day ~ and perhaps these will help.

TABLE OF CONTENTS: BAKED THINGS AND SANDWICHES

CUSTARDY POPOVERS

Crisp and puffy, full of hot air and a layer of custard on the inside, Popovers are very easy to throw together on a moment's notice, and they can lend a festive spirit to even a simple bowl of soup. The custard quotient depends on how many eggs you use. This recipe is very flexible, and will work with 2, 3, or 4 eggs.

2 to 3 Tbs. melted butter or margarine, for the pan
2, 3, or 4 large eggs
1¼ cups milk (lowfat OK)
1¼ cups flour
½ tsp. salt

1) Preheat oven to 375°F. Brush the insides of 12 muffin cups with melted butter or margarine.

2) Beat together the eggs and milk in a medium-sized bowl. Add the flour and salt, and beat with a whisk until reasonably well blended. It's fine if the batter has a few lumps.

3) Fill each muffin cup about ½ to ⅔ full. Bake 25 minutes if using 2 eggs, 30 minutes for 3 eggs, and 35 minutes for 4 eggs. Try to refrain from opening the oven during baking.

4) Remove the popovers from the pan immediately, and prick each with a fork to let the steam escape. (This helps them hold their shape.) Serve as soon as possible, either plain or with butter and/or jam.

FOCACCIA

~an easy olive oil-and-rosemary-flavored pizza bread. Great with soups, salads, pasta dishes, or chili.

> 1 cup wrist-temperature water
> 1 ½ tsp. (half a ¼-oz. packet) active dry yeast
> 1 tsp. sugar
> 1 tsp. salt
> approximately 3½ cups flour
> 2 to 3 Tbs. dried rosemary
> olive oil, for the bowl, dough, and baking tray
> extra flour, for handling the dough

1) Follow steps 1 and 2 in the directions for Pita Bread (opposite page), adding rosemary with the flour, and using olive oil to oil the bowl and the dough.

2) Punch down the dough, and transfer to a clean floured surface. Adding small amounts of extra flour as needed, to avoid stickiness, knead the dough for about 5 to 8 minutes—until it is smooth and elastic. Form the dough into a ball, and roll it into a 10- to 12-inch diameter circle. Let it rest for about 10 minutes. Meanwhile, preheat the oven to 400°F. Lightly oil a baking tray.

3) Transfer the circle of dough to the baking tray, and brush the top surface of the dough with a little more olive oil. Bake for 20 to 30 minutes, or until lightly browned. (Take it out sooner if you like it softer; later if you like it crisper.) Serve hot, warm, or at room temperature.

Pita Bread
(Arabic Pocket Bread)

Preparation time:
about 2 hours
(most of which
is rising time)

Yield: 6 larger
(or 12 smaller)
pocket breads

1 cup wrist-temperature water
1½ tsp. (half a ¼-oz. packet) active dry yeast
1 Tbs. sugar or honey
1 tsp. salt
about 3½ cups flour (1 cup of it can be whole wheat)
OPTIONAL: 1 Tbs. sesome seeds
a little oil for the dough
extra flour for rolling out
oil or cornmeal, for the baking tray

1) Place the water in a medium-sized bowl and sprinkle in the yeast. Let stand for 5 minutes – it will become foamy.
2) Add sugar or honey and salt. Stir until everything dissolves.
3) Add 3 cups of flour, one cup at a time, mixing enthusiastically with a whisk. As the dough thickens, switch to a wooden spoon and, eventually, your hand. Knead the dough in the bowl for a few minutes, adding up to ½ cup more flour, as needed, to combat stickiness. When the dough is smooth, oil both the bowl and the top surface of the dough. Cover with a clean tea towel, and let rise in a warm place for about an hour, or until the dough has doubled in bulk.
4) Punch down the dough and transfer it to a clean, floured surface. Knead it for about 5 minutes, then divide it into either 6 or 12 equal pieces (depending on what size pitas you want). Knead each little unit for a few minutes, then use a rolling pin to flatten it into a very thin circle. (Make sure there is plenty of flour underneath!) The diameter of each circle is unimportant, as long as it is no thicker than ⅛ inch. Let the circles rest for 30 minutes.
5) Preheat oven to 500°F. Place a baking tray in the oven for a minute or two, to heat it. Then brush it with oil – or dust it with cornmeal. Place as many circles on the tray as will fit without touching, and bake for just 6 to 8 minutes, or until puffed up and very lightly browned.
6) Remove from the oven, and wrap the breads in a clean, slightly damp tea towel, then place in a brown paper bag, closed up, for 15 minutes. This will keep the breads supple. (If you'd prefer the pita bread to be crisp and cracker-like, bake 10 to 12 minutes and simply cool on a rack.)

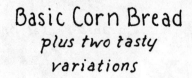

Basic Corn Bread
plus two tasty variations

10 minutes to assemble;
20 minutes to bake

Yield:
1 8-inch square
panful

butter or margarine, for the pan
1 cup cornmeal
1 cup flour
2 tsp. baking powder
½ tsp. baking soda
½ tsp. salt
1 cup buttermilk or yogurt
1 egg
3 Tbs. sugar or honey
3 Tbs. melted butter or margarine

1) Preheat oven to 350°F. Grease an 8-inch square pan (or a 9- or 10-inch cast-iron skillet) with butter or margarine.

2) Combine the dry ingredients in a medium-sized bowl. Combine the wet ingredients (including sugar or honey) separately. Stir the wet mixture into the dry, mixing just enough to thoroughly combine. Spread into the prepared pan.

3) Bake for 20 minutes, or until the center is firm to the touch. Serve hot, warm, or at room temperature.

MEXICAN CORN & CHEESE BREAD

Make the batter as described above, with the following additions:
1 cup fresh or frozen/defrosted corn
½ cup (packed) grated mild white cheese } Stir into the
3 to 4 scallions, minced } batter.
OPTIONAL: replace the melted butter with olive oil

BLUEBERRY CORN BREAD

Make the batter as described above, increasing the sugar or honey to ¼ cup. Add 1½ cups fresh blueberries, stirring them gently into the batter. (NOTE: You can also use frozen unsweetened blueberries. Defrost and drain before using.)

FLATBREADS:
FLOUR TORTILLAS, CHAPPATIS, & CHINESE GREEN ONION PANCAKES

Here are three variations on the theme of Flatbread — one Mexican, one Indian, and one Chinese. They are all basically the same — quick and easy, yet somehow exotic beyond the sum of their few simple ingredients.

FLOUR TORTILLAS   Serve with soups, salads, bean dishes, or rice.

1 cup flour   ½ cup water   a little oil, for cooking
½ tsp. salt   extra flour, for handling the dough

1) Place the flour and salt in a medium-sized bowl. Add the water, and stir until fairly well combined.
2) Transfer the dough to a clean, floured surface, and knead for a minute or two, adding extra flour, if necessary, to keep it from becoming sticky. Divide the dough into 6 equal balls, and roll each one into a very thin circle — no thicker than ⅛ inch. Use lots of flour, both on the rolling surface and the rolling pin.
3) You can either bake or pan-fry the tortillas. To bake, preheat the oven to 325°F. Place the tortillas on a lightly oiled tray, brush their top surfaces with a little more oil, and bake for 10 to 15 minutes, or until very lightly browned. (Bake them longer if you like them crisper, shorter if you like them softer.) To pan-fry, heat a heavy skillet or a griddle for a few minutes. Add a small amount of oil, and cook the tortillas for 3 to 5 minutes on each side. (Just as with baking, cooking them longer makes them crisper.)
4) Remove the tortillas from the oven, and serve hot or warm. If you need to reheat them, wrap tightly in foil, and place in a 300°F. oven for 10 to 15 minutes.

CHAPPATIS   Serve with any soup or with curries (p. 172-75).
Make Flour Tortillas as described above, but substitute ½ cup whole wheat flour for ½ cup of the white flour.

CHINESE GREEN ONION PANCAKES   Serve with any soup, with Tofu Salad (p.56), or with Duck Sauce (p.97) or Stir-Fry Sauce (p.88) for an appetizer or snack.
Make Flour Tortillas as described above, adding to the flour mixture:
3 medium-sized scallions, very finely minced. After the pancakes are cooked, sprinkle on a little extra salt.

Felafel

Felafel are small, spicy chick pea patties. They are almost always topped with Tahini-Lemon Sauce (p. 103), and served either in a sandwich with Pita Bread (p. 113), or as an appetizer, either alone, or on a Mezza (p. 100). Traditionally, Felafel are deep-fried, but they are equally good — and satisfyingly crisp — if pan-fried in a very hot skillet with a small amount of oil.

4 cups cooked chick peas (OK to use canned. Two 15-oz. cans will provide the right amount.)

4 medium cloves garlic, minced
2 tsp. cumin
1 tsp. turmeric
1 tsp. salt
½ cup finely minced onion,
  or 6 scallions, minced

¼ cup (packed) minced parsley
¼ cup water
1 Tbs. lemon juice
a few dashes of cayenne
⅓ cup flour
oil for frying

1) Rinse the chick peas, and drain them well.

2) Combine all ingredients except flour in a food processor or a medium-sized bowl and process — or mash — until you have a uniform batter.

3) Add flour, and stir until thoroughly combined. You can cook the Felafel right away, or store the batter in a tightly covered container in the refrigerator for several days.

4) Heat a heavy skillet and add about 3 Tbs. oil. When it is hot enough to sizzle a bread crumb on contact, drop tablespoonfuls of batter into the pan, flattening each slightly, like a small, thick pancake. Sauté for about 10 minutes on each side, until golden and crisp. Add small amounts of extra oil to the pan as needed throughout the cooking.

5) Place the cooked Felafel on a plate lined with paper towels, and, if necessary, keep warm in a 300°F. oven until serving time.

Celebratory Sandwich Fillings

If you pack a lunch for yourself or for members of your family, and you need some inspiration to get away from cheese, egg salad, and peanut butter and jelly, try some of these sandwich filling ideas. Remember that most of them keep for at least several days (and some for longer), so make a few fillings on a weekend, and you'll have inspiration and variety to get you through the week.

1) <u>Eggplant Dips</u> (p. 104 and 105) go perfectly in Pita Bread (p. 113) or on whole wheat bread.

2) <u>Walnut Pâtés</u> (p. 101) make a substantial sandwich with lettuce and tomato on sourdough or whole wheat bread.

3) Keep <u>Yogurt Cheese</u> (p. 102) on hand. It lasts a long time! You can use it wherever you would cream cheese. Some suggestions: ☆ with toasted cashews and minced candied ginger ☆ with minced fresh herbs (small amounts of parsley, chives, dill, marjoram, thyme, cilantro ~ in any combination) and a few slices of cucumber ☆ with pitted, chopped olives (your favorite kind), minced walnuts, and parsley

4) <u>Tahini-Lemon Sauce</u> (p. 103) — Make it thick; spread it on rye or pumpernickel, with tomato, red onion, cucumber, and possibly some minced bell pepper.

5) <u>Zingy Bean Dip</u> (p. 106) and <u>Hummus</u> (p. 100) make great sandwich fillings on any kind of bread (especially pita). Be sure to include a bag of tortilla chips with this lunch!

6) <u>Guacamole</u> (p. 108) can be a spread as well as a dip. It has a shorter shelf life than all of the above-suggested fillings, so make it no farther in advance than the day before.

7) Instead of peanut butter, try almond or cashew butter, just for variety. Instead of jam or jelly, try actual fresh fruit. The best: slices of tart apple, perfectly ripe peach, or banana. Try inserting some seedless grapes into your nut butter. You may forget you put them there, and at lunchtime you'll get a pleasant surprise.

BLUE CHEESE HEAVEN:
Two Simply Divine Blue Cheese Sandwiches

The ingredient amounts are open-ended in these two sandwich ideas, making them as much suggestions as recipes. This is for flexibility's sake, allowing you to accommodate the number of guests, plus your own tastes and refrigerator contents. ♪ Note of encouragement: It's hard to go wrong.

I. SAUTÉED VEGETABLES WITH BLUE CHEESE ON TOAST:

minced garlic
sliced red onion
grated carrot
finely shredded cabbage
grated beets
OPTIONAL: minced broccoli
      minced bell pepper
      sliced mushrooms
a little oil
salt, pepper, and dill —to taste
crumbled blue cheese

Sauté the vegetables in a small amount of oil for about 8 to 10 minutes, or until tender.
Season to taste with salt, pepper, and dill. Stir the crumbled cheese into the hot vegetables.

Take some modest slices of whole wheat, rye, or pumpernickel bread, toast them lightly, and spread them with your choice of: mayonnaise (p.44), Horseradish Sauce (p.91), thick yogurt (or Yogurt Cheese-p.102), or mustard. Spoon the vegetable-cheese filling onto the bread, and serve it open-faced or closed.

II. OPEN-FACED BLUE CHEESE SANDWICH WITH PEARS:

softened cream cheese
cottage cheese
ricotta cheese

Use any of these, or a combination. Lowfat varieties work well.

crumbled blue cheese
finely minced toasted walnuts
whole wheat bread, lightly toasted
slices of fresh pear, sprinkled lightly
    with lemon juice or raspberry vinegar

1) Combine the cheeses and the walnuts. Mix well, and spread onto whole wheat toast.
2) Arrange slices of pear on top, and serve.

❧ Salad ❧
❧ Sandwiches ❧

❧❧❧❧❧❧❧❧❧❧❧❧❧❧❧❧❧❧❧❧❧❧❧❧❧❧❧❧❧❧❧❧❧❧❧❧

Sometimes that leftover salad—not quite enough to serve again for lunch or even as a side dish for dinner—is really a sandwich filling waiting to happen. Just pile it onto some fresh or toasted bread, close it up, and lunch is ready.

Here are some good candidates for a salad sandwich:

❧ <u>Warm Salad</u> (p.40) — Maybe it's room temperature or even cold by now, and it will go beautifully on thick slices of bread or toast.

❧ <u>March Hare Salad</u> (p.49)

❧ <u>Tofu Salad</u> (p.56) in <u>Pita Bread</u> (p.113)

❧ <u>Alsatian Salad</u> (p.57) — also perfect for Pita

❧ <u>Marinated Vegetables</u> (p.63) — on toast, open-faced

❧ Various Antipasti: <u>Bell Peppers</u> (p.65), <u>Swiss Chard</u> (p.66), or <u>Marinated Mushrooms</u> (p.67) — on toast, open-faced

❧ <u>Odessa Beets</u> (p.68) — on rye or pumpernickel, with or without cream cheese

To construct a TOSSED SALAD SANDWICH:
(seems obvious, but maybe you need permission to leave out the sliced meat or cheese)

   ❧ slices of great bread
   ❧ spread of choice (mayonnaise—p.44; any dip—p.100-108)
   ❧ clean, crisp fresh leafy greens (lettuces, spinach, arugula, herbs)
   ❧ sliced cucumber
   ❧ sliced tomato
   ❧ sliced mushrooms
   ❧ sliced red onion
   ❧ grated carrot
   ❧ slices of avocado
   ❧ salt and pepper

Broiled and Grilled Sandwiches

Here are some ideas for broiled or grilled sandwiches that can be served for lunch or dinner. You can adjust the amounts and proportions according to your taste, your guests, and what you have on hand. With the exception of Ideas for Cheese, these sandwiches are dairy-free.

IDEAS FOR CHEESE:
☆ Tomato Chutney (p.98) spread on rye, pumpernickel, or whole wheat toast. Place some cheese on top and broil.

☆ Coleslaw (p.72) and/or apple slices on rye, pumpernickel, or whole wheat, with cheese broiled on top.

☆ Chinese Mustard (see below) and/or Horseradish Sauce (p.91) with slices of tomato and Swiss cheese on any kind of bread. Leave open-faced and broil -OR- close up the sandwich and grill on a lightly oiled skillet.

GRILLED PEPPER, ONION, CHINESE MUSTARD & TOFU SANDWICH:

For 4 servings:
a little oil for sautéing
1 small red onion, thinly sliced
1 small bell pepper, in thin strips
salt and pepper, to taste
8 slices whole wheat bread
Chinese Mustard (recipe opposite)
1 cake firm tofu, thinly sliced
a little oil for grilling

CHINESE MUSTARD

2 Tbs. Dijon mustard
2 tsp. Chinese sesame oil
1 tsp. cider vinegar
1 tsp. honey or sugar
optional: a little bit of freshly minced cilantro

} Combine

1) Heat a little oil in a small skillet. Add the onion and bell pepper, sprinkle lightly with salt and pepper, and sauté over medium heat until the vegetables are tender (8 to 10 minutes).

2) Lightly toast the bread, and spread each slice with Chinese Mustard. Arrange the sautéed vegetables and slices of tofu on 4 of the slices, and place the remaining mustard-spread bread on top.

3) Grill on a lightly oiled skillet on each side until crisp and brown and heated through. Serve hot.

BROCCOLI & FRIENDS:
For 4 servings:
1 tsp. oil
1 cup thinly sliced onion
3 cups chopped broccoli
salt and pepper, to taste
6 to 8 slices of your favorite bread
Greek Lemon Sauce (p. 91)
freshly minced parsley

1) Heat the oil in a small skillet. Add the onion and broccoli, salt lightly, and sauté over medium heat until tender (8 to 10 minutes). Sprinkle generously with black pepper.
2) Toast the bread, and spread it with a little Greek Lemon Sauce. Spoon on some sautéed broccoli, and top with more sauce.
3) Broil for just a few minutes — until bubbly. Garnish with minced parsley, and serve.

BROILED EGGPLANT WITH FAUX AIOLI AND TOMATOES:
For 4 servings:
a little olive oil for the baking tray
1 small eggplant (about 6 inches long), sliced into ¼-inch-thick rounds
6 to 8 slices (depending on their size and shape) sourdough bread
      (or Italian bread)
Faux Aioli (p. 91)
a medium-sized ripe tomato (or 2), sliced
salt and pepper
freshly minced parsley

1) Heat the broiler. Lightly oil a baking tray, and add the eggplant slices. Broil about 10 minutes, or until tender. Remove the tray, but leave the broiler on.
2) Toast the bread, and spread it with Faux Aioli. Add some tomato slices. Layer the broiled eggplant on top, and add salt and pepper. Spoon a little extra Aioli on top, and return to the broiler for just a minute or two — until the sauce is bubbly. Garnish with parsley and serve hot.

Pepper & Onion Shortcake

~ Sautéed peppers and onions in a lightly seasoned yogurt sauce
over warm corn bread

Make a batch of Corn Bread (p. 114) ahead of time. You can warm
it in a 300°F. oven while preparing the topping, or toast corn bread
chunks or slices just before serving. This makes a perfect lunch on
a chilly day, especially when served with Spicy Tomato Soup (p. 4).

       1 batch Corn Bread (p. 114)
       2 Tbs. olive oil, butter, or margarine
       2 cups thinly sliced onion
       ½ tsp. salt
       3 medium-sized bell peppers (any color), in thin strips
       ½ tsp. cumin (optional)
       black pepper } to taste
       cayenne
       3 medium cloves garlic, minced
       ½ cup yogurt (OPTIONAL: add 1 to 2 Tbs. sour cream)
          — at room temperature
       freshly minced dill, if available
       paprika

1) Heat oil (or melt butter or margarine) in a medium-large skillet.
2) Add onion and salt, and sauté over medium-low heat for 10 to 15
minutes, or until the onion is very soft and beginning to brown.
3) Add bell peppers, cumin, black pepper, and cayenne, and continue to
sauté until the peppers are tender (about 10 more minutes).
4) Add garlic, and cook just a minute or 2 more. Remove from heat
and stir in yogurt (and optional touch of sour cream).
5) Serve immediately, spooned over split chunks of warmed or toasted
corn bread and garnished with dill and paprika.

ENTRÉES

In this chapter you will find recipes for casseroles, chili, crêpes, stuffed vegetables, vegetable pies, strudels, Mexican dishes, Italian dishes, curries, stews, and more. (Pasta dishes and a stir-fry method can be found in the Sauce chapter, which begins on p. 73.) Most of the old standards from the original edition are still here, lightened up a bit in the butter, oil, cheese, and egg departments. In fact, of approximately 60 entrée recipes, only 15 now contain any eggs at all, and of these, many are egg- or yolk-optional. Where dairy products are used, lowfat alternatives are given, so you can trim these recipes even further.

TABLE OF CONTENTS : ENTRÉES

ᘓᘓᘓ Macaroni & Cheese Lite ᘒᘒᘒ

This is an adaptation of "Whole Wheat Macaroni~Russian-Style," which appeared in earlier editions. In this new version, there are more vegetables, the seasoning is intensified, and the sour cream has been replaced by lighter, zippier buttermilk. You can improvise further by increasing or varying the vegetables. Try modest amounts of chopped cauliflower, broccoli, and/or carrots (always colorful).

½ lb. (approximately 3 cups) dry pasta ~ a short, substantial
shape, like fusilli, penne, macaroni, 1-inch shells, etc.

2 Tbs. butter or margarine

2 cups chopped onion

2 medium cloves garlic, minced

½ lb. mushrooms, sliced

4 cups shredded cabbage (about ½ an average head)

1 tsp. salt

1 tsp. caraway seeds

1 bunch fresh spinach ~ stemmed and coarsely chopped

1 lb. (2 cups) cottage cheese (can be lowfat)

½ cup buttermilk or yogurt

2 Tbs. fresh (or 2 tsp. dried) dill, finely minced

fresh black pepper, to taste

2 cups (packed) grated cheddar

a handful of sunflower seeds (optional)

1) Preheat oven to 350°F. Lightly grease a 9 × 13-inch baking pan.

2) Cook the pasta until just barely tender. Drain thoroughly, and transfer to a large bowl.

3) Melt the butter in a large, deep skillet, and add the onions. After sauté-ing for about 5 minutes, add garlic, mushrooms, cabbage, salt, and car-away. Stir, cover, and cook until the cabbage is just tender (10 minutes). Stir in spinach, and remove from heat. Add to the pasta.

4) Stir in cottage cheese, buttermilk, dill, black pepper, and half the cheddar. Taste to adjust seasonings, and spread into the prepared pan. Sprinkle with the remaining cheddar and a few sunflower seeds, and bake uncovered for 20 to 30 minutes, or until heated through.

Broccoli Mushroom Noodle Casserole

30 minutes
to prepare;
45 minutes
to bake.

Yield:
about 6
servings

1 1-lb. (or 12-oz.) package wide flat egg noodles
2 Tbs. butter or margarine
2 cups chopped onion
3 medium cloves garlic, minced
1 large bunch fresh broccoli, chopped
1 lb. mushrooms, sliced or chopped
½ tsp. salt (more, to taste)
lots of fresh black pepper
optional: ¼ cup dry white wine
optional: 3 eggs, beaten
3 cups (1½ lbs.) cottage cheese (may be lowfat)
1 cup sour cream (may be lowfat) or buttermilk
1½ cups fine bread crumbs and/or wheat germ
optional: 1 cup (packed) grated medium or sharp cheddar

1) Preheat oven to 350°F. Butter or oil a 9 x 13-inch baking pan.

2) Cook the noodles in plenty of boiling water until about half-done. Drain and rinse under cold water. Drain again and set aside.

3) Melt the butter or margarine in a large skillet, and add onions and garlic. Sauté for about 5 minutes over medium heat, then add broccoli, mushrooms, salt, and pepper. Continue to cook, stirring frequently, until the broccoli is bright green and just tender. Remove from heat and possibly add optional white wine.

4) In a large bowl, beat together optional eggs (or not) with cottage cheese and sour cream or buttermilk. Add noodles, sautéed vegetables, and 1 cup of the bread crumbs. Mix well.

5) Spread into the prepared pan, and top with remaining bread crumbs and, if desired, grated cheese. Bake covered for 30 minutes; uncovered for 15 minutes more.

noodle kugel

You can make this recipe richer or lighter. Options
for both persuasions are listed below.

1 1-lb. (or 12-oz.) package wide egg noodles

2 to 3 Tbs. butter or margarine (optional)

3 eggs (yolks can be omitted)

2 cups (1 lb.) cottage cheese (lowfat OK)

3/4 cup sour cream or yogurt

8 oz. cream cheese (lowfat OK) - optional

1 tsp. vanilla extract

1 to 2 tsp. cinnamon

1/4 to 1/2 cup sugar (to taste)

1/2 to 1 tsp. salt (to taste)

OPTIONAL ADDITIONS: 1 to 2 Tbs. lemon juice (to taste)
                      1/2 cup (packed) raisins
                      1 tart apple, peeled and sliced
                      2 ripe peaches, peeled and sliced

TOPPING (ALSO OPTIONAL):   1 cup bread crumbs and/or wheat germ
                           1 1/2 tsp. cinnamon
                           1/4 cup (packed) brown sugar

1) Preheat oven to 375°F. Lightly grease a 9 x 13-inch baking pan.

2) Cook the noodles until about half-done. Drain, and toss with butter or margarine (or simply rinse in cold water and drain again). Transfer to a large bowl.

3) Combine eggs, cottage cheese, sour cream or yogurt, cream cheese, cinnamon, sugar, and salt in a blender or food processor and whip until smooth. (Do this in several batches, if necessary.) Stir this into the noodles, along with whatever optional additions you choose. Transfer to the baking pan.

4) Combine the topping ingredients and sprinkle them over the top. Bake uncovered for about 40 minutes. Serve hot, warm, or at room temperature.

I hour to prepare,
including baking.
(Sauté vegetables
while millet cooks.)

Cauliflower Marranca

Yield:
4 to 6
servings

~a simple cauliflower· mushroom· millet casserole~

oil for the pan
1½ cups raw millet
2½ cups water
1 Tbs. butter or oil
2 cups chopped onion
1 lb. mushrooms, sliced
black pepper, to taste

1½ tsp. salt
1 tsp. basil
1 large cauliflower, in 1-inch pieces (or smaller)
3 medium cloves garlic, minced
2 to 3 Tbs. lemon juice
OPTIONAL: 1 to 2 cups grated cheese (your choice)
paprika, for the top

PRELIMINARY: Preheat oven to 350°F. Oil a 9 x 13-inch pan.
1) Place the millet and water in a small saucepan. Bring to a boil, cover,
and simmer until tender (15 to 20 minutes). Transfer to a large bowl,
and fluff with a fork to let steam escape.
2) Melt butter or heat oil in a large skillet. Add onion, mushrooms, pepper,
salt, and basil, and sauté about 5 minutes — until the onions soften.
Add cauliflower and garlic, and sauté about 10 minutes more — until
the cauliflower is tender. Add lemon juice.
3) Stir the sautéed vegetables into the millet, along with the optional
cheese, and mix well. Spread into the prepared pan, dust with paprika,
and bake for 30 minutes.

yum yum

Mushroom Moussaka

This is a meatless and eggless version of the famous Greek eggplant casserole, with two deceptively rich-tasting sauces. One is tomato-based and loaded with mushrooms; the other is a traditional Béchamel.

The mushroom sauce can be prepared well ahead of time. You can make the Béchamel while the eggplant slices bake, then assemble the casserole, using the same hot oven for the final baking.

3 medium eggplants (about 7 inches long), peeled or not, depending
   on your preference and the condition of the eggplants
salt

Mushroom-Tomato Sauce

2 Tbs. olive oil
2 cups chopped onion
1 ¼ tsp. salt
1 ½ lbs. (or even 2 lbs.) mushrooms, coarsely chopped
5 medium cloves garlic, sliced or minced
1 14½-oz. can tomatoes, including all the liquid
1 6-oz. can tomato paste
1 tsp. cinnamon
lots of black pepper
1 tsp. each: oregano and basil
1 packed cup freshly minced parsley
½ cup fine bread crumbs, plus extra for the top
½ cup grated parmesan cheese

Béchamel Sauce

3 Tbs. butter or margarine
6 Tbs. flour
2 ½ cups hot milk (lowfat works fine!)
½ cup grated parmesan cheese, plus extra for the top
nutmeg

1) Slice the eggplants into quarter-inch-thick rounds. Salt the slices lightly on both sides, then layer them gently in a colander, and place over a sink or bowl. Let stand for 20 to 30 minutes. This will allow them to sweat out their bitter juices. (Meanwhile, you can work on the mushroom sauce.)

2) Lightly oil a baking sheet, and preheat oven to 375°F. Retrieve the eggplant slices from their spa, and pat them dry with a clean towel. Spread the slices on the tray (it's ok if they pile up a little) and bake until tender (20 to 25 minutes). Meanwhile, prepare the Béchamel sauce.

. . . . .

MUSHROOM-TOMATO SAUCE:

1) Heat the olive oil in a large, deep skillet or a Dutch oven. Add onions and salt, and cook over medium heat, stirring, for 8 to 10 minutes, or until the onions become translucent. Add mushrooms and garlic, stir, and cover. Cook over medium heat another 8 to 10 minutes.

2) Add tomatoes, tomato paste, cinnamon, pepper, oregano, and basil. (Use a spoon or a dinner knife to break the tomatoes into bite-sized pieces.) Bring to a boil, then lower heat, and simmer, uncovered, another 12 to 15 minutes. Remove from heat, and stir in parsley, bread crumbs, and parmesan. Set aside.

. . . . .

BÉCHAMEL SAUCE:

1) In a medium-sized saucepan, melt the butter or margarine over low heat. Whisk in 4 Tbs. of the flour, keeping up a steady motion with the whisk even after the flour is added. Cook for several minutes, whisking still.

2) Slowly pour in the hot milk, whisking even yet. Cook and stir over low heat another 5 to 8 minutes, or until the sauce is very smooth and thickened slightly. Sift in the remaining 2 Tbs. flour, whisking yet some more, to prevent lumps. After another 5 to 8 minutes of cooking with occasional stirring, add the parmesan and a few shakes of nutmeg. Remove from heat. The sauce should be smooth and quite thick.

. . . . .

ASSEMBLY: Preheat oven to 375°F. Oil a very large casserole or a deep oblong baking pan with dimensions of at least 9 x 13 inches. Place a double layer of eggplant on the bottom, and add the entire batch of mushroom sauce. Lay the remaining eggplant slices over the mushroom sauce, and spread the Béchamel over the top. Dust lightly with fine bread crumbs and a small handful or two of parmesan. Bake uncovered for 35 to 40 minutes, or until bubbly on the bottom and ever so lightly browned on top. Serve hot.

Lasagne

Preparation time:
1½ hours

~~~~~~~~

Yield:
6 to 8 servings

Have ready:
1) 1 batch Italian Tomato Sauce ~ any variation (p. 80)
2) 12 lasagne noodles, half-cooked or even uncooked (it _will_ work!)
3) 1½ to 2 cups ricotta or cottage cheese (lowfat OK)
4) 1 lb. grated or thinly sliced mozzarella cheese
5) at least ½ cup grated parmesan, romano, or asiago cheese
6) a 9 x 13-inch pan

Proceedings:
1) Preheat oven to 375°F.
2) Spread a little sauce over the bottom of the pan.
3) Cover with a single layer of noodles (⅓ of them. Break as necessary, to fit.)
4) Place mounds of ricotta/cottage cheese here and there. Use half.
5) Add ⅓ the sauce, followed by
6) ½ the mozzarella, randomly scattered, then
7) another ⅓ the noodles, and
8) the remaining ricotta (cottage), followed by
9) another ⅓ the sauce, which gets covered by
10) the remaining mozzarella.
11) Add every last noodle, and
12) the final sauce.
13) Sprinkle the parmesan (romano/asiago) over the top.

Bake for 45 minutes. Cover loosely with foil toward the end of the baking, if it is getting too brown. Let stand 10 minutes before serving.

1¼ hours to prepare (most of
which is baking time). This
assumes the tomato sauce
is already made.

 Eggplant
Parmesan

Yield:
at least
8 servings

Eggplant is highly absorbent, and when fried, it soaks up oil like a sponge. Because it is usually fried for Eggplant Parmesan, this dish ends up being much heavier than it needs to be. Here is a way to prepare crispy eggplant without frying ~ I suppose you could call it the shake-and-bake method. It is easier and much neater than frying, in addition to being lighter and better for you ~ and all those things you are possibly tired of hearing about. But people seem not to get tired of things tasting good, and this does taste really good.

2 medium eggplants (about 7 inches long)
¾ cup milk (more, as needed)
2 cups fine bread crumbs or wheat germ (or a combination)
1 tsp. basil
½ tsp. each: oregano and thyme
1 batch Italian Tomato Sauce (p.80)
1 lb. mozzarella cheese, thinly sliced or grated
parmesan cheese ~ about ½ cup (amount = flexible)

1) Preheat oven to 375°F. Lightly oil a baking tray and a 9 x 13-inch pan.

2) Cut the eggplants into ⊙'s ½ inch thick. Place the milk in a shallow bowl; combine bread crumbs (wheat germ) with herbs on a plate. Dip each eggplant slice in the milk, moistening both sides, then coat it thoroughly with the crumb mixture. Spread the prepared slices on the baking tray and the pan, and bake until tender (about 20 to 30 minutes). Remove from oven, and pile them gently on the baking tray.

3) Without cleaning the 9 x 13-inch pan, ladle some tomato sauce into the bottom. Add a layer of eggplant slices, and cover with more sauce. Arrange some mozzarella over the sauce, then repeat the layering until you run out of something or you run out of room, whichever comes first. Generously sprinkle the top with parmesan.

4) Bake uncovered at 375°F. for about 40 minutes, or until heated through and bubbly around the edges. Remove from oven and let sit about 10 minutes before serving. Serve hot or warm.

Tart & Tangy Baked Beans

Preparation time:
Presoaked beans need
up to 1½ hours to cook.
Get everything else
ready during
this time.

Yield:
6 to 8
servings

A version of this recipe appeared in earlier editions as "Cheese-Beans." This one is more deeply seasoned, but basically the same. Cheese is optional.

Serve this with rice, corn bread (p. 114), or warmed tortillas (p. 115).

NOTE: The beans need to soak for at least 4 hours ahead of time.

3 cups dry pinto beans, soaked
4 cups chopped onions
2 Tbs. olive oil
1½ to 2 tsp. salt
1 Tbs. chili powder
2 tsp. cumin
1½ tsp. dry mustard
6 to 8 medium cloves garlic, minced
6 Tbs. dry white wine (optional)

6 to 8 Tbs. cider vinegar (to taste)
3 to 4 Tbs. molasses (to taste)
2 cups grated mild cheese (optional)
lots of black pepper
crushed red pepper, to taste
3 medium-sized tart apples, cut
 into medium-sized chunks
4 medium-sized ripe tomatoes,
 chopped

1) Place the presoaked beans in a kettle and cover them with plenty of water. Bring to a boil, lower to a simmer, partially cover, and cook slowly until tender (1¼ to 1½ hours), checking the water level during cooking. Drain off any excess when the beans are done. (This can be saved for soup stock.)

2) Begin cooking the onions in olive oil in a medium-sized skillet. Add salt, chili powder, cumin, and mustard, and sauté over medium heat for about 8 to 10 minutes. Add garlic, and sauté for another 5 minutes or so. Add this sauté to the cooked beans, along with all remaining ingredients.

3) Preheat oven to 350°F. Mix the beans well and transfer to a deep casserole or a 9 × 13-inch baking pan. Cover tightly with foil, and bake 1 hour.

Spinach-Rice Casserole

The original version contained 4 eggs. This one has only 2, and they're optional. Also, you can experiment by replacing some or all of the spinach with other greens: mustard, kale, collard, etc.

2 cups uncooked brown rice (long- or short-grain)
1 Tbs. butter or margarine — or olive oil
2 cups minced onion
2 lbs. fresh spinach, stemmed and finely chopped
1 tsp. salt
4 to 5 medium cloves garlic, minced
¼ tsp. nutmeg
¼ tsp. cayenne
black pepper, to taste
optional: 1 to 2 tsp. prepared mustard
½ cup sunflower seeds
2 beaten eggs (optional)
1 cup lowfat milk (optional)
1½ cups (packed) grated cheddar (optional)
paprika

1) Place the rice in a medium-sized saucepan with 3 cups water. Cover, bring to a boil, then lower to the slowest possible simmer. Cook, covered and undisturbed, for 35 to 40 minutes. Remove from heat, transfer to a medium-sized bowl, and fluff with a fork.

2) Preheat oven to 350°F. Oil a 9 X 13-inch baking pan.

3) Heat the butter, margarine, or oil in a deep skillet. Add onion, and sauté 5 to 8 minutes ~ until soft. Add spinach, salt, and garlic, and cook about 5 minutes more over medium heat, stirring frequently. Add this to the rice, along with the seasonings and half the sunflower seeds. Mix well.

4) PURELY OPTIONAL: Beat together eggs and milk, and stir this into the spinach-rice mixture, along with the grated cheese.

5) Spread into the prepared pan, sprinkle with the remaining sunflower seeds and dust with paprika. Bake uncovered for 35 to 40 minutes ~ until heated through and lightly browned on top.

Solyanka

1¼ hours to prepare
(including baking)

Serves about 6

Very simple ingredients comprise this tasty casserole. Serve it with Beet Borscht (p. 35) or Odessa Beets (p. 68) and Balkan Cucumber Salad (p. 69).

4 medium potatoes (about 2 lbs.)
1½ cups cottage cheese (lowfat ok)
1 cup firm yogurt
1 Tbs. butter or margarine
2 cups chopped onion
¾ to 1 tsp. salt
1 tsp. caraway seeds
1 small head green cabbage, shredded (about 6 cups)

2 medium carrots, shredded
4 to 5 medium cloves garlic, minced
1 Tbs. dill (3 Tbs., if using fresh)
lots of black pepper, to taste
3 Tbs. cider vinegar
½ cup sunflower seeds } toppings
paprika

1) Preheat oven to 350°F. Lightly grease a 2-quart casserole or its equivalent.
2) Scrub the potatoes, cut them into small pieces, and boil until mashable. (You can do Steps 4 and 5 while the potatoes boil.) Drain and transfer to a large bowl.
3) Mash the potatoes while still hot, adding cottage cheese and yogurt.
4) Melt the butter or margarine in a large, deep skillet. Add onions and salt, and sauté about 5 minutes. Add caraway and cabbage, and sauté about 10 more minutes, stirring occasionally and covering in between.
5) When the cabbage is tender, add carrots, garlic, and dill. Cook about 5 more minutes, and remove from heat.
6) Add the sautéed vegetables and all remaining ingredients -except toppings- to the mashed potatoes. Mix well and spread into the prepared pan. Sprinkle the sunflower seeds and paprika on top.
7) Bake uncovered 35 to 45 minutes, or until heated through and lightly browned on top. Serve hot.

MEXICAN PEPPER CASSEROLE

The original version of this recipe contained butter in addition to the oil, plus more oil, 4 eggs, sour cream, and ½ lb. cheese. This trimmed-down version deletes the butter, reduces the oil and eggs, replaces sour cream with yogurt (if desired), and makes the cheese optional. The seasonings are intensified.

If you want to serve this with beans and rice, don't forget to get them ready beforehand.

1 Tbs. olive oil
2 cups sliced onion
6 to 8 medium-sized bell peppers (a mix of colors, if available), thinly sliced
4 to 5 medium cloves garlic, minced
1 tsp. salt
1½ tsp. cumin
optional: 1 tsp. dried coriander
1 tsp. dry mustard

black pepper, to taste
cayenne, to taste
2 Tbs. flour
2 to 3 eggs
2 cups yogurt and/or sour cream
optional: a handful of freshly minced cilantro
2 cups sliced jack or cheddar cheese (optional)
paprika, for the top

1) Lightly grease a 10-inch square pan or its equivalent. Preheat oven to 375°F.

2) Heat the olive oil in a deep skillet or Dutch oven. Add onions and sauté about 5 to 8 minutes over medium heat, until the onions begin to soften.

3) Add peppers, salt, cumin, dried coriander, mustard, black pepper, and cayenne. Sauté another 8 to 10 minutes, then sprinkle in the flour. Cook and stir another 5 minutes, or until the peppers are very tender. Transfer to the baking pan.

4) Beat together the eggs and yogurt or sour cream. Stir in the minced fresh cilantro. Pour this custard over the peppers. Top with slices of cheese, if desired, and dust with paprika.

5) Bake uncovered for 40 to 45 minutes until firm in the center and bubbly around the edges. Serve hot with rice and beans and/or warmed tortillas.

BULGARIAN PEPPER CASSEROLE

Garlicky herbed sautéed peppers and onions are blended with feta cheese, dilled lemon rice, and whipped cottage or ricotta cheese, then topped with tomatoes, olives, and more garlic, and baked until bubbly hot.

The peppers can be sautéed and the rice prepared several days in advance. Assemble and bake the casserole just before serving.

NOTE: In earlier editions, a version of this casserole was called Bulgarian Pepper and Cheese Delight. It had bulgur instead of rice, contained 4 eggs, and was far less intensely seasoned than this one, which is eggless.

❋ ❋ ❋ ❋ ❋ ❋ ❋ ❋ ❋ ❋ ❋ ❋ ❋ ❋ ❋ ❋

1½ cups uncooked brown rice
2¾ cups water
1 Tbs. lemon juice
2 to 3 Tbs. freshly minced dill (or 2 tsp. dried dill)
1½ Tbs. olive oil
2 cups minced onion
4 to 5 medium green and/or red bell peppers, chopped into ½-inch pieces
¾ tsp. salt (more, to taste)
fresh black pepper
½ tsp. oregano
2 tsp. basil
8 medium cloves garlic, half of them minced, half of them sliced
   (keep minced and sliced garlic separate)
1 cup crumbled feta cheese
1½ cups cottage or ricotta cheese (may be lowfat)
2 medium-sized fresh, ripe tomatoes
1 cup whole Niçoise olives (or sliced, pitted Kalamata olives)
   (possibly more, to taste)

... continued on next page →

1) Place rice and water in a saucepan. Cover and bring to a boil. Turn the heat down as low as possible, and simmer without interruption for about 40 minutes, or until the rice is tender. Remove from heat, fluff with a fork, and stir in lemon juice and dill. Set aside.

2) Meanwhile, heat the olive oil in a large skillet. Add onions, and sauté over medium heat 5 to 8 minutes, or until the onions become soft. Add peppers, salt, pepper, and herbs, and continue to cook, stirring occasionally, for about 10 more minutes, or until the peppers are tender. Stir in the minced garlic (save the sliced garlic for later) and cook for just a minute more. Remove from heat, and stir in the feta cheese.

3) When you are ready to assemble the casserole, preheat the oven to 375°F. Lightly oil a 9 x 13-inch baking pan.

4) Place the cottage or ricotta cheese in a blender or food processor fitted with the steel blade, and whip until smooth.

5) Combine rice, pepper sauté, and whipped cheese in a large bowl, and mix until very well combined. Transfer to the prepared pan, and spread into place. Top with tomato slices, then scatter olives and slices of garlic in a liberated, random fashion over the tomatoes.

6) Bake uncovered at 375°F. until bubbly ~ about 30 to 40 minutes. Serve hot or warm.

Arabian Squash Casserole

Preparation time: about
1 hour, after the squash
is cooked and puréed

Good served with Tabouli
Salad (p.46), or with warmed
pita bread and a spinach
salad with ripe tomatoes.

Yield
4 to 5 servings

4 cups cooked squash or pumpkin, mashed or puréed
1 Tbs. olive oil
1½ cups chopped onion
1 tsp. salt
2 small bell peppers (one red and one green, if possible), minced
4 or 5 medium cloves garlic, minced
black pepper and cayenne, to taste
½ cup firm yogurt
1 cup crumbled feta cheese
OPTIONAL: sunflower seeds and/or minced walnuts, for the top

PRELIMINARY: Preheat oven to 375°F.

1) Place the mashed or puréed squash in a large bowl.

2) Heat the olive oil in a medium-sized skillet. Add onion, and sauté
over medium heat for about 5 minutes. Add salt and bell peppers.
Sauté about 5 more minutes, or until the peppers begin to get soft.

3) Add garlic, black pepper, and cayenne, and sauté a few more minutes.

4) Add the sauté, along with yogurt and feta, to the squash, and mix well.
Spread into an ungreased 9-inch square baking pan; sprinkle the top
lightly with sunflower seeds and/or minced walnuts.

5) Bake uncovered for 25 to 30 minutes, or until bubbly.

Chilean Squash (a variation)

Delete: yogurt, feta, sunflower seeds, walnuts.

Add to step 2: 1 tsp. cumin, ½ tsp. dried coriander (optional), 1 tsp.
chili powder, 2 cups corn (frozen/defrosted = OK)

Top with: 1 cup grated cheddar

Preparation time:
1¼ hours after
soybeans are soaked

SCHEHERAZADE CASSEROLE

This is one of my favorite recipes, and I strongly recommend it: ground soybeans baked with bulgur, vegetables, garlic, tomatoes, feta cheese. The texture is deeply satisfying, and the seasonings are bold. It tastes great!

Few changes have been made from the original, other than to intensify the seasonings. It was — and remains — eggless.

You can assemble the casserole a day or 2 in advance of baking it. Also, it can be frozen before or after baking. It doesn't mind being reheated.

PRELIMINARY: The soybeans need at least 4 hours to soak beforehand.

1 cup raw bulgur	black pepper and cayenne, to taste
1 cup boiling water	1 large bell pepper, diced
1 Tbs. olive oil	¾ cup dry soybeans, soaked
2 cups minced onion	1 14½-oz. can tomatoes, drained
3 large cloves garlic, minced	3 Tbs. (half a small can) tomato paste
½ tsp. salt	½ cup (packed) finely minced parsley
2 tsp. cumin	1½ to 2 cups crumbled feta cheese
1½ tsp. basil	

1) Preheat oven to 375°F. Lightly oil a 9 x 13-inch baking pan.

2) Place the bulgur in a small bowl. Add boiling water, cover with a plate, and let stand at least 15 minutes.

3) Meanwhile, heat the olive oil in a large skillet. Add onion, garlic, salt, and seasonings. Stir occasionally as you sauté over medium heat for 5 to 8 minutes. Add bell pepper and sauté about 5 minutes more.

4) Drain the soybeans, if necessary, and place them in a blender or food processor with 1 cup fresh water. Grind until the soybeans resemble a coarse batter. Transfer to a large bowl.

5) Add the soaked bulgur and sautéed vegetables to the soybeans. Stir in the tomatoes, breaking them up into bite-sized pieces. Add tomato paste, parsley, and 1 cup of the feta. Mix well.

6) Spread into the baking pan and sprinkle the remaining feta on top. Cover and bake for 30 minutes at 375°F, then uncover and bake 15 minutes more with the oven turned down to 350°F. Serve hot.

Preparation time:
The batter takes
a few minutes.
Cooking the crêpes
takes about 15
minutes.

Crêpes

Yield: 8 to 10
7-inch crêpes

Elegant, but not extravagant, these thin pancakes are at the same time sturdy and delicate. You can make them just to have around. Keep them stacked on a plate, tightly covered and refrigerated. They will last at least a week —just fill and heat as desired. Wrap crêpes around many varieties of foods (a great way to use leftovers!) for different occasions, different times of day. They can quickly transform otherwise ordinary food into something special.

1 large egg
1 ¼ cups milk (can be lowfat)
1 cup flour
¼ tsp. salt
a few drops of oil for the pan

NOTE: You will need a 6-or 7-inch crêpe or omelette pan – ideally a
heavy one with a nonstick surface.

1) Place egg, milk, flour, and salt in a blender or food processor, and whip until smooth.

2) Heat a crêpe or omelette pan. After a few minutes, lightly brush its entire inside surface with oil. When the pan is hot enough to sizzle a drop of water instantly on contact, pour in approximately ¼ cup batter. Slowly tilt the pan in all directions until the batter thoroughly coats the bottom. Pour off any excess batter (the pancake should be thin). Cook on one side over medium heat until set (about 20 seconds), then turn over and cook for just another second or two on the other side.

3) Turn the crêpe out onto a clean, dry dinner plate, and repeat the procedure until you have used up all the batter. (If you keep the pan hot, you won't have to add any additional oil.) You can pile the finished crêpes on the plate — they won't stick together.

4) Cover the plate tightly with plastic wrap, and refrigerate until use. The crêpes will keep well for at least several days.

5) To fill, simply place a small amount of whatever filling at one end of the crêpe and fold over sides and end to make a neat little packet. Filled crêpes can be heated gently — covered, in a 325° oven — or sautéed in a little butter just before serving.

SUGGESTED FILLINGS

FOR DESSERT:
- Sauté in butter, fold in quarters, and sprinkle with powdered sugar.
- Lightly sauté some slices of tart apple; drizzle with lemon juice, cinnamon, and a little maple syrup or honey. Fill the crêpes and serve warm — plain, or with ice cream or whipped cream.
- Heat crêpes gently and serve with room-temperature Berry Sauce (p.207) — with or without ice cream.

VEGETABLES:
- Steamed whole green beans with almonds
- Steamed asparagus or broccoli spears with Zippy Cheese Sauce (p. 92), Rarebit (p.93), or a Vegetable Purée (p.86)
- Steamed carrot sticks with Cashew-Ginger Sauce (p.90)

LEFTOVERS:
- White Rabbit Salad (p.48) — inside room-temperature crêpes
- Ratatouille (p.179) or Vegetable Stew (p.177)
- Stellar Mushroom Sauce (p.78)
- Asparagus-Mushroom Sauce (p.77) — delete water
- Caramelized Onion Sauce (p.78)
- Etc. (whatever ideas you come up with are probably just brilliant)

Zucchini-Feta Pancakes

...Light and very satisfying (also quite attractive, with lovely flecks of green). A food processor will grate the zucchini in seconds flat.

NOTE: This recipe calls for 4 eggs. Some or all of the yolks can be deleted.

○○

4 eggs, separated (yolks optional)
4 packed cups coarsely grated zucchini (about 4 7-inchers)
1 cup finely crumbled feta cheese
½ cup finely minced scallions
1 tsp. dried mint (or 1 Tbs. fresh, finely minced)
a little salt (optional, to taste)
lots of black pepper
⅓ cup flour
oil for frying
sour cream or yogurt for topping

1) Beat the egg whites until stiff.

2) In a medium-sized bowl, combine zucchini, egg yolks (or not), feta, scallions, seasonings, and flour. Mix well.

3) Fold the egg whites into the zucchini mixture.

4) Heat a little oil in a heavy skillet. When it is very hot, add spoonfuls of batter, and fry on both sides until golden and crisp.

5) Serve immediately, topped with sour cream or yogurt.

Cottage Cheese & Apple Pancakes

Preparation time:
30 minutes

Yield: serves
about 4

Great for brunch!

The batter keeps well for days, so you can have it on hand for breakfast cheer on an otherwise depressing weekday. (And these pancakes are equally uplifting for dinner.)

- 4 eggs, separated (yolks optional — use all, some, or none)
- 1 cup cottage cheese (lowfat OK)
- 1 cup (packed) grated tart apple
- ¾ cup flour
- 1 to 2 tsp. lemon juice
- optional: 1 Tbs. honey
- ½ tsp. cinnamon
- ½ tsp. salt
- optional: 2 to 3 Tbs. finely minced walnuts or almonds
- oil or butter for frying
- real maple syrup ⎫
- sour cream or yogurt ⎬ optional toppings
- Berry Sauce (p. 207) ⎭

1) Beat the egg whites until stiff.
2) Combine all other ingredients (except toppings and frying oil) in a medium-sized bowl and mix well. Fold in the egg whites.
3) Heat oil or melt butter in a skillet. When it is hot enough to sizzle a drop of batter on contact, add spoonfuls of batter. Fry on both sides until firm and lightly browned. Serve right away, topped with syrup, sour cream or yogurt, and/or Berry Sauce.

SWEET POTATO PANCAKES

30 minutes to prepare   Yield: 4 to 6 servings

These can be for breakfast, brunch, lunch, or supper, depending on what you serve them with (and, of course, what time of day or night it is).

The sweet potatoes and onion can be grated by hand or in a food processor fitted with the grating attachment. Peeling the sweet potatoes is optional. If you choose not to peel, scrub.

NOTE: The batter stores well for several days if kept in a tightly covered container in the refrigerator.

4 cups (packed) coarsely grated sweet potatoes or yams
        (approximately 1 large or 2 medium)
½ cup grated onion
3 to 4 Tbs lemon juice
1 tsp. salt
black pepper, to taste
4 beaten eggs (yolks optional)
⅓ cup flour
optional: ¼ cup minced parsley
oil for frying
TOPPINGS: sour cream or yogurt
              applesauce

1) Combine all ingredients and mix well.

2) Heat a small amount of oil in a skillet until it is very hot. (It should sizzle a fleck of batter upon contact.)

3) Use a non-slotted spoon to form thin pancakes, patting the batter down. Fry on both sides until brown, adding small amounts of additional oil, if/as needed.

4) Serve hot, with toppings.

35 minutes to prepare;
1 hour to chill;
15 minutes to cook

Yield:
4 to 6
servings

Lentil-Walnut Burgers

These are delicious fried or broiled, with or without some cheese melted on top. Try serving Lentil-Walnut Burgers with thickly sliced, very ripe homegrown tomatoes and Faux Aioli (p. 91).

NOTES: ☆ You can sauté the vegetables while the lentils cook. ☆ The burgers can be made up to several days in advance and stored in the refrigerator until just before cooking. ☆ Uncooked burgers can be individually wrapped and frozen. Defrost before cooking.

¾ cup dry lentils
1½ cups water
2 Tbs. cider vinegar
1 Tbs. peanut or olive oil
1 cup finely minced onion
4 to 5 large cloves garlic, minced
about 10 large mushrooms, minced
½ cup very finely minced walnuts
1 tsp. salt
OPTIONAL: ½ lb. fresh spinach, finely minced
1 tsp. dry mustard
fresh black pepper, to taste
½ cup fine bread crumbs or wheat germ

1) Place lentils and water in a small saucepan and bring to a boil. Lower the heat and simmer, partially covered, for about 30 minutes, or until the lentils are soft and the liquid is gone. Transfer to a medium-sized bowl, add vinegar, and mash well.
2) Heat oil in a medium-sized skillet. Add onions and sauté over medium heat for about 5 minutes. Add all remaining ingredients except wheat germ or bread crumbs, and sauté 5 to 10 minutes, or until all the vegetables are tender. Add the sauté and crumbs to the lentils and mix well. Chill for about 1 hour before forming patties.
3) Form 4-inch-diameter burgers. Fry in a small amount of hot oil on both sides until heated through and crispy on the outside, or broil for 5 to 8 minutes on each side.

Greek Pilaf

45 minutes to prepare

Yield: about 6 servings

Greek Pilaf is a simple rice preparation that can be used as a filling for grape leaves or artichokes (following page), or for eggplant (p.151). It is also delicious all by itself.

1½ cups raw brown rice (long- or short- grain)
2¼ cups water
1 to 2 Tbs. olive oil
1½ cups minced onion
1 small stalk celery, minced
½ tsp. salt
½ cup lightly toasted sunflower seeds or pine nuts
black pepper, to taste
4 to 5 medium cloves garlic, minced
2 Tbs. lemon juice
¼ cup freshly minced parsley
1 Tbs. dried mint (or 3 Tbs. fresh, minced)

1) Place rice and water in a small saucepan. Bring to a boil, cover, and simmer until tender (about 40 minutes).
2) Meanwhile, heat the olive oil in a small skillet. Add onion, celery, and salt, and sauté until the vegetables are tender (5 to 8 minutes). Add sunflower seeds or pine nuts, black pepper, and garlic. Sauté for 5 minutes.
3) Stir the sautéed mixture into the cooked rice along with the lemon juice and herbs. Mix well.

Stuffed Grape Leaves

These can be served with an assortment of other dishes to make an appetizer sampler that is really main-course material (see Mezza, p. 100). You can also serve Stuffed Grape Leaves as a light entrée with any soup, especially Lentil Soup (p. 25).

If you have grapevines in your yard, pick leaves for stuffing early in the season, when they are large enough to stuff, but still tender. You can also buy preserved leaves in specialty shops or in the imported foods section of a good grocery store.

1 recipe Greek Pilaf (preceding page)
about 24 grape leaves (3 to 4 inches across)
1 batch Greek Lemon Sauce (p. 91)

1) Preheat oven to 325°F. Lightly oil a baking tray.
2) Place each leaf down flat on a clean surface. Add a heaping tablespoon of filling near the stem end. Roll tightly, folding in the sides.
3) Arrange the stuffed leaves on the prepared tray. Bake about 20 minutes or until heated through. You can also skip this step and just serve them cold, with the sauce on top or on the side. Serves 4 to 6.

to Stuff an Artichoke

1 recipe Greek Pilaf (preceding page)
6 medium artichokes
1 batch Greek Lemon Sauce (p. 91) or
   Horseradish Sauce (also on p. 91)

1) Trim and cook the artichokes as you normally would. Drain and cool until handleable.
2) Pull off the centermost leaf cluster. Use a teaspoon to scoop out the fibrous choke, being careful not to scoop out the tender heart beneath it. Fill the cavity with pilaf. Serve at room temperature, with sauce for dipping. Serves 6.

150 ENTRÉES

STUFFED EGGPLANT

45 minutes to prepare;
30 to 40 minutes to bake

Yield: 6 servings
per recipe

I. 1970s ALTERNATIVE LIFESTYLE-STYLE — still good!

3 medium eggplants
(about 7 inches long)

2 Tbs. olive oil

2 cups minced onion

½ lb. mushrooms, chopped

1 tsp. salt (or more, to taste)

2 tsp. basil

a dash of thyme

1 tsp. oregano

fresh black pepper, to taste

5 to 6 medium cloves garlic, minced

2 cups cooked brown rice

1½ cups cottage cheese (lowfat OK)

1 cup grated cheddar

½ cup (packed) freshly minced parsley

Tabasco and soy sauce, to taste

a handful of sunflower seeds

a handful of sesame seeds

paprika

Red Pepper Purée (p.86) - optional

1) Cut the eggplants in half lengthwise. Use a spoon to scoop out the insides, leaving a ½-inch shell. Mince the eggplant scoopings.

2) Heat the olive oil in a large skillet. Add onion, mushrooms, salt, herbs, and pepper. Sauté over medium heat for about 5 minutes, then add the minced eggplant. Cook until the eggplant is tender (about 15 minutes), stirring occasionally. Add garlic, and sauté for about 5 more minutes. Transfer to a large bowl.

3) Add rice, cheeses, parsley, Tabasco, and soy sauce, and mix well. Taste to correct seasonings.

4) Preheat oven to 375°F. Fill the eggplant shells, and top with seeds and a fine dusting of paprika. Bake for 30 to 40 minutes — until heated through. Serve hot, with room-temperature Red Pepper Purée drizzled on top, for a lovely effect.

II. MEDITERRANEAN STYLE

3 medium eggplants (about 7 inches long)

a double recipe Greek Pilaf (p. 148)

1 cup crumbled feta cheese

3 medium-sized ripe tomatoes

1) Preheat oven to 375°F. Slice eggplants in half lengthwise, and bake face-down until tender (20 to 30 minutes). Scoop out and mince the insides.

2) Combine chopped eggplant with Greek Pilaf. Stir in the feta. Stuff the eggplant shells and top with slices of tomato.

3) Turn oven down to 350°, and bake until heated through (about 30 minutes).

ENTRÉES 151

```
                    ┌··················┐
                    :                  :
1 hour to prepare   :  Stuffed         :    Yield: at least 4 servings
                    :  Squash          :
                    :                  :
                    └··················┘
```

Each of these filling recipes makes plenty for 4 servings of Stuffed Squash — half a medium-sized squash apiece. Any winter squash will work; the most common are acorn and butternut.

The 2 squash need to be prebaked. Preheat the oven to 350°F. Split the squash lengthwise down the middle and remove the seeds. Bake face-down on an oiled tray for about 30 minutes or until very soft (a fork should slide in easily). Make your choice of fillings while the squash bake.

··

I. SAVORY FRUIT-STUFFED SQUASH

2 medium-sized winter squash, halved lengthwise and prebaked
1 cup raw brown rice (long- or short-grain) + 1¾ cups water

1 Tbs. butter	1 tsp. salt
1½ cups minced onion	1 to 2 Tbs. honey or brown sugar
2 medium cloves garlic, minced	1 cup chopped almonds and/or pecans
2 medium-sized tart apples, diced	TOPPINGS:
3 large navel oranges, sectioned	Orange-Ginger Sauce (p. 90)
½ tsp. cinnamon	yogurt
½ tsp. allspice or cloves	

1) Place rice and water in a small saucepan. Bring to a boil, cover, and let simmer undisturbed for 30 to 40 minutes — until tender. Transfer to a medium-sized bowl.

2) Meanwhile, melt butter in a medium skillet. Add onion and sauté for about 5 minutes, or until translucent.

3) Add garlic, apples, oranges, and spices, and sauté over medium heat about 5 minutes more. The orange sections may fall apart, but that's OK.

4) Add the sauté to the rice and mix well. Season to taste with salt and honey or brown sugar.

5) Preheat oven to 350°F. Fill the prebaked squash halves, and top with chopped nuts. Bake uncovered until heated through — about 20 to 30 minutes (depending on how warm the ingredients were to begin with).

. . . .

II. COMPREHENSIVELY STUFFED SQUASH

Perfect for a holiday meal, especially Thanksgiving. For a colorful accompaniment, choose Odessa Beets (p.68) or Vegetable Purées (Beet or Red Pepper - p.86) to go alongside or on top.

2 medium-sized winter squash, halved and prebaked
2 Tbs. butter
1 cup minced onion
½ lb. mushrooms, minced
1 large clove garlic, minced
1 stalk celery, minced
½ tsp. salt
lots of black pepper
½ tsp. sage
½ tsp. thyme
2 Tbs. lemon juice
¼ cup minced walnuts
¼ cup sunflower seeds
¼ cup raisins (optional)
2 cups good bread crumbs (from good bread)
6 to 8 dried apricots
1 cup (packed) grated cheddar (entirely optional)

1) Melt the butter in a large skillet. Add onion, and sauté over medium heat for about 5 minutes, or until the onion is translucent.

2) Add mushrooms, garlic, celery, and seasonings, and sauté about 10 minutes — until everything is tender and well mingled.

3) Stir in remaining ingredients and mix well. Taste to correct seasonings.

4) Preheat oven to 350°F. Fill the prebaked squash and bake, covered, until heated through (20 to 30 minutes).

⌣Zuccanoes⌣
(Stuffed Zucchini)

About 1¼ hours
to prepare
(including baking)

Yield:
4 to 6
servings

PRELIMINARY: You'll need 1½ cups cooked rice.

4 medium-sized zucchini (about 7 inches long)
1 Tbs. olive oil
1½ cups minced onion
1 tsp. salt
½ lb. mushrooms
6 medium cloves garlic, minced
1½ cups cooked rice
1½ cups finely minced (or ground) almonds
3 Tbs. lemon juice
black pepper and cayenne, to taste
small handfuls of freshly minced herbs, if available
    (parsley, basil, thyme, dill, chives, marjoram)
optional: 1 cup (packed) grated Swiss cheese
optional: 1 batch Vegetable Purée (Beet or Red Pepper- p. 86)

1) Cut the zucchini lengthwise down the middle. Use a spoon to scoop
   out the insides, leaving a canoe with ¼-inch shell. Finely mince
   the scrapings; set the canoes aside.

2) Heat the olive oil in a medium-sized skillet. Add onion and salt, and
   sauté over medium heat 5 to 8 minutes, or until the onion is soft.

3) Add zucchini innards and mushrooms, and sauté another 8 to 10 minutes. Add the garlic during the last few minutes.

4) Place rice and almonds in a medium-sized bowl. Stir in the sauté and
   lemon juice and mix well. Season to taste with black pepper, cayenne,
   and optional fresh herbs.

5) Preheat oven to 350°F. Fill the zucchini shells, top with cheese (optional),
   and bake for 30 to 40 minutes ~ until heated through. Serve hot,
   sublimely augmented by room-temperature Beet or Red Pepper Purée.

154 ENTRÉES

Preparation time:
1½ hours
(This includes time
for making the sauce.)

Stuffed Cabbage

Yield:
6 servings
(2 rolls apiece)

Serve over rice.

1 large head green cabbage	salt and black pepper, to taste
1 Tbs. butter	2 cups (1 lb.) ricotta cheese
1 cup minced onion	1 small tart apple, finely chopped
1 small clove garlic, minced	¼ cup raisins or currants
1 stalk celery, minced	3 to 4 Tbs. lemon juice
1 small carrot, diced	1 to 2 Tbs. soy sauce
¾ cup minced cashews (optional)	1 Tbs. honey (optional)
¼ cup sunflower seeds	1 batch Cashew-Ginger Sauce (p.90)

1) Heat a large kettleful of water to boiling. Core the head of cabbage, and carefully lower it into the water. Turn the heat down to a simmer, and leave the cabbage in there for about 10 to 15 minutes, or until the outer leaves can be removed easily. Retrieve the cabbage from the water, and pull off the 12 outermost leaves. Make sure the cabbage is cooked well enough so the leaves will not break when rolled, but not so well done that they disintegrate. Set aside the 12 leaves, and save the rest of the cabbage to use for another dish. (It's great for soup!)

2) Melt the butter in a medium-sized skillet and add the onion, garlic, celery, and carrot. Sauté over medium heat for about 10 minutes, then add nuts, seeds, salt, and pepper. When the vegetables are tender, remove from heat.

3) Place the ricotta in a medium-large bowl. Add the sauté, plus the apple, raisins, lemon juice, soy sauce, and optional honey. Mix well, and taste to adjust seasonings. Meanwhile, preheat oven to 325°F.

4) Place 3 to 4 Tbs. filling near the base of each cabbage leaf. Roll firmly, folding in the sides. Arrange the cabbage rolls in an oblong baking pan, pour Cashew-Ginger Sauce over the top and bake, covered, until heated through — about 30 minutes.

✦✦✦ Spinach-Ricotta Pie ✦✦✦

The Crust: 6 Tbs. butter or margarine, cut into small pieces
1½ cups flour
about 4 Tbs. cold water, milk, or buttermilk

The Filling: 1 tsp. butter or margarine
1 cup minced onion
1 lb. spinach, stemmed and finely chopped
½ tsp. salt
freshly ground pepper, to taste
1 tsp. basil
1 lb. ricotta cheese
2 or 3 beaten eggs
3 Tbs. flour
½ cup (packed) grated sharp cheese of your choice
a dash of nutmeg (optional)

Optional topping: 1 cup sour cream (may be lowfat), lightly beaten
paprika

CRUST

1) Use a pastry cutter, two forks, or a food processor to cut together the butter and flour until the mixture is uniformly blended and resembles coarse cornmeal. (The food processor will do this in just a few spurts.)

2) Add just enough liquid (water, milk, or buttermilk) to hold the dough together. Roll out the dough and form a crust in a 9- or 10-inch pie pan. Set aside.

3) Preheat oven to 375°F. Melt the butter or margarine in a medium-sized skillet, add the onion, and sauté for 5 minutes over medium heat. Add spinach, salt, pepper, and basil, and cook, stirring, over medium-high heat until the spinach is wilted. Remove from heat.

4) Combine all filling ingredients in a large bowl, and mix well. Spread into the unbaked pie shell. For an extra rich pie, top with sour cream, spread to the edges of the crust. Dust generously with paprika.

5) Bake 40 to 45 minutes, or until firm to the touch at the center. Serve hot, warm, or at room temperature.

Swiss Cheese & Mushroom Quiche

Preparation time:
about 1¼ hours,
including baking

Yield:
1 10-inch pie
(4 to 6 servings)

1 10-inch pie crust (recipe on preceding page), pressed into either
    a pie pan or a springform tart pan

1 tsp. butter or margarine

1½ cups chopped onion

¼ lb. mushrooms, sliced or minced

½ tsp. salt

black pepper

a pinch of thyme

½ tsp. dry mustard

4 large eggs (or 2 whole eggs plus 2 egg whites)

1½ cups milk (can be lowfat)

2 Tbs. flour

1½ cups (packed) grated Swiss cheese

paprika

OPTIONAL VARIATIONS:
    ★ substitute other delicious cheeses for the Swiss
    ★ add fresh tomato slices (no need to sauté first)
    ★ minced fresh herbs (chives, parsley, chervil,
       marjoram, basil, dill, etc.)
    ★ a hint of Hot: 1 tsp. prepared horseradish
       and/or cayenne or Tabasco

1) Preheat oven to 375°F.

2) Melt the butter in a small pan. Add onions, and sauté over medium heat for a few minutes. When they begin to soften, add mushrooms, salt, pepper, thyme, and mustard. Sauté about 5 minutes more and remove from heat.

3) Combine eggs, milk, and flour in a blender or food processor, and beat well.

4) Spread the grated cheese over the bottom of the unbaked crust, and spread the onion-mushroom mixture on top. Pour in the custard, and sprinkle the top with paprika.

5) Bake for 35 to 45 minutes, or until solid in the center. Serve hot, warm, or at room temperature.

Old Country Pie

1 unbaked 9- or 10-inch pie crust (see 2 pages back)
1 Tbs. butter, margarine, or oil
1½ cups minced onion
1 tsp. caraway seeds
1 tsp. salt
½ lb. mushrooms, chopped or sliced
1½ cups shredded cabbage
1 medium stalk broccoli, chopped
1 medium carrot, thinly sliced
2 tsp. dill
lots of black pepper
3 medium cloves garlic, minced
2 Tbs. flour
½ cup cottage cheese (lowfat ok)
2 eggs (one or both yolks can be omitted)
2 medium scallions, finely minced
OPTIONAL: ¾ cup sour cream and/or yogurt; paprika

1) Prepare pie crust. Preheat oven to 350°F.
2) Melt butter (or heat oil) in a medium-sized skillet. Add onion, caraway, and salt, and sauté over medium heat until the onions begin to brown (10 to 15 minutes).
3) Add mushrooms, cabbage, broccoli, carrot, and dill, and sauté until everything is just tender — about 8 more minutes.
4) Stir in black pepper, garlic, and flour, and cook, stirring, for just a few minutes more. Remove from heat.
5) Beat together cottage cheese and eggs. Add this to the sauté along with the scallions and mix well.
6) Spread into the unbaked crust and, if desired, top with a layer of sour cream and/or yogurt. Sprinkle with paprika, and bake for 40 minutes or until set. Serve hot, warm, or at room temperature.

Cauliflower-Cheese Pie
with Grated Potato Crust

1 hour
to prepare

1 9-inch pie
(4 to 5 servings)

CONVENIENCE TIPS: ☆ Use food processor with grating attachment to grate cheese, potato, and onion in that order. (No need to clean in between.)
☆ Prepare the filling while the crust bakes.

CRUST:

2 cups (packed) grated raw potato
¼ cup grated onion
½ tsp. salt

1 egg white, lightly beaten
flour for your fingers
a little oil

FILLING:

1 Tbs. olive oil or butter
1 cup chopped onion
2 medium cloves garlic, minced
½ tsp. salt
black pepper, to taste
½ tsp. basil

¼ tsp. thyme
1 medium cauliflower, in small pieces
2 eggs (or 1 whole egg plus 1 egg white)
¼ cup milk (lowfat OK)
1 cup (packed) grated cheddar
paprika

1) Preheat oven to 400°F. Oil a 9-inch pie pan.

2) Combine grated potato and onion, salt, and egg white in a small bowl and mix well. Transfer to the pie pan and pat into place with lightly floured fingers, building up the sides into a handsome edge.

3) Bake for 30 minutes, then brush the crust with a little oil and bake it 10 more minutes. Remove from oven, and turn the temperature down to 375°.

4) Heat the olive oil or butter in a large skillet. Add onion, garlic, salt, pepper, and herbs, and sauté over medium heat for about 5 minutes. Add cauliflower, stir, and cover. Cook until tender, stirring occasionally (about 8 to 10 minutes).

5) Spread half the cheese onto the baked crust (OK if it's still hot). Spoon the sautéed vegetables on top, then sprinkle on the remaining cheese. Beat the eggs and milk together, and pour this over the top. Dust lightly with paprika.

6) Bake 35 to 40 minutes, or until set. Serve hot or warm.

CALZONE

A calzone is a savory Italian pastry resembling a large overstuffed turnover made with pizza dough. Traditionally, the filling is a mixture of cheeses, contrasting perfectly with the crispy crust.

I've included a cheese filling, plus a few ideas for nondairy ones as well.

One calzone per person plus a green salad make a very satisfying dinner.

Preparation time:
about 2 hours

Yield:
6 servings

- Make the filling while the dough rises, to save time.
- The dough can be made in advance and refrigerated or even frozen until use. Let come to room temperature before assembling, then knead for a few minutes to warm it up.

THE DOUGH:

1 cup wrist-temperature water
1½ tsp. active dry yeast
1 Tbs. honey or sugar
1½ tsp. salt
2½ to 3 cups flour
olive oil

1) Place the water in a medium-sized bowl. Sprinkle in the yeast, and stir in the honey or sugar until everything dissolves.

2) Use a whisk to stir in the salt and flour. When it gets too thick to whisk, mix with one floured hand. Knead in the bowl for about 5 minutes.

3) Brush a little olive oil over the dough, cover the bowl, and let rise in a warm place until doubled in bulk (about 1 hour). In the meantime, you can get the filling ready.

SPINACH-CHEESE FILLING:

1 Tbs. olive oil
1 cup minced onion
1 lb. spinach, stemmed and minced
about ½ tsp. salt
lots of black pepper

4 or 5 medium cloves garlic, minced
1 Tbs. dried (or 3 Tbs. minced fresh) basil
1 lb. ricotta or cottage cheese
2 cups (packed) grated mozzarella
about ¼ cup grated parmesan

1) Heat the olive oil in a medium-sized skillet. Add onion, and sauté over medium heat until translucent — about 5 minutes.
2) Add spinach, salt, and pepper. Cook, stirring, over high heat for several minutes — until the spinach wilts. Stir in the garlic and basil and cook for about 2 more minutes.
3) Place the cheeses in a medium-sized bowl. Add the spinach sauté and mix very well. Taste to correct seasonings.

TO ASSEMBLE:

1) Preheat oven to 450°F. Oil a baking tray.
2) Punch down the risen dough. Divide it into 6 equal sections, and roll out on a floured surface into circles ¼ inch thick.
3) Place ½ to ¾ cup filling on one half of the circle, leaving a ½-inch rim. Use your fingers or a brush to moisten the rim with a little water. Fold over the empty side and crimp the edges with your favorite fork. Use that same fork to prick little holes here and there on the top surface.
4) Arrange the completed calzones on the oiled tray, and bake for 15 to 20 minutes, or until crisp and lightly browned. OPTIONAL: You can brush each pastry with a little melted butter or some olive oil during the last 5 minutes of baking. Serve hot.

ALTERNATIVE FILLINGS:

- 1 batch Eggplant Scallopini Marsala (p.83) — it's nondairy.
- 1 batch Asparagus-Mushroom Sauce (p.77). Replace the butter with olive oil; reduce wine to ½ cup; delete water. (Also nondairy.)
- Thick slices of fresh tomato — with mozzarella and Pesto (p.84). [If you don't have pesto made, just add a few cloves of sliced garlic, some freshly minced basil, and a drizzle of olive oil.]

SAVORY FILO PASTRIES

40 minutes to prepare;
30 minutes to bake

Yield: 2 rolls (about
6 servings) per recipe

Once you get past the mystique of filo pastry, you will see how easy it is to make delicious, mouthwateringly crisp, savory vegetable strudels. Buy the pastry (sometimes called "Fillo Leaves" or "Greek Phyllo") in a long rectangular package in the frozen foods section of most good grocery stores. Let it thaw out thoroughly while still wrapped (this will take an hour or two). Unwrap just before using, take out a pile of however many sheets you will need, and rewrap (airtight!) and refrigerate the rest until next time. Cover the sheets you are about to use with a slightly damp tea towel — they dry out quickly!

When I first learned to make strudels, I always brushed melted butter between the pastry layers. In recent years, however, I discovered I like using olive oil much better. You don't have to mess around with melting it; it goes further, so you can use much less of it; and it is lighter, has a great flavor, and is cholesterol-free. But if you just love butter so much that it would break your heart to substitute olive oil, try adding some melted butter to the oil, to flavor it.

Broccoli Strudel

- In the earlier version of Broccoli Strudel, there were 2 eggs and 3 Tbs. butter in the filling. Now there are no eggs and only 1 Tbs. butter or olive oil in the filling. You can choose to eliminate the cheese.
- Try making your own bread crumbs by grating some good bread in the food processor. The better-tasting the bread, the better.
- Each of these strudels uses about 10 sheets of filo pastry, which is approximately half a 1-lb. package.

1 Tbs. butter or olive oil
1 cup minced onion
1 large bunch broccoli, finely chopped
½ tsp. salt
lots of black pepper
2 medium cloves garlic, minced

2 cups good bread crumbs
2 cups grated cheddar (optional)
2 Tbs. lemon juice (more, to taste)

10 sheets of filo pastry
3 to 4 Tbs. olive oil (for the filo)

1) Preheat oven to 375°F. Oil a baking tray.

2) Melt butter or heat 1 Tbs. olive oil in a large skillet. Add onion, and sauté for about 5 minutes over medium heat.

3) Add broccoli, salt, and pepper, and cook, stirring, for about 5 more minutes. Add garlic, and sauté until the broccoli is just tender (about 5 more minutes). Remove from heat.

4) Stir in bread crumbs, cheese, and lemon juice. Taste to adjust seasonings.

5) TO ASSEMBLE: Place one sheet of filo on a clean, dry countertop. Brush the top lightly with oil, then add another sheet. Brush with oil, then add another. Continue until you have a pile of 5 leaves. Add half the filling (as illustrated), fold in the sides, and gently roll until you have a neat little log. Brush the top with more oil, then carefully lift the pastry, and place it on the oiled baking sheet. Repeat this procedure to make a second roll, and place it next to the first one on the tray.

filling

6) Bake 25 to 30 minutes, until golden and exquisitely crisp. Cut with a serrated knife, using a gentle sawing motion. Serve hot or at room temperature.

꒰ ꒱ ꒰ ꒱ ꒰ ꒱ ꒰ ꒱ ꒰ ꒱

Mushroom Strudel

1 lb. mushrooms, chopped
1 cup (8 oz.) cream cheese or
    cottage cheese (lowfat OK)
1 cup sour cream and/or yogurt
1 tsp. salt
lots of black pepper
1 tsp. dill
1 cup good bread crumbs

2 scallions, finely minced (whites & greens)
¼ cup (packed) minced parsley
3 Tbs. lemon juice
    . . . . .
10 sheets of filo pastry
3 to 4 Tbs. olive oil, for the filo
optional: poppy seeds, for the top

1) Preheat oven to 375°F. Oil a baking tray.

2) Place the mushrooms in a saucepan, and cook them all by themselves over medium heat for about 10 minutes. Drain them, squeezing out all the excess liquid, and transfer the mushrooms to a medium-sized bowl. (You can save the discarded liquid for a great soup stock.)

3) Add cream cheese, cut into small pieces, or cottage cheese to the hot mushrooms. Mix well. Stir in remaining filling ingredients.

4) Follow directions in steps 5 and 6 above. A very nice optional touch: sprinkle some poppy seeds on top before baking.

Spanakopita

Heavenly Greek Spinach Pastry

1½ hours
to prepare
and bake

Yield:
about 8
servings

New! NO EGGS and NO BUTTER Revised!

2 Notes ♪: ♪Stores well (unbaked) for up to several days. Cover tightly and refrigerate. ♪Detailed information about filo pastry on p. 162.

FILLING:
1 Tbs. olive oil
2 cups minced onion
¼ to ½ tsp. salt
1 tsp. basil
1 tsp. oregano

2½ lbs. fresh spinach, stemmed and finely chopped
5 medium cloves garlic, minced
3 Tbs. flour
2 to 3 cups (packed) crumbled feta cheese (about 1 lb.)
1 cup cottage or pot cheese
black pepper, to taste

⅓ to ½ cup olive oil, for the filo
1 lb. filo pastry leaves (approximately 20 leaves) — thoroughly defrosted (unwrap just prior to step 5)

1) Preheat oven to 375°F. Oil a 9 x 13-inch baking pan.
2) Heat 1 Tbs. olive oil in a Dutch oven. Add onion, salt, and herbs, and sauté for about 5 minutes, or until the onion softens. Add spinach, turn up the heat, and cook, stirring, until the spinach wilts (5 to 8 minutes). Stir in the garlic.
3) Sprinkle in the flour, stir, and cook over medium heat 2 to 3 more minutes. Remove from heat.
4) Mix in the cheeses. Taste to correct seasonings, adding lots of black pepper.
5) Place a sheet of filo in the oiled pan, letting the pastry edges climb up the sides. Brush lightly with oil, and add another sheet. Keep going until you have a pile of 8 oiled sheets. Add half the filling, spreading it to the edges, then repeat with 8 more sheets of oiled filo, followed by the remaining filling. Layer the rest of the filo over the filling, brushing oil in between. Oil the top, tuck in the edges, and bake uncovered for about 45 minutes or until golden and crispy. Cut into squares and serve hot or warm.

POLENTA PIE

Easy deep-dish pizza
with a thick and crunchy
cornmeal crust

1¼ hours to prepare
(most of which is
crust-baking time)

Yield:
1 10-inch pie
(serves 4)

FILLING:

CRUST:

1½ cups coarse cornmeal
1 tsp. salt
1½ cups cold water
2 cups boiling water
a little olive oil

1 Tbs. olive oil
1 small onion, thinly sliced
½ cup thinly sliced bell pepper
about 10 mushrooms, sliced
1 small zucchini, thinly sliced
5 to 6 medium cloves garlic, sliced
2 tsp. dried basil (or 2 Tbs. minced fresh basil)
½ tsp. oregano
fresh black pepper
¼ lb. mozzarella cheese, grated
2 small – or 1 medium – ripe tomato(es), sliced

1) Combine cornmeal, salt, and cold water in a small bowl. Have the boiling water on the stove in a saucepan, and add the cornmeal mixture, whisking. Cook about 10 minutes over low heat, stirring frequently. It will get very thick. Remove from heat, and let cool until handleable.

2) Preheat oven to 375°F. Oil a 10-inch pie pan. Add the polenta, and use a spatula and wet hands to form it into a smooth, thick crust over the bottom and sides of the pan. Brush the surface with olive oil, and bake uncovered for 45 minutes.

3) While the crust bakes, heat 1 Tbs. olive oil in a medium-sized skillet. Add the onion, and sauté for 5 to 8 minutes, or until it begins to soften. Add bell pepper, mushrooms, and zucchini, and sauté until everything is tender. Stir in the garlic and herbs, and sauté just a few minutes more.

4) Turn up the oven to broiling temperature. Sprinkle half the cheese onto the bottom of the baked crust, then add the tomato slices. Spread the sautéed mixture over the tomatoes, and sprinkle the remaining cheese on top. Broil until brown (about 5 minutes), and serve hot.

Zucchini-Crusted Pizza

🌱🌱🌱🌱🌱🌱🌱🌱🌱🌱🌱🌱🌱🌱🌱🌱🌱🌱🌱🌱

~ a normal pizza on top, with a beautiful, substantial-yet-tender crust: golden, with flecks of green and a slight crunch.

~ If possible, use a food processor with the grating attachment for the zucchini and mozzarella.

~ You can make the crust up to several days in advance.

🌱🌱🌱🌱🌱🌱🌱🌱🌱🌱🌱🌱🌱🌱🌱🌱🌱🌱🌱🌱🌱🌱🌱🌱🌱🌱🌱🌱

olive oil and flour for the pan
2 cups (packed) grated zucchini (about 2 7-inchers)
2 eggs, beaten (OK to delete one or both yolks)
¼ cup flour
½ cup grated mozzarella
½ cup grated parmesan
OPTIONAL: pinches of basil, marjoram, and/or rosemary
2 Tbs. olive oil

TOPPING SUGGESTIONS:

extra olive oil
1 large ripe tomato, sliced
extra mozzarella, sliced or grated
2 to 3 large cloves garlic, thinly sliced
sautéed mushrooms
thinly sliced bell peppers
sliced olives

1) Preheat oven to 400°F. Generously oil a 10-inch pie pan and coat lightly with flour.
2) Combine zucchini, eggs, flour, mozzarella, parmesan, herbs, and 1 Tbs. olive oil in a bowl and mix well.
3) Spread into the prepared pan and bake for 35 to 40 minutes, or until golden brown. About halfway through the baking, brush with the remaining tablespoon of olive oil (optional). Remove from oven. When it has cooled for about 10 minutes, use a spatula to loosen the crust from the pan, so it won't break later.
4) Top with your favorite pizza items and bake at 400°F. until heated through.

Eggplant-Almond Enchiladas

... slightly different enchiladas, with deep flavor
and wonderful textural contrasts

Serve with rice and plain beans or Refritos (following page). You'll
need a batch of Mexican Red Sauce (p.95) made in advance.

1 Tbs. olive oil
1 cup minced onion
6 cups diced eggplant (approximately 1 large or 2 small)
1 tsp. salt (possibly more, to taste)
lots of black pepper   *Cumin & Chili Powder*
4 medium cloves garlic, minced
1 medium green bell pepper, minced
1 cup lightly toasted almonds, minced
1 packed cup grated jack cheese (or a similar mild white cheese)
6 ~~12~~ corn tortillas
1 batch Mexican Red Sauce (p.95)

1) Heat olive oil in a deep skillet or Dutch oven. Add onion, and sauté for
about 5 minutes over medium heat.

2) Add eggplant, salt, and pepper, and mix well. Cover and cook for about
10 minutes over medium heat, stirring occasionally, until the eggplant
is soft.

3) Add garlic and bell pepper. Stir and cook 5 to 8 more minutes, or until
the pepper is just tender. Taste to correct salt.

4) Remove from heat; stir in almonds and cheese.

5) Preheat oven to 350°F. Moisten each tortilla briefly in water, then place
approximately ¼ cup *Big Spoon* of filling on one side and roll up. Gently situate
the filled enchiladas in a baking pan. Pour a batch of sauce over the
top. Bake uncovered for about 30 minutes.

REFRITOS
(REFRIED BEANS)

The beans need to soak
for at least 4 hours;
then to cook for about
1¼ hrs. Do other preparations
while the beans cook.

ꝺ ꝺ ꝺ ꝺ ꝺ ꝺ ꝺ ꝺ

Yield:
6 to 8
servings

Serve Refritos in Tostadas (see below) or stuffed into bell peppers and baked, then served over rice with Nachos Sauce (p.94). Or, for a plain and inexpensive dinner, serve with rice, green salad, and warm tortillas.

       2 cups dry pinto beans, soaked
       2 to 3 Tbs. olive oil
       2 cups minced onion
       5 to 6 (or even more) medium cloves garlic, minced
       2 tsp. cumin
       1½ tsp. salt
       black pepper
       optional: 1 small bell pepper, minced

1) Cook the presoaked beans in plenty of boiling water until very soft. Drain and set aside.

2) Heat the olive oil in a large skillet. Add onion, half the garlic, cumin, and salt. Sauté over medium heat about 10 minutes, or until the onions are soft. Add (or don't add) the optional bell pepper, and sauté another 5 minutes. Add remaining garlic; season with black pepper.

3) Turn heat to low, add beans, and mix well. Mash with a fork or a potato masher, and cook for just a few minutes more. Serve right away, or store in refrigerator or freezer until time to reheat. (Refritos reheat beautifully.)

ϭ ϭ ϭ ϭ ϭ ϭ ϭ ϭ ϭ   TOSTADAS   ꝺ ꝺ ꝺ ꝺ ꝺ ꝺ ꝺ ꝺ ꝺ

A tostada is a kind of open-faced Mexican sandwich, with many contrasting layers of food piled onto a crispy corn tortilla. Invite your friends over for a tostada-building party. Spread a large table with dishes of tostada components, and do it buffet-style. (Continued →)

168   ENTRÉES

Tostada Components:

1) DEEP-FRIED TORTILLAS: Fry corn tortillas in hot oil until crisp. Drain well on paper towels, and serve in a basket.

2) REFRITOS (preceding page)

3) ACCESSORIES: (use all or some ~ or add your own inspired ideas)

shredded lettuce	minced olives	chopped hardboiled egg
finely shredded cabbage	grated cheese	minced mild chilies
Guacamole (p.108)	chopped tomatoes	sour cream

4) HOT SAUCE (p.95) or NACHOS SAUCE (p.94) or SALSA FRESCA (p.96).

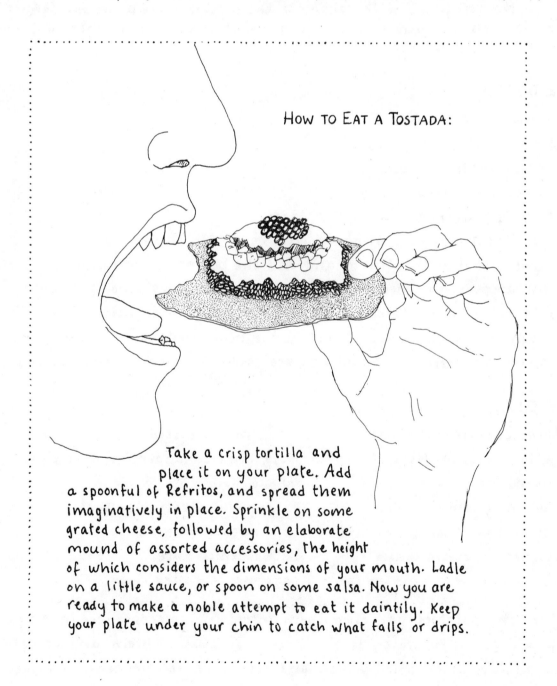

HOW TO EAT A TOSTADA:

Take a crisp tortilla and place it on your plate. Add a spoonful of Refritos, and spread them imaginatively in place. Sprinkle on some grated cheese, followed by an elaborate mound of assorted accessories, the height of which considers the dimensions of your mouth. Ladle on a little sauce, or spoon on some salsa. Now you are ready to make a noble attempt to eat it daintily. Keep your plate under your chin to catch what falls or drips.

SAMOSAS

1½ hours to prepare;
25 minutes to bake

Yield: 15 or 16 medium-sized,
very satisfying pastries (enough
to feed 6 to 8 people, at least)

Samosas are flaky pastries filled with spicy potatoes and peas. In traditional Indian cuisine, they are deep-fried (and that is still an option). But baking them works very well, and is easier and more healthful.

All components can be made well ahead of time. Finished Samosas can be stored for days in the refrigerator or freezer. Make the Dipping Sauce while the Samosas bake.

Serve Samosas with any curry, or as a simple supper with Gingered Carrot Soup (p.22) and Raita (p.99).

THE DOUGH:

2½ cups flour
½ tsp. salt
1 cup buttermilk or yogurt
extra flour, as needed

1) Place the flour in a medium-sized bowl. Mix in the salt.
2) Make a well in the center, and add the buttermilk or yogurt. Mix first with a spoon and then with your hand, to make a smooth dough.
3) Add extra flour, as needed, to keep the dough from being sticky. The dough will be quite soft. Knead in the bowl for about 5 minutes. Cover tightly and refrigerate until you are ready to assemble the pastries.

THE FILLING:

2 large potatoes (the size of a large person's fist)
1 Tbs. butter
1 cup finely minced onion
2 medium cloves garlic, minced
1 Tbs. freshly grated ginger

1 tsp. mustard seeds
1 tsp. dried coriander (if available)
¾ tsp. salt
1½ cups uncooked green peas (frozen, thawed = fine)
2 Tbs. lemon juice
cayenne, to taste

1) Peel the potatoes and chop them into 1-inch pieces. Place in a sauce-pan, cover with water, and boil until very soft. Drain and transfer to a medium-sized bowl. Mash and set aside. (continued on next page...)

2) Melt the butter in a heavy skillet. Add onion, garlic, ginger, mustard seeds, coriander, and salt. Sauté over medium heat about 8 to 10 minutes, or until the onions are quite soft. Add this to the mashed potatoes, along with the remaining ingredients. Mix well, but try not to smash the peas. Cool for at least 15 minutes before filling the pastries.

THE DIPPING SAUCE:

½ cup cider vinegar
½ cup water
3 Tbs. brown sugar
1 small clove garlic, minced
1 tsp. salt

1) Place all ingredients in a small saucepan. Stir until the sugar dissolves.
2) Heat to boiling, then let simmer uncovered for about 10 minutes. It will reduce slightly.
3) Serve warm or at room temperature with hot Samosas.

TO ASSEMBLE AND BAKE:

1) Preheat the oven to 425°F. Generously oil a baking sheet.
2) Keep a small container of flour, a fork, a small bowl of water, and a pastry brush close at hand. Flour a clean surface, and, one by one, roll 1-inch balls of dough into 5-inch circles, using a rolling pin.
3) Place approximately 1½ Tbs. filling in the center of each circle, and fold over, just like a turnover. Brush the inside edges of each circle with a little water, and fold the edges together to make a small hem. Crimp the edges firmly with the fork.
   NOTE: If you are storing the Samosas to bake later on, place them on a heavily floured plate or tray, dust the tops with more flour, and cover tightly. Store in the refrigerator or freezer until baking time.
4) To bake: Place the Samosas on the oiled baking sheet. Brush the tops with oil. Bake 15 minutes at 425°F., then reduce heat to 375°F. and bake for 10 minutes more. For maximum crispiness, turn the Samosas over when you turn the oven down.
5) Serve within 15 minutes of baking, with Dipping Sauce. A nice way to serve the sauce is in individual saucers or tiny bowls, so each person can hold both Samosa and sauce directly under his or her face while eating, and the sauce bowl can catch the drips. (It does drip, but that's one of the charms of this ritual.)

EGGPLANT CURRY

Preparation time: 45 minutes
(Put up rice when you begin.)

Yield: 6 to 8 servings

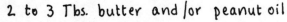

2 to 3 Tbs. butter and/or peanut oil
1 Tbs. mustard seeds
2 Tbs. sesame seeds
2 tsp. cumin seeds
1½ cups chopped onion
1½ to 2 tsp. salt
2 tsp. turmeric
¼ tsp. cayenne (possibly more, depending on your tolerance / preference)
2 medium eggplants (7 to 8 inches long; 4-inch diameter at roundest
    point), cut into 1-inch cubes
water, as needed
2 cups frozen or fresh green peas
optional: 1 small bunch fresh cilantro, minced

1) Heat butter or oil over medium heat in a very large, deep skillet or
   Dutch oven. Add seeds, and sauté until they begin to pop (5 minutes).

2) Add onion, salt, turmeric, and cayenne. Cook, stirring occasionally,
   for 8 to 10 minutes, or until the onion is translucent.

3) Add eggplant and salt. Cook, stirring from the bottom regularly,
   for 15 to 20 minutes—until the eggplant is soft. You might need
   to add a little water if the mixture is too dry. Cover the pan between stirrings.

4) Steam the peas until they are just tender and bright green. Serve
   the curry over rice, topped with peas and freshly minced cilantro.

సత్యమ్మ ప్రసిద్ది గోపి పువ్వు కూర

(Satyamma's Famous Cauliflower Curry)

30 to 40 minutes
to prepare

Yield:
about 6 servings

ON THE SIDE

Begin cooking some rice at around the same time you start preparing the curry.

2 cups brown rice in 3 cups water will be the right amount.

2 medium-small (3-inch diameter) potatoes, cut into small chunks
½ cup shredded unsweetened coconut
1 Tbs. mustard seeds
3 medium cloves garlic, peeled
1½ Tbs. minced fresh ginger
½ cup lightly toasted peanuts
1 tsp. turmeric
½ tsp. ground cloves or allspice
2 Tbs. toasted cumin seeds
1 to 2 Tbs. toasted sesame seeds
¼ tsp. cayenne
½ cup water (more, as needed)
1 to 2 Tbs. peanut oil
1½ cups chopped onion
1 tsp. salt
1 large cauliflower, cut in 1-inch pieces
1 medium carrot, thinly sliced
optional: 1 cup cooked chick peas
3 to 4 Tbs. lemon juice

ON THE SIDE

Your choice of condiments:

Raita (p.99)
Lemon slices
Orange slices
Toasted Nuts
Toasted Coconut
Raisins
Sliced Cucumbers
Sliced Tomatoes
Thin Strips of Bell Pepper (assorted colors)

1) Boil the potatoes until just tender. Drain and set aside.
2) Place the next 11 ingredients in a blender and purée until fairly homogenous. Add extra water, as needed, to form a soft, workable paste.
3) Heat the oil in a large, deep skillet or Dutch oven, and add onion and salt. Sauté for 5 minutes over medium heat, then add cauliflower and carrot and mix well. Cover and cook about 10 minutes, then add the paste. Mix well. Cook, covered, over low heat until the cauliflower is tender, stirring every few minutes. Add more water, if necessary, to prevent sticking.
4) Add the cooked potatoes, chick peas, and lemon juice, and cook a few more minutes. Taste to adjust salt, and serve hot, with rice and condiments.

✿ ★ Mushroom Curry ✿

50 minutes to prepare
(put up rice when you
begin)

Yield:
4 to 6
servings

There are a few surprises in this tart-savory-sweet curry. Try sautéing chopped almonds in a little butter or margarine for the topping.

The tomatoes work best if peeled and seeded ahead of time. It's easy: just core them and plunge them into boiling water for 10 seconds. Pull off the peel, then cut them open and squeeze out the seeds. Chop the remaining pulp.

2 Tbs. butter or margarine
2 cups chopped onion
3 medium cloves garlic, minced
1 tsp. cumin
1 tsp. cinnamon
1 tsp. turmeric
1 tsp. powdered ginger
1 tsp. mustard seeds
½ tsp. cloves or allspice

1½ tsp. salt (possibly more, to taste)
1 cup chopped celery
1½ lbs. mushrooms, coarsely chopped
3 medium-sized tomatoes, chopped
2 medium-sized tart apples, chopped
½ cup shredded unsweetened coconut
1 Tbs. honey (optional, to taste)
3 to 4 Tbs. lemon juice
cayenne, to taste

optional toppings { yogurt
sautéed or toasted almonds

1) Melt the butter in a large, deep skillet or a Dutch oven. Add onions and garlic, and sauté over medium heat. After a few minutes add spices and salt. Sauté another 5 to 8 minutes ~ until onions are soft.

2) Add celery and mushrooms. Mix well, cover, and simmer another 8 to 10 minutes, stirring occasionally. You can add up to ½ cup water during this time, to prevent sticking. (It makes a nice broth.)

3) When the celery is slightly tender, add tomatoes, apples, coconut, honey, and lemon juice. Cover, and continue to cook until everything is tender, but not mushy. (Additional water may be needed. Use small amounts at a time.) Add cayenne to taste, cover, and let sit for about 10 minutes before serving. Serve over rice.

Yield:
4 or 5
servings

TOMATO CURRY

...delicious on rice, with chutney (p.98) and Raita (p.99) or plain yogurt. Good, also, as an accompaniment to other curries. The eggs go well with the tomatoes, or you can use tofu, which is very similar to the Indian cheese, panir.

PRELIMINARY: Peel and seed the tomatoes beforehand. First, core the tomatoes, and drop them into a saucepanful of boiling water for 10 seconds. Then hold them over a sink and pull off the skins. (They will come right off.) Cut the tomatoes open; squeeze out and discard the seeds. Coarsely chop the remaining pulp.

1 Tbs. butter or oil
1½ cups chopped onion
1 tsp. salt
1 small bell pepper, minced
6 medium-sized ripe tomatoes, peeled and seeded (see above)
2 cups tomato purée
½ tsp. cinnamon
2 tsp. cumin
optional: ½ tsp. ground fenugreek
           ½ tsp. dried coriander
¼ tsp. cayenne (more, to taste)
optional: 3 hardboiled eggs, peeled and cut into wedges
           ½ lb. very firm tofu, cut into small cubes
           fresh cilantro, minced

2 tsp. mustard seeds
2 tsp grated ginger
3 to 4 medium cloves garlic, minced

1) Melt butter (or heat oil) in a Dutch oven. Add onion, salt, and mustard seeds. Sauté over medium heat for 8 to 10 minutes, or until the onions soften and the seeds begin to pop.
2) Add ginger, garlic, and minced bell pepper, and cook another 5 minutes, or until the pepper begins to be tender.
3) Add remaining ingredients, mix well, and heat just to boiling, stirring frequently. Turn the heat down to a simmer, cover, and cook for 15 to 20 minutes.
4) Serve hot, over rice, with wedges of egg or cubes of tofu artfully arranged on top, and a final sprinkling of minced cilantro.

Preparation time:
about 1¾ hours
after beans are soaked

Vegetarian Chili

A traditional chili, except with bulgur and without ground meat. Although the concept of "meat substitutes" is hardly compelling, the bulgur really does give a ground-beef-like texture. It also enhances the protein content.

Soak the beans for at least 4 hours (preferably overnight) before cooking. Prepare all other ingredients while the beans are cooking, to save time.

2½ cups dry kidney beans, soaked	2 tsp. basil
1 cup tomato juice	2 tsp. chili powder (more, to taste)
1 cup uncooked bulgur wheat	1½ tsp. salt (more, to taste)
2 Tbs. olive oil	black pepper and cayenne, to taste
2 cups chopped onion	1 medium bell pepper, chopped
6 to 8 large cloves garlic, minced	1 14½-oz. can tomatoes
1 medium carrot, diced	3 Tbs. tomato paste (half a small can)
1 medium stalk celery, diced	finely minced parsley } optional toppings
2 tsp. cumin	grated cheese

1) Place the soaked beans in a Dutch oven or kettle, cover with water, and bring to a boil. Partially cover, turn heat down to a simmer, and cook until tender (about 1¼ hours). Watch the water level during cooking, adding more if necessary. Drain off any excess water when the beans are done.

2) Heat the tomato juice to boiling. Add it to the bulgur in a small bowl, cover, and let stand 15 minutes. Add this to the cooked beans.

3) Heat the olive oil in a medium-sized skillet. Add onion, half the garlic, carrot, celery, and seasonings. Sauté over medium heat about 5 minutes, add bell pepper, and sauté until all the vegetables are tender.

4) Add the sautéed vegetables, tomatoes (au jus), and tomato paste to the beans. Simmer over lowest possible heat, stirring occasionally, for 20 to 30 minutes or longer. After about 15 minutes, add remaining garlic. Taste to adjust seasonings, and serve hot, topped with parsley and/or cheese.

VEGETABLE STEW

Preparation time:
about 50 minutes

Yield:
about 6 servings

2 Tbs. olive oil and/or butter
3 cups minced onion
3 medium cloves garlic, minced
2 medium potatoes, diced
1 medium (7-inch or so) eggplant, diced
1 tsp. salt (more, to taste)
fresh black pepper, to taste
2 medium stalks celery, chopped
1 healthy stalk broccoli, chopped small
2 to 3 medium carrots, sliced or diced
½ cup dry red wine (optional)
2 small (6-inch) zucchini, diced
3 Tbs. (half a small can) tomato paste
½ lb. mushrooms, coarsely chopped
3 Tbs. molasses
2 tsp. dill
sour cream or yogurt } optional
finely minced parsley } toppings

1) Heat oil (or melt butter) in a Dutch oven. Add onion, garlic, potatoes, eggplant, salt, and pepper. Cover and cook over medium heat, stirring often, until the potatoes are tender. Add small amounts of water, as needed, to prevent sticking.

2) Add celery, broccoli, and carrots, along with optional red wine. Continue to cook over medium heat, covered but occasionally stirring, until all the vegetables begin to be tender (8 to 10 minutes).

3) Add remaining ingredients (except toppings) and stir. Cover and simmer very quietly about 15 minutes more, stirring every once in a while. Taste to correct seasonings.

Serve piping hot, topped
with sour cream or yogurt
and minced parsley.

Polenta

Cornmeal mush with Class

For a super-easy, super-fast meal, serve Polenta in a bowl topped with a little olive oil or butter and some cheese. Or top it with Pesto (p.84), Gorgonzola (or any blue cheese), chopped fresh tomatoes, and a generous amount of coarsely ground black pepper. You can also serve Polenta under or next to Ratatouille or its Spicy Variation (see following page) or paired with any kind of chili or bean dish (see pages 176 and 134).

5 cups water
1 1/2 cups coarse cornmeal
1/2 tsp. salt
OPTIONAL TOPPINGS: See above

1) Place 4 cups of water in a medium-sized saucepan and bring to a boil.

2) Combine the cornmeal with the remaining cup of water in a small bowl, and mix until uniform.

3) Spoon the cornmeal mixture into the boiling water, add salt, and whisk until smooth.

4) Turn the heat down to a simmer, and cook, stirring often, for about 10 minutes, or until very thick.

Ratatouille

Mediterranean vegetable stew

3 Tbs. olive oil
4 medium cloves garlic
2 cups chopped onion
1 bay leaf
1 medium eggplant (7 to 8
   inches long; 4 to 5-inch
   diameter), cubed
1½ tsp. salt
1½ tsp. basil
1 tsp. marjoram or oregano
½ tsp. rosemary
½ tsp. thyme
1 medium (6- to 7-inch)
   zucchini, cubed

2 medium bell peppers, in strips
fresh black pepper
1 14½-oz. can tomatoes
freshly minced parsley } optional
minced olives

FOR SPICY VARIATION:
- omit bay leaf, marjoram, rosemary,
- add in their place:
   1½ tsp. cumin
   2 tsp. chili powder
   cayenne, to taste
- (optional): add 1 cup pitted,
   sliced oil-cured olives

1) Heat olive oil in a deep skillet or Dutch oven. Add garlic, onion, and
bay leaf, and sauté over medium heat for about 5 minutes.

2) Add eggplant, salt, and herbs, and stir. Cover and cook over medium
heat, stirring occasionally, for 15 to 20 minutes, or until the eggplant
is soft.

3) Add zucchini, bell peppers, black pepper, and tomatoes. (Break the
tomatoes into smaller pieces with a spoon.) Cover and simmer for
about 10 more minutes, or until the zucchini and bell peppers are
tender.

4) Serve hot, warm, or at room temperature – plain, or topped with parsley
and/or olives.

Gado Gado

Preparation time: about 1 hour
(Much of this can be made
in advance.)

Yield: approximately
6 servings

... an Indonesian extravaganza: yellow rice on a bed of spinach, topped
with an assortment of delicately cut vegetables, topped with delicious
peanut sauce, topped with exuberant condiments, garnished with
wedges of fruit. And it's all quite easy – even for beginners.
   All the ingredients can be prepared in advance, and can be served
warm or at room temperature. Have fun with this!

UNDERNEATH THE SAUCE:

NOTE: These components are all flexible. The vegetables can be cooked or raw,
   or some of each. The vegetables can be varied – what follows is just
   a suggestion. Arrange everything on a large platter or on individual
   plates.

1) a bed of fresh <u>spinach</u>
2) <u>rice</u> (2 cups raw cooked in 3 cups simmering water until tender)
      Adding ½ tsp. turmeric to the rice as it cooks will turn it a
      lovely shade of yellow.
3) <u>assorted vegetables</u>, such as:
         mung bean sprouts – uncooked or lightly steamed
         2 to 3 medium carrots, thinly sliced
         ½ small head each: red and green cabbage, very finely
            shredded
         ½ lb. fresh green beans, lightly steamed
         a small bunch of broccoli, cut into small spears and steamed
4) <u>tofu</u> – about ¾ lb., in small cubes
5) <u>hardboiled eggs</u> – chopped

THE SAUCE:

1 Tbs. peanut oil

1 cup minced onion

1 Tbs. freshly grated ginger

1½ cups good peanut butter

1½ to 2 cups hot water

2 to 3 Tbs. cider vinegar (to taste)

2 Tbs. soy sauce

1 tsp. salt (or, to taste, if peanut butter is salted)

1 Tbs. brown sugar or honey

2 to 3 Tbs. lemon juice (to taste)

1) Heat the oil in a medium-sized saucepan. Add onion and ginger, and sauté over medium-low heat for about 10 minutes, or until the onion is very soft.

2) Add remaining ingredients and whisk until smooth. Simmer over very low heat for about 15 minutes. Taste to adjust seasonings. Set aside until serving time. Serve at any temperature.

ON TOP OF THE SAUCE (this is the fun part):

• about 1 Tbs. peanut oil

• a 1-inch knob of fresh ginger, peeled and sliced into tiny thin strips with your sharpest paring knife

• 1 cup very, very finely minced onion

• 10 to 12 medium cloves garlic, minced or thinly sliced

• crushed red pepper flakes

• 1 cup shredded unsweetened coconut

• squeezable wedges of lemon or lime ⎫

• apple and/or orange slices ⎬ optional garnishes

• small wedges of fresh pineapple ⎭

1) Heat 1 tsp. of the oil in a small frying pan. Sauté the ginger over medium heat for a minute or two, then transfer to a small bowl. Repeat with the onion and the garlic, sautéing each in about 1 tsp. of oil for about 5 minutes (onion) and just a minute or two (garlic). Place each in a separate small bowl and set aside.

2) To serve, drizzle the sauce over the vegetables and rice. Arrange all of these toppings (or just toss them randomly) on top. Garnish with slices of fruit, and serve to your eager and appreciative guests.

VEGETABLE KEBABS

MARINADE: (can be doubled, if you like lots of extra for basting)

2/3 cup olive oil

1/4 cup red wine vinegar

5 medium cloves garlic, minced

1/2 tsp. salt

lots of freshly ground black pepper

1/2 tsp. marjoram or oregano

1/2 tsp. thyme

1/2 tsp. basil

a pinch or two of rosemary

1 medium (6-to 7-inch long) eggplant, cut into 1 1/2-inch cubes

about a dozen cherry tomatoes

about a dozen medium-sized mushrooms

1 or 2 bell peppers (any color), cut into 2-inch strips

1 medium onion, cut into 1 1/2-inch wedges

1 1/2 lbs. very firm tofu, cut into 1 1/2-inch cubes

OPTIONAL ADDITIONS:

1-inch slices of corn-on-the-cob, parboiled 5 minutes

1 1/2-inch chunks of potato or sweet potato, parboiled about 8 minutes
   (until just tender)

1-inch chunks of zucchini or any summer squash

1) Prepare marinade in a long, shallow baking pan.

2) Add all other ingredients and stir gently. Let marinate, stirring occasionally, for at least 2 hours, and as long as overnight. (You don't have to get up and stir in the middle of the night.)

3) Arrange the marinated tidbits on 9- or 10-inch skewers in an imaginative sequence. Grill over hot coals or broil, basting frequently with the marinade and turning every few minutes. The cooking time is not exact, so watch them carefully, and remove from the heat as soon as they seem done (tender, browned, perfect). Baste one more time, and serve hot to your delighted guests, not forgetting to mention that the skewers, if metal, might be hot. Serve with rice or pasta.

Szechwan Eggplant & Tofu

Most of the preparation for this deeply seasoned stir-fry can be done well ahead of time. In addition, put up some rice to cook about 30 to 40 minutes before beginning the stir-fry.

3 Tbs. soy sauce
¼ cup dry sherry or Chinese rice wine
1 Tbs. white or brown sugar
1 Tbs. cider vinegar
3 Tbs. cornstarch

2 Tbs. peanut oil
1 medium onion, thinly sliced
1 large eggplant, cut into strips
   (thin slices lengthwise, then
   cut across. This should make
   about 7 to 8 cups of strips.)

¾ tsp. salt
2 Tbs. minced garlic
1 Tbs. minced fresh ginger
¼ tsp. black pepper

cayenne pepper, to taste
3 cakes (about ¾ lb.) firm tofu, cut into strips
8 scallions: greens minced, whites in strips (keep separate)
1 medium bunch fresh cilantro, minced (optional)

1) Combine soy sauce, sherry, sugar, and vinegar in a liquid-measuring cup. Add enough water to make 1 cup. Place cornstarch in a small bowl, pour in the liquid, and whisk until dissolved. Set aside, keeping the whisk handy.

2) Heat a large wok over a high flame. Add oil and onion, and stir-fry for about a minute. Add eggplant and salt, and stir-fry for 8 to 10 minutes, until the eggplant is soft. Add garlic, ginger, black pepper, and cayenne. Cook a few minutes more.

3) Add tofu and scallion bottoms. Stir the bowl of liquid (step1) from the bottom, using the whisk, and add to the wok. Mix well, and stir-fry another few minutes, until the sauce is thick.

4) Remove from heat, and serve over rice, topped with minced scallion greens and fresh cilantro.

Carrot-Mushroom Loaf

30 minutes to assemble;
45 minutes to bake

Yield: 6 to 8 servings

I don't know why this is called a loaf, since it is baked in a 9 x 13-inch pan. But it's been called a loaf for so long, I hate to tamper with tradition. The original version had 4 Tbs. butter and 5 eggs. Now it's been pared down to 1 Tbs. butter and 2 eggs. Also, the amount of vegetables has been increased, keeping the yield at a good 6 to 8 servings — although it's a hard dish to stop eating, especially if it comes out of the oven when everyone is hungry.

A food processor fitted with the grating attachment makes short work of this casserole. Use it first to make the bread crumbs, then to grate both the carrots and the cheese — without cleaning it in between.

You can use store-bought bread crumbs, but homemade ones will make this dish taste exceptional. To make superb bread crumbs, the trick is to use superb bread.

NOTE: Once baked, this casserole can be frozen. It reheats beautifully.

2 cups minced onion	3 to 4 medium cloves garlic, minced
1 Tbs. butter	1½ lbs. carrots, grated (about 6 cups)
1 lb. mushrooms, chopped	2 cups superb bread crumbs
1½ tsp. salt	1 cup (packed) grated cheddar
1 tsp. basil	2 eggs, beaten
1 tsp. thyme	black pepper, to taste
1 tsp. dill	OPTIONAL TOPPINGS: extra dill, cheese, bread crumbs; a sprinkling of sesame seeds } any, some, or all (ALL = GREAT!)

1) Lightly oil a 9 x 13-inch baking pan. Preheat the oven to 350°F.

2) In a large skillet, sauté onions in butter over medium heat for about 5 minutes. Add mushrooms, salt, herbs, and garlic, and continue to sauté for about 10 more minutes.

3) In a large bowl, combine carrots, bread crumbs, cheese, eggs, and pepper. Add the sautéed mixture and mix well. Spread into the prepared pan and sprinkle with your choice of toppings. Cover the pan with foil.

4) Bake for 30 minutes covered, then uncover and bake 15 minutes more. Serve hot or warm.

DESSERTS

I've tried to include something for everyone — or at least for most people — in this collection of desserts. There is a range of cakes from Cardamom Coffee Cake and Pound Cake (both rich and buttery) to Apple Cloud Cake (no egg yolks, butter, oil, or dairy). There are Fruited Yogurt Desserts, containing simply yogurt and fruit, and Berry Sorbet, containing mostly just berries, but also a rich Banana-Cream Cheese Pie and Crunchy-Top Peach Pie. The Rice Pudding is eggless and optionally dairyless, and there is a range of cheesecakes from the very intense Montana's Mom's to the much lighter Ricotta Cake and Yogurt Pie. The old stand-bys are still here: Moosewood Fudge Brownies, Ukrainian Poppy Seed Cake, Carrot Cake, No-Fault Pumpkin Pie — plus some new ones: Poor Person's Trifle, Lemon Meringues, Danish Cherries, Bittersweet Chocolate Custard, and more. I hope you find something here to love!

TABLE OF CONTENTS: DESSERTS

Date-Nut Cake

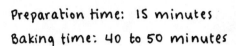

Preparation time: 15 minutes
Baking time: 40 to 50 minutes

Yield: about 6 servings

butter and flour for the pan
3 eggs, separated and
   at room temperature
1/4 cup sugar
1/2 tsp. vanilla extract

1/3 cup flour
1/4 tsp. salt
3/4 cup very finely chopped
   nuts (walnuts, almonds, or pecans)
1 cup chopped dates

TOPPING
1/2 pint heavy cream or 1 cup ricotta cheese
1/2 tsp. vanilla extract
2 to 3 Tbs. powdered sugar (or, to taste)

1) Preheat oven to 350°F. Generously butter and flour a 9-inch round pan.

2) In a medium-sized bowl, beat the egg whites with an electric mixer at high speed until stiff but not dry.

3) In a second medium-sized bowl, beat the egg yolks with sugar and vanilla for several minutes — until smooth and thick.

4) Stir the flour, salt, nuts, and dates into the yolk mixture and blend well. Gently fold in the beaten egg whites.

5) Transfer to the prepared pan and bake for 40 minutes, or until the surface of the cake springs back when touched lightly. Remove from the oven and allow to cool in the pan. Invert onto a serving plate.

6) Combine the cream or ricotta with vanilla and powdered sugar, and whip to your favorite consistency. Spread over the top of the cake, and chill. Serve cold.

Orange Cake

Preparation time: 30 minutes
Baking time: 50 to 60 minutes
-Allow time to cool and glaze.

Yield: 1 large cake,
serves 12 to 16

butter for the pan
1½ cups (3 sticks) butter, softened
1¾ cups sugar
4 eggs

1 tsp. grated orange rind
1 tsp. vanilla extract
3 cups flour
1 Tbs. baking soda

½ tsp. salt
1 cup sour cream or yogurt } whisked together
½ cup orange juice

ORANGE GLAZE:
½ cup orange juice
1 to 2 Tbs. sugar
1 Tbs. lemon juice
optional: 2 to 3 Tbs. dry sherry or orange liqueur

1) Preheat oven to 350°F. Butter a 10-inch tube or bundt pan.
2) In a large bowl, beat together the butter and sugar until light and fluffy.
3) Add the eggs, one at a time, beating well after each.
4) Stir in the orange rind and vanilla. Set aside.
5) Sift together the dry ingredients in a separate bowl. Add this to the butter mixture alternately with the combined sour cream (or yogurt) and orange juice, beginning and ending with the dry ingredients. Mix by hand after each addition — just enough to combine well.
6) Turn into the prepared pan. Bake 50 to 60 minutes, or until a knife inserted all the way down comes out clean. Cool for about 15 minutes, then invert onto a plate. Allow to cool completely.
7) Combine the glaze ingredients in a small saucepan and bring to a boil. Lower heat and simmer uncovered for about 3 minutes. Pour the hot glaze onto the cooled cake. Let stand at least 10 minutes before slicing.

Ukrainian Poppy Seed Cake

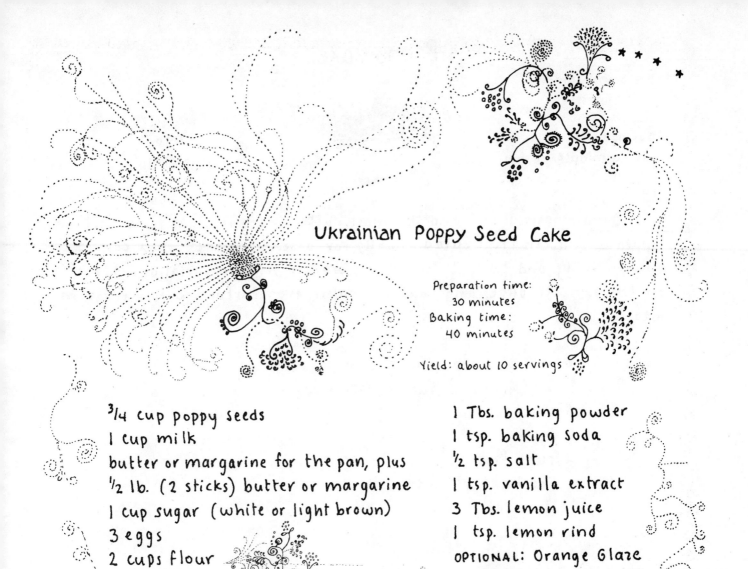

Preparation time:
30 minutes
Baking time:
40 minutes

Yield: about 10 servings

³/₄ cup poppy seeds
1 cup milk
butter or margarine for the pan, plus
½ lb. (2 sticks) butter or margarine
1 cup sugar (white or light brown)
3 eggs
2 cups flour

1 Tbs. baking powder
1 tsp. baking soda
½ tsp. salt
1 tsp. vanilla extract
3 Tbs. lemon juice
1 tsp. lemon rind
OPTIONAL: Orange Glaze
(preceding page)

1) Place poppy seeds and milk in a small saucepan. Heat just to the boiling point, but remove from heat before it actually boils. (This is called scalding.) Set aside and allow to cool for at least 15 minutes.

2) Preheat oven to 350°F. Butter a 10-inch tube or bundt pan.

3) Cream the butter and sugar in a large mixing bowl. Add eggs, one at a time, beating well after each.

4) Sift together the dry ingredients in a separate bowl. Add this to the butter mixture alternately with the poppy seed-milk, beginning and ending with the dry mixture. Stir just enough to blend thoroughly, adding the vanilla, lemon juice, and lemon rind at the end.

5) Spread the batter into the prepared pan, and bake for about 40 minutes, or until a cake tester comes out clean. Cool for 10 minutes, then invert onto a plate. Allow to cool completely before adding the Orange Glaze (same method as on preceding page) and/or slicing.

Pound Cake

The most basic cake - and the most buttery. Try it plain for dessert, or topped with fresh Fruit Salad (p. 54) for a serious snack. You can also slice it thinly and toast it for tea or brunch. A few variations appear on the opposite page, and you can explore even further with your own ideas.

butter and flour for the pans
1 lb. (4 sticks) butter, softened
3 cups sugar
6 eggs
4 cups flour
1 Tbs. baking powder
½ tsp. salt
1 cup milk
2 tsp. vanilla extract

1) Preheat oven to 350°F. Butter and flour the bottom and sides of a 10-inch tube or bundt pan.

2) In a large bowl, cream together butter and sugar with an electric mixer at high speed until light and fluffy.

3) Add eggs, one at a time, beating well after each. Set aside.

4) Sift together the dry ingredients in a separate bowl. Mix together the milk and vanilla. Add dry and wet alternately to butter mixture, beginning and ending with dry. Mix by hand — just enough to blend thoroughly without excess beating.

5) Spread the batter into the prepared pan. Bake 50 to 60 minutes, or until a sharp knife inserted all the way down comes out clean. Allow to cool for 10 minutes in the pan, then turn out onto a plate. Cool completely before slicing.

Pound Cake Variations

Here are some delightful adulterations you can perform in your own kitchen. For each of these variations, follow the pound cake recipe on the opposite page, with the following changes:

Lemon Pound Cake

1) Replace vanilla with lemon extract.

2) Add ¼ cup fresh lemon juice.

3) Add 1 tsp. freshly grated lemon rind.

Blueberry Pound Cake

~ Same changes as for Lemon Pound Cake, plus:
2 cups fresh blueberries, folded in gently with the last addition of dry ingredients

Mocha-Swirl Pound Cake

1) Replace the milk with 1 cup strong black coffee.

2) After the batter is all assembled, transfer about ⅓ of it to a small bowl, and add 1 oz. (1 square) melted unsweetened chocolate. Mix thoroughly.

3) Spread the plain batter into the prepared pan and spoon clumps of chocolate batter on top. Using a humble dinner knife, cut through to the bottom of the pan and swirl the dark and light together to create a marbled effect. Bake as directed.

Carrot Cake

butter, margarine, or oil for the pan(s)
optional: about ¼ cup poppy seeds

1½ cups (3 sticks) butter or margarine, softened
1¾ cups (packed) brown sugar
4 eggs
3 tsp. vanilla extract
1 tsp. grated lemon rind
4 cups flour
1 tsp. salt
½ tsp. baking soda
1 Tbs. baking powder
1 tsp. allspice
2 tsp. cinnamon
2½ cups (packed) finely shredded carrot } combined
¼ cup lemon juice

OPTIONAL ADDITIONS: ¾ cup raisins or currants
¾ cup chopped pecans or walnuts
½ cup shredded unsweetened coconut

1) Preheat oven to 350°F. Generously grease 2 standard-sized loaf pans or 1 oblong pan (9 x 13, or 10 x 14). Sprinkle in the poppy seeds; tilt and shake the pan(s) to distribute the seeds. They will stick nicely.
2) Beat together butter or margarine and sugar in a large bowl. Add eggs, one at a time, beating well after each. When the mixture is fluffy, stir in the vanilla and lemon rind.
3) Sift together the dry ingredients. Add this to the butter mixture alternately with the carrots, beginning and ending with the dry mixture. Mix just enough after each addition to combine—don't overmix. Stir in the optional items (or not) with the last flour addition.
4) Spread the batter evenly in the pan(s), and bake 40 to 50 minutes (loaf pans) or 35 minutes (oblong pan) — or until a probe inserted into the center comes out clean. For loaf pans: cool 10 minutes in the pan, then rap the pan sharply, and dislodge and remove the cake. Transfer to rack, and let it cool at least 1 hour before slicing.

Banana Bread

Banana Bread is basically the same recipe as Carrot Cake (opposite page), but with the following changes:

1) Replace the poppy seeds with sesame seeds.

2) Use 2½ tsp. vanilla extract and ½ tsp. almond extract.

3) Use orange rind, instead of lemon.

4) Substitute ½ tsp. nutmeg for the allspice.

5) Replace the carrot with 2 cups puréed ripe banana (3-4 bananas) soaked in 1 cup strong black coffee (can be decaf).

6) Omit the raisin/currant and coconut options.

Apricot-Almond Bread

40 minutes to prepare;
about 1½ hours to bake   Yield: 1 large loaf

Moist and tart with apricots and crunchy with almonds, this bread is ideal for brunches and teas. It's also good as a mid-evening semi-dessert, when you want <u>Something</u> — sweet, but not too — and you don't know exactly what. Try this bread at such times.

butter for the pan	1 tsp. salt
1½ cups thinly sliced	2 Tbs. softened butter
dried apricots	½ cup honey or real maple syrup
1½ cups water	1 egg, beaten
2½ cups flour	1 tsp. vanilla extract
1 tsp. baking soda	½ to 1 tsp. orange rind
2 tsp. baking powder	1 cup finely chopped almonds

1) Preheat oven to 350°F. Butter a large loaf pan.

2) Place apricots and water in a medium-sized saucepan and bring to a boil. Lower the heat, cover, and simmer for 10 minutes. Transfer to a medium-sized bowl, and allow to cool for about 15 minutes.

3) Sift together dry ingredients (except almonds) in a separate bowl.

4) Stir the butter plus honey or syrup into the cooled apricot mixture. Beat in the egg and vanilla.

5) Add the dry ingredients, orange rind, and almonds. Mix minimally but well.

6) Spread into the prepared pan, and bake about 1½ hours, or until a probe inserted all the way down comes out clean. Let cool for 10 minutes in the pan, then rap the pan firmly a few times on its sides and bottom. The bread should slip right out. Cool at least 15 minutes more before attempting to slice.

Cardamom Coffee Cake

Very rich ~ very delicious

1¾ hours to prepare and bake

16 servings

oil or butter for the pan
1 lb. (4 sticks) butter or margarine
  (or a combination), softened
2 cups (packed) light brown sugar
4 eggs
2 tsp. vanilla extract
4 cups flour
2 tsp. baking powder
2½ tsp. baking soda

½ tsp. salt
1 Tbs. powdered cardamom
2 cups sour cream, yogurt, or buttermilk

NUT MIXTURE:
¼ cup (packed) light brown sugar
1 Tbs. cinnamon
½ cup finely chopped walnuts

1) Preheat oven to 350°F. Butter or oil a 10-inch tube or bundt pan.
2) In a large mixing bowl, beat butter or margarine with sugar until light and fluffy. Add eggs, one at a time, beating well after each. Stir in the vanilla.
3) Sift together the dry ingredients (not including nut mixture ingredients) in a separate bowl.
4) Add the flour mixture, ⅓ of it at a time, to the butter mixture, alternating with the sour cream (or yogurt or buttermilk). Stir just enough to blend after each addition. Don't beat or otherwise overmix.
5) Combine the nut mixture ingredients in a separate small bowl.
6) Spoon approximately ⅓ the batter into the prepared pan. Sprinkle with half the nut mixture, then add another third of the batter. Cover with remaining nut mixture, then top with remaining batter. Lightly spread into place.
7) Bake approximately 1¼ hours or until a knife inserted all the way in comes out clean. Allow to cool in the pan for 20 minutes, then invert onto a plate. Cool at least 30 minutes more before wildly devouring.

Apple Cloud Cake

20 minutes to prepare;
30 minutes to bake

Yield: 1 9-inch
square cake

As its name suggests, this cake is very light and fluffy, thanks to the presence of 8 beaten egg whites (and the absence of egg yolks, butter, oil, or any dairy products).

A few tips:
- Separate the eggs when cold, then let the whites come to room temperature before beating them.
- You can grate the apples in a food processor with the grating attachment.
- Be generous when you oil and flour the pan. This cake has a tendency to stick.
- If you can't bring yourself to throw out all those egg yolks, save them (they do freeze well) for brushing onto unbaked bread loaves — they make a rich, shiny crust.

NOTE: You can make a larger cake by doubling the recipe and baking it in a well greased and floured tube or bundt pan. Add 10 minutes to the baking time.

oil and flour, for the pan
8 egg whites
3 cups grated peeled apple
~roughly the equivalent
of 2 large apples

2 Tbs. lemon juice
½ cup sugar
1½ tsp. cinnamon
½ tsp. vanilla extract
1½ cups sifted flour
½ tsp. salt

OPTIONAL ADDITIONS: ½ cup finely chopped nuts
1 cup minced cranberries (add 3 Tbs. sugar)
powdered sugar, for the top

1) Preheat oven to 350°F. Generously oil a 9-inch square pan and dust with flour.
2) Place the egg whites in a large bowl, and beat with an electric mixer at high speed until they form sturdy peaks.
3) In another large bowl, combine apples with all remaining ingredients (including optional nuts and cranberries) and mix well.
4) Use a rubber spatula to fold the beaten egg whites into the apple mixture until fairly well combined. Transfer to the prepared pan, and bake about 30 minutes — until a probe comes out clean. Cool before slicing. Serve plain or dusted lightly with powdered sugar.

MERINGUES

Meringues have the great ability to satisfy all longings for a rich dessert, yet they contain no butter, oil, egg yolks, or flour.

These two versions provide a contrast of textures: an ethereal crunch on the first bite, followed by full-bodied chewiness. The baking process is slow and gradual — almost more of a drying-out than an actual baking.

TO BAKE MERINGUES: Preheat oven to 250°F. Lightly grease a baking tray — OR line it with parchment or waxed paper. Bake the meringues for 2½ to 3 hours without opening the oven. Then turn off the oven, and leave them in there for at least 15 minutes. (You can also leave them in for up to an hour or two. This part is flexible!) Cool completely before removing them from the tray.

Meringues will turn out softer or firmer, depending on the humidity in your kitchen. Store them in an airtight bin lined with waxed paper.

ONE MORE THING: Separate the eggs while they're cold, then let the whites come to room temperature. See the opposite page for a few ideas for the unused yolks.

---

10 minutes to prepare
3 hours to bake

CHOCOLATE MERINGUES

Yield: 1½ dozen
(easily doubled)

1 cup powdered sugar
2 Tbs. cocoa
a pinch of salt

OPTIONAL:
¼ cup hazelnuts,
    pecans, or almonds

4 egg whites
½ tsp. vanilla
optional: ½ cup chocolate chips

1) Sift together powdered sugar, cocoa, and salt. If you're adding nuts, place them in a blender or food processor with the sugar mixture, and grind in a series of spurts until the nuts and sugar form a fine powder.
2) Beat together the egg whites and vanilla at high speed until they form stiff peaks. Fold in the sugar-nut mixture (or just the cocoa-sugar) and the chocolate chips.
3) Drop by rounded tablespoonfuls onto the prepared tray. Bake as described above.

---

15 minutes to prepare;
3 hours to bake

LEMON MERINGUES

Yield: 1 dozen
(easily doubled)

2 Tbs. cornstarch
½ cup powdered sugar

¼ cup fresh lemon juice
¼ cup water
½ tsp. grated lemon rind

3 egg whites
1 Tbs. granulated sugar

1) Place cornstarch and powdered sugar in a small saucepan.
2) Combine the lemon juice and water, and whisk this into the cornstarch-sugar. Stir in the lemon rind.
3) Heat to boiling, whisking frequently. Lower heat to a simmer; cook and whisk until very thick. (This will only take about a minute.) Cool for 15 minutes.
4) Beat the egg whites at medium speed until they get foamy. Add the granulated sugar, then beat at high speed until the egg whites form stiff peaks.
5) Add the lemon mixture, and fold until fairly well mixed. (It won't be uniform.) Drop by rounded tablespoons onto the prepared tray. Bake as described above.

STOVETOP RICE PUDDING

~ Eggless, and possibly even dairy-free!

Eggs are not going to be missed in this good rice pudding - it's as rich-tasting as one could desire. Use lowfat or even nonfat milk - or make a dairy-free version with rice milk (plain or vanilla) or soy milk. Both of these are available in most natural foods stores.

To make this recipe with leftover cooked rice: place 2 cups cooked rice in a saucepan with 1 cup milk. Heat to boiling, lower heat to a simmer, and cook, covered, for 20 to 30 minutes, or until the milk is mostly absorbed. Add remaining ingredients and mix well.

1 cup short-grain brown rice
3 to 3½ cups milk (low-or nonfat, rice, or soy)
½ to ¾ tsp. salt
3 to 5 Tbs. sugar, honey, or real maple syrup
½ tsp. vanilla extract

½ tsp. cinnamon
a dash of nutmeg
a handful of raisins ⎫
2 to 3 tsp. lemon juice ⎬ OPTIONAL
extra cinnamon or ⎭
    nutmeg

possible toppings: yogurt
chopped fresh or dried fruit
chopped nuts

1) Rinse the rice in a strainer. Drain well, and place in a saucepan with 3 cups milk. Bring to a boil, cover, and lower heat as much as possible. Simmer until the rice is very tender. This will take up to 1½ hours.

2) About 1 hour into the cooking, stir in salt, sweetening, vanilla, spices, and optional raisins. (When adding the sweetening, start with about 3 Tbs. This dish is naturally sweet, and it's easy to overdo it.)

3) Optional Step: If you want an extra-thick and creamy rice pudding, purée about 1 cup of the rice in a blender with ½ cup additional milk. Return the purée to the rest of the rice; mix well.

4) Stir in lemon juice to taste, if desired, and adjust sweetening. Optional: sprinkle a little extra cinnamon and/or nutmeg on top (go easy!) for a finishing touch. Serve at room temperature or cold, possibly topped with yogurt, fresh or dried fruit, and/or nuts.

old-fashioned
BREAD PUDDING

Humble and easy, yet very rewarding. And transcendent served warm, with ice cream!

This is one of the few instances where ordinary white bread is actually preferable to whole grain.

3 to 4 packed cups cubed bread
   (OK if stale or frozen)
3 eggs
3 cups milk (lowfat OK)
⅓ cup sugar (more or less, to taste)
½ tsp. salt
2 tsp. vanilla extract

OPTIONAL TOPPINGS: {
ice cream
Berry Sauce (p.207)
sliced fresh peaches and/or strawberries
}

1) Preheat oven to 350°F. Have ready a 9 x 13-inch baking pan.
2) Spread the bread in the pan.
3) Beat together remaining ingredients. Pour this custard over the bread.
4) Bake about 35 minutes, or until firm but not dry. Serve warm or at room temperature.

VARIATIONS

POOR PERSON'S TRIFLE

add to custard {
¼ cup rum
1½ cups crushed pineapple au jus (canned-in-juice = fine)
1½ cups berries or pitted cherries (frozen unsweetened = fine. No need to defrost.)
}
OPTIONAL: 1 cup chopped walnuts

BREAD & CHOCOLATE PUDDING

Add to the bread: 1½ cups semisweet chocolate chips

BANANA BREAD PUDDING

Add to the bread: 1 or 2 ripe bananas, sliced.
OPTIONAL: a few dashes of cinnamon and nutmeg.

○ Baked Custard ○
(Bittersweet Chocolate; Maple; Maple-Peach)

Easy super-comfort food

Yield: 6
custard cups

BITTERSWEET CHOCOLATE CUSTARD:

Preparation time:
20 minutes
(45 minutes to bake)

2½ cups milk (lowfat works just fine)

¾ to 1 cup semisweet chocolate chips (depending on how deeply chocophilic you are)

4 eggs

½ tsp. salt

1 tsp. vanilla extract

1) Preheat oven to 350°F. Have ready six ovenproof custard cups and a 9 X 13-inch baking pan.

2) Place the milk and chocolate chips in a small saucepan. Heat gently, stirring occasionally, until all the chips are melted. Remove from heat and stir until blended. Allow to cool for about 15 minutes.

3) Place remaining ingredients in a blender or food processor. Add the milk mixture, scraping in all the wayward clumps of chocolate, and whip until frothy.

4) Divide the batter among the custard cups. Place them in the baking pan, and half-fill it with water. Bake 40 to 45 minutes, or until the custards are solid in the center when shaken.

5) Carefully remove the cups from the baking pan. Cool to room temperature, then cover each one tightly with plastic wrap and chill.

MAPLE CUSTARD

Preparation time:
10 minutes

omit chocolate chips

add ⅓ cup real maple syrup

optional: a dash each of cinnamon and nutmeg

~ Skip Step 2. Blend all ingredients together in Step 3. Bake as directed.

MAPLE-PEACH CUSTARD

Preparation time:
15 minutes

1½ to 2 cups sliced fresh peaches

~ Make Maple Custard batter. Divide the peaches among the custard cups, pour the custard over the peaches, and bake as directed.

STRAWBERRY·RHUBARB CRISP

Preparation time: 15 minutes   Baking time: 35 to 40 minutes   Yield: about 6 servings

...An easy cobbler with a very crunchy top. Use the smaller amount of sugar if you like it tart. It would be a good idea to have some vanilla ice cream on hand, since you might decide that you can't bear not to have this dessert à la mode.

2 lbs. fresh rhubarb,
   cut into 1-inch chunks
3 to 4 cups sliced strawberries
⅓ to ½ cup white sugar

1 cup rolled oats
1 cup flour
2 to 3 Tbs. brown sugar
½ tsp. cinnamon
a dash or two of each: allspice
   and nutmeg
¼ tsp. salt
5 Tbs. melted butter or margarine

1) Preheat oven to 375°F.
2) Combine the rhubarb and strawberries in a 9-inch square pan. Sprinkle with white sugar.
3) Mix together the remaining ingredients in a medium-sized bowl. Distribute over the top of the fruit and pat firmly into place.
4) Bake uncovered for 35 to 40 minutes, or until the top is crisp and lightly browned and the fruit is bubbling around the edges. Serve hot, warm, or at room temperature, plain or à la mode.

variations using other fruits:
APPLE CRISP
• Use 6 to 8 cups peeled and sliced tart apples
• 2 to 3 Tbs. lemon juice
• ¼ cup white sugar
• increase cinnamon (use up to 1 tsp.)
• optional: add ½ cup finely chopped walnuts to the topping

PEACH (or APRICOT)·CHERRY CRISP
• Use about 4 cups peeled and sliced peaches or apricots, plus
   2 cups pitted, halved dark cherries (OK to use frozen unsweetened)
• Same adjustments as in Apple Crisp. In addition, you can increase the nutmeg to ¼ tsp. and use almonds instead of walnuts in the topping.

Apple

Custard

Pie

Preparation time: 25 minutes

Baking time: 45 minutes

Yield: 4 to 6 servings

2 cups peeled and thinly sliced tart apples

1 unbaked 9-inch pie crust (see p. 156)

4 eggs (ok to omit 2 of the yolks)

¼ to ⅓ cup brown sugar or honey

1 cup yogurt

1 tsp. vanilla extract

½ tsp. cinnamon

¼ tsp. salt

OPTIONAL VARIATIONS:
- Replace the sugar or honey with real maple syrup.
- Replace the apples with sliced peaches or pitted, halved dark cherries.
- Sprinkle a small handful of chopped nuts on top.

---

1) Preheat oven to 375°F.

2) Spread the apple slices evenly over the unbaked pie crust.

3) Combine all remaining ingredients in a food processor or blender and whip until frothy. Pour this custard over the apples.

4) Bake for 45 minutes, or until solid in the center. Cool for at least 1 hour before slicing. This pie tastes best at room temperature or cold.

20 minutes to prepare
(including crust);
50 minutes to bake

No-Fault Pumpkin Pie

FILLING:

3 cups cooked, puréed pumpkin or squash (or 1 29-oz.
    can of pumpkin purée)
3 Tbs. white sugar
3 Tbs. brown sugar
2 Tbs. molasses
½ tsp. cloves or allspice
1½ to 2 tsp. cinnamon
1½ to 2 tsp. powdered ginger
½ tsp. salt
2 beaten eggs
1½ cups evaporated milk (lowfat ok)

1 unbaked 9-inch pie crust (recipe on p. 156)

OPTIONAL TOPPINGS:
whipped cream with a little sugar and rum
whipped cream with a little sugar and vanilla extract
vanilla ice cream

1) Preheat oven to 375°F.
2) Place pumpkin or squash purée in a medium-sized bowl, and add
   all other filling ingredients. Beat until smooth.
3) Spread into the pie crust and bake at 375° for 10 minutes. Turn
   the oven down to 350°, and bake another 40 minutes, or until
   the pie is firm in the center when shaken lightly.
4) Cool at least to room temperature before serving. This pie tastes
   very good chilled, with rum- or vanilla-spiked whipped cream, or
   some high-quality vanilla   ice cream.

Maple - Walnut Pie

Delicious - and very easy!

Preparation time:
20 minutes

Baking time:
30 minutes

Yield:
about 6
servings

4 large eggs
3/4 cup real maple syrup
2 Tbs. lemon juice
1/4 to 1/2 tsp. cinnamon (to taste)
1 1/2 tsp. vanilla extract
1/4 tsp. salt
2 cups chopped walnuts
1 unbaked 9-inch pie crust (p.156)
OPTIONAL: whipped cream, for the top

1) Preheat oven to 375°F.

2) Beat together all ingredients, except walnuts and pie crust, until
light and frothy.

3) Spread the walnuts into the unbaked crust. Pour in the batter.

4) Bake for 30 minutes or until solid in the center. Remove from oven
and allow to cool for at least 30 minutes before serving.

5) Serve warm, at room temperature, or cold, with or without
whipped cream.

Crunchy-Top Peach Pie

Preparation time: about 40 minutes
Baking time: about another 40 minutes

Yield: 6 servings

Make this at the height of peach season, with the finest, ripest peaches available. Or, you can freeze some of those same fine, ripe peaches (peel and slice them first; spread on a tray and freeze, then transfer to a plastic bag, seal, and store in the freezer), and surprise everyone with this delightful pie in November.

If you have access to some equally fine and ripe apricots, they will work equally well.

6 cups sliced ripe peaches
1/4 to 1/3 cup sugar
3 Tbs. fresh lemon juice
3 Tbs. flour
1 tsp. cinnamon
a few dashes of nutmeg
1 unbaked 9-inch pie crust (p. 156)

TOPPING:
2 cups rolled oats
1/4 cup flour
1/2 tsp. salt
1/2 tsp. cinnamon
1/2 cup minced almonds
3 Tbs. brown sugar
5 Tbs. melted butter

POSSIBLE ACCOMPANIMENTS:
ice cream (recommended: vanilla, almond, or amaretto)
whipped cream
nothing at all

1) Preheat oven to 400°F.
2) Place peaches in a medium-sized bowl and sprinkle with sugar and lemon juice.
3) Combine 3 Tbs. flour and spices, and sprinkle this into the peaches. Mix gently but thoroughly. Spread this filling into the unbaked crust.
4) Combine topping ingredients in the same bowl (no need to wash it first), and mix well. Apply the topping evenly over the top, patting it firmly into place.
5) Bake for 10 minutes at 400°F, then turn the oven down to 375° and bake for about 30 minutes more. Serve warm or cold, with ice cream or whipped cream, or just plain.

Lowfat Berry Pie

Preparation time (after crust is made): 10 minutes, plus time to chill.

Yield: about 6 servings

The only fat is the butter in the crust. For a nonfat dessert, try the pudding variation that follows. The crust gets prebaked, and this can be done up to several days in advance. No further baking is necessary.

- 1 9-inch pie crust (see p.156)
- 6 to 8 cups fresh raspberries and/or blackberries
- 1/3 to 1/2 cup sugar
- 1 1/2 Tbs. cornstarch

1) TO PREBAKE THE CRUST: Preheat oven to 375°F. Place a piece of foil or waxed paper on the unbaked crust and add about 2 cups dried beans or grains, spreading them evenly. Bake for 15 minutes, then remove the foil and beans and bake another 10 minutes or so — until the crust is lightly browned. Remove from the oven and allow to cool completely.

2) Place about 2 cups of berries in a food processor or blender. Add 1/3 cup sugar and purée. Taste to adjust the amount of sugar. Set aside.

3) Place the remaining berries in the cooled crust, gently spreading them into place.

4) Put the cornstarch into a small saucepan, and whisk in the puréed berries. Bring to a boil, then lower heat and simmer, whisking frequently, for 5 minutes or until thickened slightly. Remove from heat and pour over the berries in the crust. Cool to room temperature (or chill) before serving.

FRESH BERRY PUDDING: Same as above, but without the crust.

OPTIONAL SIMPLIFICATION: The cornstarch and the cooking can be eliminated (i.e., you can just pour the purée over the berries). Chill in an attractive serving bowl or in individual dessert dishes.

Berry Sauce

Preparation time:
5 minutes

Yield: about ¾ cup
(easily multiplied)

Lovely, light, and easy, this sauce consists purely of berries, lightly sweetened and sieved to smoothness. Serve it as an elegant complement to many other desserts. It is incredibly good on vanilla ice cream with pieces of bittersweet chocolate on top.

This sauce can also be made with frozen unsweetened berries. Look for them in the supermarket. They usually come in sealed plastic bags.

1 cup fresh (or frozen, defrosted) berries
    (rasp-, black-, or straw-)
1 to 2 Tbs. sugar
a few drops of fresh lemon or lime juice

1) Place all ingredients in a blender or food processor, and purée.
2) Strain through a fine sieve to separate out and discard the seeds. Taste to adjust sugar and lemon juice.
3) Transfer to a container, cover tightly, and refrigerate. This sauce keeps very well for a week or longer.

Berry Sorbet or Ice

~ a wonderful nonfat dessert! Try pairing Berry Sorbet or Ice with Meringues (p.197), to make an even more wonderful, equally nonfat treat.

1) Make Berry Sauce as described above.
2) Place the sauce in an ice cream maker, and follow the instructions for your particular machine.

If you are not the proud owner of an ice cream maker (I've never owned one myself), you can make Berry Ice:

Make Berry Sauce, place it in a tightly covered container; put it in the freezer for 30 minutes. Take it out and stir, then return it to the freezer for another 30 minutes. This would be an ideal time to serve it, but if you must wait longer, keep it frozen until about 20 minutes before serving time. Let it sit at room temperature for those 20 minutes, and stir before serving.

Ricotta Cake
~Italian-style cheesecake~

15 minutes to prepare;
50 minutes to bake

Yield: about 8 servings

Simple and plain, but full of soul.
Low in fat!

butter or margarine for the pan
flour, fine crumbs, or ground nuts − for the pan
4 large eggs, separated (OK to omit yolks)
2 lbs. ricotta cheese (lowfat OK)
½ cup sugar
⅓ cup flour
1½ tsp. vanilla extract
¼ tsp. almond extract
¼ tsp. salt
½ tsp. each: orange and lemon rinds
2 Tbs. lemon juice
OPTIONAL: Berry Sauce (p.207)

1) Preheat oven to 375°F. Butter a 10-inch springform pan, then dust lightly with flour, fine crumbs, or ground almonds (made by processing − almost to a powder − with a series of short bursts in a food processor or a blender).

2) Beat the egg whites until stiff but not dry. Set aside.

3) Without cleaning the beaters, beat together ricotta, egg yolks (or not), sugar, flour, extracts, salt, rinds, and juice in a large bowl.

4) Gently fold in the beaten egg whites. Transfer to the prepared pan.

5) Bake for 50 minutes, or until solid in the center. Cool completely before serving. This tastes best cold, with room-temperature Berry Sauce.

Montana's Mom's Dynamite Cheesecake

"Loved by millions from coast to coast" — Montana

Preparation time: 15 minutes

Baking time: 25 minutes, then
   a cooling period, then
   8 minutes more

Yield: enough
for 8 to 10

Basic cheesecake: unadorned and unabashed.

Make it a day ahead, so it will have plenty of time to set.

NOTE: Use a food processor or blender to make the graham cracker crumbs.

CRUST:

2 cups graham cracker crumbs

½ stick butter or margarine, melted

~Combine, and press firmly into the bottom of a 10-inch springform pan.

FILLING:

16 oz. (2 packages) cream cheese, softened

⅓ cup sugar

4 eggs

1½ tsp. vanilla extract

3 Tbs. lemon juice

½ tsp. lemon rind

1) Preheat oven to 375°F.

2) Beat all filling ingredients together until smooth.

3) Pour onto crust and bake for 25 minutes, or until set. Remove from oven and cool to room temperature. You will need the oven again, so you can either leave it on, or reheat it.

TOPPING: No- PER MARTH

1½ cups sour cream

3 Tbs. sugar

½ tsp. vanilla extract

1) Reheat oven to 375°F.

2) Blend topping ingredients well, and pour on top of cooled cake.

3) Bake for 8 minutes. Remove from oven and cool to room temperature, then cover tightly (still in the pan) and chill at least 12 hours.

YOGURT PIE

The earlier version of this pie, called Yogurt-Cream Cheese Pie, had aspirations of being a purely yogurt pie, but needed a large proportion of cream cheese to hold it together. I have since discovered how to thicken nonfat yogurt, not by adding anything, but by slowly squeezing out much of the water. The result is a luxuriously rich-textured yogurt cheese, which can hold this pie together all by its nonfat self.

This is how you do it:

1) Place 6 layers of cheesecloth about 16 inches long in a large (12-inch diameter) colander. (If you haven't one that large, you can use 2 smaller colanders, and cut slightly shorter pieces of cheesecloth.) Place the colander(s) over a bowl or in the sink.

2) Add 2½ quarts nonfat yogurt, and wrap the cheesecloth around it tightly, securing the cloth with a clip or a bagtie.

3) Place a 3- or 4-lb. bag of beans on top, and let it sit there for 6 to 8 hours. The yogurt will solidify as its water content slowly drips out the bottom. When you unwrap it, you will find about 5 cups of thick, creamy yogurt cheese.

> 1 9-inch graham cracker crust (see opposite page)
> approximately 5 cups yogurt cheese (see above)
> 5 Tbs. sugar (or more, to taste)
> 1¼ tsp. vanilla extract
> OPTIONAL TOPPINGS:
> fresh fruit (berries, pitted cherries, sliced peaches)
> Berry Pudding (p. 206)
> Berry Sauce (p. 207)

1) Make the crust as directed. Bake and cool.

2) Place the yogurt cheese in a medium-sized bowl with the sugar and vanilla, and beat lightly with a whisk until completely blended.

3) Turn into the prepared crust. Optional: top with leftover crust mixture. Cover tightly and chill. Serve plain or with a topping.

Banana-Cream Cheese Pie

About 40 minutes
to prepare- plus
time to chill

Yield: 1
rich
9-inch pie

CRUST:

2½ cups crushed graham crackers (easily done in a food processor)
½ cup (1 stick) butter or margarine, melted
OPTIONAL: a dash of cinnamon
OPTIONAL: •2 Tbs. sesame seeds
          •replace up to ½ cup of the graham crackers with ground
           almonds

1) Preheat oven to 375°F.
2) Combine all ingredients and mix well. Press firmly into the bottom
and sides of a 9-inch pie pan, building up a handsome ½-inch ridge
around the edge. You will have more than enough to fill the pie pan;
spread the rest loosely in another pan. Place both in the oven and bake
for 10 minutes. Remove and cool.

FILLING:

12 oz. (1½ packages) cream cheese, softened (lowfat ok)
3 to 4 Tbs. sugar (to taste)
¼ cup yogurt
2 large bananas (perfectly—not overly-ripe)— one mashed, one
   thinly sliced
2 Tbs. fresh lemon or lime juice
¼ tsp. almond extract
1 tsp. vanilla extract

1) Place everything except the sliced banana in a food processor and
purée until smooth. (Or, place everything in a bowl, and whip it
up at high speed with an electric mixer.)
2) Fold in the sliced banana. Spread into the cooled crust, top with
the toasted extra crumbs, wrap tightly, and chill 24 hours.

Ginger-Brandy Cheesecake

Preparation time: 20 minutes

Baking time: 40 minutes

Yield: 8 to 10 servings

I. CRUST: 2 cups ginger snap crumbs (make them in a food processor or a blender. Or the old-fashioned way, with a rolling pin)

5 Tbs. melted butter

Mix together well. Press firmly into the bottom of a 10-inch springform pan.

II. FILLING: 12 oz. (1½ packages) cream cheese, softened (lowfat OK)

1½ cups sour cream or yogurt (or a combination)

4 eggs (some or all yolks can be omitted)

¼ cup honey or sugar (or, to taste)

¼ cup brandy

2 Tbs. finely grated fresh ginger

a dash of salt

Wild Ginger

1) Preheat oven to 350°F.

2) Whip everything together until very smooth. Taste to adjust sweetening.

3) Pour onto the crust in the springform pan. Bake for 40 minutes, or until the center is firm to the touch and the edges are slightly brown. Cool completely before removing the rim of the pan and glazing.

III. GLAZE: 2 Tbs. cornstarch

¾ cup orange juice

2 Tbs. honey or sugar

1 Tbs. brandy

½ tsp. orange rind

optional: candied ginger, cut into thin strips

1) Place cornstarch in a small saucepan. Whisk in the orange juice.

2) Cook over medium heat, whisking constantly, until smooth and glossy (about 5 minutes).

3) Remove from heat, and whisk in the remaining ingredients, except the candied ginger. Pour the hot glaze onto the cooled cheesecake, spreading it evenly. If desired, decorate in an expansive pattern with strips of candied ginger. Chill thoroughly before serving.

... Moosewood Fudge Brownies ...

On a brownie-intensity scale of 1 to 10, these are about an 11; in other words, not for the faint-hearted. You should probably have some good vanilla or coffee ice cream on hand, or you'll find yourself running out to the store to get some as soon as you take a bite, and this will rudely interrupt your dessert hour.

butter for the pan
5 oz. (5 squares) unsweetened chocolate
½ lb. (2 sticks) butter or margarine, softened
1¾ cups (packed) light brown sugar (white sugar also OK)
5 eggs
1½ tsp. vanilla extract
1 cup flour (use ¾ cup for fudgier brownies)
MANY OPTIONAL EMBELLISHMENTS:
1 cup chopped walnuts or pecans
1 tsp. freshly grated orange rind
½ tsp. cinnamon
a small ripe banana, mashed
2 to 4 Tbs. strong black coffee
1 cup semisweet chocolate chips
OR anything else you might think of
OR, for purists, none of the above

1) Butter a 9 X 13-inch baking pan. Preheat oven to 350°F.
2) Gently melt the chocolate. Let it cool for about 10 minutes.
3) Cream the butter and sugar in a medium-sized bowl until light and fluffy.
4) Add the eggs, one at a time, beating well after each. Stir in the vanilla.
5) Stir constantly as you drizzle in the melted chocolate. After all the chocolate is in, beat well for a minute or two.
6) Stir in flour and possible embellishments. Mix just enough to blend thoroughly.
7) Spread the batter into the prepared pan. Bake 20 to 25 minutes, or until a knife inserted into the center comes out clean. Cut into squares while still hot, then allow to cool for at least 10 minutes, if you can wait that long.

Iced Carob Brownies

If you think of carob as itself and not as a chocolate substitute, you'll appreciate these lovely brownies even more than you would anyway.

butter or margarine for the pan
½ cup (1 stick) melted butter or margarine
¼ cup carob powder
2 eggs
½ cup (packed) light brown sugar
1 tsp. vanilla extract
¼ cup water
1 cup flour
1 tsp. baking powder
¼ tsp. salt
½ cup raisins or currants
½ cup finely chopped walnuts
optional: a dash or two of cinnamon and/or allspice

1) Preheat oven to 350°F. Butter an 8-inch square pan.

2) Beat together butter, carob, eggs, sugar, and vanilla in a medium-sized bowl. Stir in the water.

3) Sift together flour, baking powder, and salt. Stir this into the first mixture along with raisins, nuts, and optional spices. Mix just enough to blend thoroughly.

4) Spread into the prepared pan, and bake 20 to 25 minutes, or until a probe comes out clean. Cool completely before icing.

. . . .

ICING: ¼ cup carob powder
          8 oz. (1 package) cream cheese, softened
          ¼ cup powdered sugar
          ½ tsp. vanilla

Beat everything together until very smooth. Spread on top of the cooled brownies.

LEMON MOUSSE

Ethereal, yet it packs a tangy punch. Serve Lemon Mousse by itself or topped with Berry Sauce (p. 207). It also goes beautifully served in tandem with many different cakes, especially Ukrainian Poppy Seed Cake (p. 189).

Lemon Mousse will keep well for several days if tightly covered and refrigerated.

1/4 cup cornstarch
1/2 cup sugar
1/2 cup freshly squeezed lemon juice
1/2 cup water
1 tsp. grated lemon rind
2 egg whites, at room temperature
1/2 pint heavy cream
OPTIONAL VARIATIONS:
1 cup berries or sliced peaches
orange rind, instead of lemon

1) Place cornstarch and sugar in a small saucepan. Add lemon juice and water and whisk until smooth.

2) Cook, whisking constantly, over medium heat until thick (5 to 8 minutes). Remove from heat, transfer to a medium-sized bowl, and stir in the lemon rind. Let cool to room temperature.

3) Place the egg whites in a medium-sized mixing bowl and beat at high speed with an electric mixer until stiff but not dry. Fold this into the lemon mixture, cover tightly, and chill at least 1 hour (longer = also ok).

4) Without cleaning the beaters, whip the cream until it is firm but still fluffy. Fold this into the mousse (add optional berries or peaches at this point), cover tightly again, and chill until serving time.

♪ DANISH CHERRIES ♪

Make this delicious, beautiful, and very simple stovetop dessert well in advance OR right before serving. You can get fine results from frozen cherries (they come pitted and unsweetened in sealed plastic bags), if fresh are unavailable. No need to defrost before using.

NOTES: ♪ To blanch almonds, place them in a colander over a sink. Pour boiling water over them, and rub off the skins. Cut vertically with a sharp knife to sliver them.

♪ To whip ricotta, beat it vigorously with a whisk, or at high speed with an electric mixer.

4 cups pitted cherries
1½ Tbs. cornstarch
3 to 4 Tbs. sugar
¼ cup lemon juice
½ tsp. grated lemon rind
¾ tsp. almond extract
OPTIONAL: ½ cup blanched, slivered almonds
TOPPINGS: whipped cream
    or
  whipped ricotta cheese
    or
  plain yogurt
} with a few blanched, slivered almonds folded in

1) Place cherries in a heavy medium-sized saucepan, and cook over medium heat, covered, for 10 minutes.

2) Meanwhile, combine cornstarch and sugar in a small bowl. Add lemon juice and whisk until smooth. Stir this into the hot cherries, and cook over medium heat, stirring frequently, until thick (5 to 8 minutes).

3) Remove from heat and stir in lemon rind, almond extract, and slivered almonds. Serve hot, warm, room temperature, or cold, topped with whipped cream, whipped ricotta, or yogurt.

Fruited Yogurt Desserts

Almost any combination of fruit and yogurt will taste delicious - and make a filling lowfat dessert. Here are a few suggestions. Combine as close to serving time as possible.

I.

3 cups plain yogurt
1 cup fresh blueberries
1 cup seedless grapes
1 cup pitted, halved cherries
sugar, maple syrup, or honey
~to taste

Combine and chill.

II.

3 cups plain yogurt
1 cup fresh strawberries, halved
1 to 2 medium-sized ripe
    peaches, sliced
1 perfectly ripe banana, sliced
sugar, honey, or maple syrup
~to taste

Combine and chill.

III.

3 cups plain yogurt
1 to 2 medium-sized apples,
    grated
1/2 cup lightly toasted minced
    almonds
a dash of cinnamon
sugar, maple syrup, or honey
~to taste

Combine and chill.

🍎 APPLE STRUDEL 🍎

This is a delicious and straightforward strudel, minimally sweetened, and made without butter. You can add some cheddar cheese to the apples, or make it plain and dairy-free. It's very good both ways.

Apple Strudel can be made several days in advance, and stored unbaked, tightly wrapped in the refrigerator. Baked strudel keeps very well in the refrigerator or freezer, provided it is thoroughly wrapped. Defrost completely, and reheat in a 350°F. oven for 20 minutes before serving.

To make fine bread crumbs, let 2 or 3 slices of white or whole wheat bread dry out for a few hours. Then toast them lightly, and grind to a fine meal in a blender or food processor.

NOTE: See p. 162 for detailed information about filo pastry.

oil for the baking tray
8 medium (3-inch diameter) tart apples, peeled and chopped
4 to 5 Tbs. sugar
1 tsp. cinnamon
2 Tbs. lemon juice
½ tsp. grated lemon rind
½ cup finely minced walnuts

¼ cup (packed) raisins (optional)
½ cup fine bread crumbs
1 cup (packed) grated mild cheddar (optional)
18 sheets of filo pastry (most or all of a 1-lb. package)
about 6 Tbs. vegetable oil

1) Preheat oven to 375°F. Generously oil a baking tray.
2) Combine all ingredients except filo and oil in a medium-large bowl. Toss gently.
3) To assemble: Place 1 sheet of filo on a dry surface, and brush lightly with oil. Place another sheet on top, and brush with oil. Continue until you have a pile of 6. Distribute ⅓ the filling here, fold over the sides→, and roll up this way.
4) Brush the top of the roll with a little more oil, then transfer to the prepared tray. Repeat with remaining ingredients to make 2 more rolls.
5) Bake about 35 minutes, or until lightly browned and exquisitely crisp. Serve warm. (Reheat, if necessary: 20 minutes, uncovered, at 325°F.)

✿ Afterword: Reflections, Hopes, and a Reading List ✿

It is an honor to have the opportunity to revise a work that has been in circulation for fifteen years. During this time, I have been thinking about more than just recipes, trying to understand the broader history we are living through. When I first began work on the Moosewood Cookbook, the Vietnam War was still raging, and Roe v. Wade had just been passed. The epidemics of AIDS and homelessness, as well as the concept of global warming, still years in the future, were unimagined. The first edition of the Moosewood Cookbook was born into a very different world, and in just fifteen years, life has become much more complex. During those seemingly more innocent times, many of us had a vague feeling that personal choices, such as the decision to live simply, to "tread lightly on the earth" — which usually included cutting meat out of one's diet — could make a positive difference in the world. And although that type of thinking might seem simplistic or grandiose, it has turned out to be true that what's healthy for us really is healthy for the environment. I have come to understand that when we make conscious decisions in favor of personal health and enrichment, this can help us make sense of the rest of our lives, which, in turn, can actually lead us to become more effective in the larger world.

In previous editions of the Moosewood Cookbook, as well as in my two subsequent books, I didn't venture into discussions of dietary ethics. I simply presented collections of recipes to give people options, without preaching or recommending one style of living over another. Continuing in that spirit, I am offering a list of reading materials that deal with the relationship between food choices and the environment. My first hope is that the recipes in this book will promote confidence in cooking and pleasure in eating. Beyond that, I hope that people who use and enjoy these recipes will be inspired to think about where the food comes from, and perhaps to investigate the possibility that ordinary people working together can move the world toward ecologically sound methods of food production. My greatest hope is that future generations will live in a world where health of all kinds and for all beings is not only possible, but a right and not a privilege.

✿ READING LIST ✿

Diet for a Small Planet - 20th Anniversary Edition, by Frances Moore Lappé (Ballantine, 1991). This is the latest edition of the extraordinary book that inspired millions to see the connection between personal choices and broader responsibility. Using well-documented data on agriculture and economics,

Frances Moore Lappé bravely analyzes world hunger on a deep political level, leading us to reconsider the very meaning of democracy. Essential reading, now more than ever! For an update on Frances Moore Lappé's current work, write to her C/o The Institute for the Arts of Democracy, 36 Eucalyptus Lane, Suite 100, San Rafael, CA 94901.

Food First: Beyond the Myth of Scarcity, by Frances Moore Lappé and Joseph Collins (Ballantine, 1977, 1978) and World Hunger: Twelve Myths (same authors- A Food First Book / Grove Press, 1986). Each of these books provides a thorough look at the root causes of world hunger, outlining the shifts in power that are necessary to bring about change. The latter book includes a resource guide, reference books, and suggestions for action.

Other materials from Food First Books include school curriculums, guides to graduate studies, a directory of options for voluntary service, plus a long list of reference books. Send for a catalogue: Food First Books, 145 Ninth St., San Francisco, CA 94103. Phone: (800) 888-3314. Fax: (415) 864-3909.

Rainforest in Your Kitchen, by Martin Teitel (Island Press, 1992)—written by an environmental activist. Simple strategies for wielding consumer power.

"Taking Stock" (Worldwatch Paper #103, July 1991) and "Fat of the Land" (Worldwatch Magazine, June 1991). To order, send $5.00 per article or back issue plus $3.00 mailing to Worldwatch Institute, 1776 Massachusetts Ave. NW, Washington, D.C. 20036. Phone: (202) 452-1999.

Diet for a New America, by John Robbins (Stillpoint Press, 1987)—an emotionally moving book, which has influenced many people to become vegetarians.

"Eating as if the Earth Mattered: How Food Choices Affect the Environment" (E Magazine, January/February 1992) To order a copy, send $3.95 to E/ The Environmental Magazine, 28 Knight St., Norwalk, CT 06851. To subscribe, send $20.00 for 6 issues (1 year).

50 Simple Things You Can Do to Save the Earth (EarthWorks Press)- the best-selling environmental how-to book. For a catalogue of other EarthWorks publications, write to EarthWorks Press, 1400 Shattuck Ave. #25, Berkeley, CA 94709. Phone: (510)652-8533.

APPENDIX

Lowfat Soups

(less than 2 tablespoons oil or butter per 5 or more servings)

Brazilian Black Bean, 26
Cream of Asparagus, 3
Cream of Spinach, 30
Curried Squash and Mushroom, 15
Gingered Carrot, 22
Herbed Carrot (also has nonfat option), 23
Light Cream of Celery, 6
Mushroom-Barley, 28
Mushroom Bisque, 19
Potato-Fennel, 29
Russian Cabbage Borscht, 27
Succotash Chowder, 11
Vegetable Chowder, 12

Nonfat Soups:

Cascadilla, 34
Chilled Beet Borscht, 35
Chilled Berry, 36
Chilled Cucumber-Yogurt, 32
Chinese Vegetable Chowder, 13
Hot & Sour, 8
Lentil, 25
Miso, 9
Split Pea, 17
Summer Vegetable, 10

Oil-Free Salads and Dressings

Balkan Cucumber Salad, 69
Carrot-Yogurt Salad, 72
Lowfat Creamy Garlic, 43
Lowfat Creamy Roquefort, 43
Lowfat Ranch, 43
March Hare, 49
Nonfat Gazpacho Dressing, 43
Odessa Beets, 68
Pickled Red Onions, 60
Very Green Dressing, 41
White Rabbit, 48

Oil-Free Sauces and Dips

Apple Chutney, 98
Beet Purée, 86
Carrot Purée, 87
Chinese Duck Sauce, 97
Faux Aioli, 91
Greek Lemon Sauce, 91
Guacamole (no added oil), 108
Horseradish Sauce, 91
Mango Salsa, 96
Mondo Bizarro, 84-85
Orange-Ginger Sauce, 90
Pasta Mediterranée, 81
Pesto Impersonation, 87
Pineapple Salsa, 96
Plain Fake Mayo, 91
Raita, 99
Red Pepper Purée, 86
Sauce Puttanesca, 81
Spinach Purée, 87
Tomato Chutney, 98
Yogurt Cheese, 102
Zingy Bean Dip, 106

Entrées without Eggs

Arabian Squash Casserole, 140
Broccoli-Mushroom-Noodle Casserole
  (eggs optional), 127
Broccoli Strudel, 162
Bulgarian Pepper Casserole, 138
Calzone, 160
Cauliflower Marranca, 129
Chilean Squash, 140
Eggplant Curry, 172
Eggplant Parmesan, 133
Eggplant-Almond Enchiladas, 167
Gado Gado (eggs optional), 180
Greek Pilaf, 148
Lasagne, 132
Lentil-Walnut Burgers, 147
Macaroni and Cheese Lite, 126
Mushroom Curry, 174

Mushroom Moussaka (eggless!), 130
Mushroom Strudel, 163
Polenta, 178
Polenta Pie, 165
Ratatouille, 179
Refritos (Refried Beans), 168
Samosas, 170
Satyamma's Famous Cauliflower Curry, 173
Savory Filo Pastries, 162-63
Scheherazade Casserole, 141
Solyanka, 136
Spanakopita, 164
Spinach Rice Casserole (eggs optional), 135
Stuffed Artichokes, 149
Stuffed Cabbage, 155
Stuffed Eggplant, 151
Stuffed Grape Leaves, 149
Stuffed Squash, 152-53
Szechwan Eggplant & Tofu, 183
Tart and Tangy Baked Beans, 134
Tomato Curry, 175
Tostadas, 168
Vegetable Kebabs, 182
Vegetable Stew, 177
Vegetarian Chili, 176
Zuccanoes (Stuffed Zucchini), 154

Desserts without Oil or Butter:

Apple Cloud Cake, 196
Baked Custards, 200
Berry Pudding/Sauce/Sorbet, 207
Bread Pudding and variations, 199
Danish Cherries, 216
Date-Nut Cake, 187
Fruited Yogurt Desserts, 217
Meringues, 197
Poor Person's Trifle, 199
Rice Pudding, 198
Ricotta Cake, 208

Desserts without Eggs (or with egg whites only):

Apple Cloud Cake, 196
Apple Strudel, 218
Banana-Cream Cheese Pie, 211
Berry Pie/Pudding/Sauce/Sorbet, 206-7
Crunchy-Top Peach Pie, 205
Danish Cherries, 216
Fruited Yogurt Desserts, 217
Lemon Mousse, 215
Meringues, 197
Rice Pudding, 198
Ricotta Cake, 208
Yogurt Pie, 210

INDEX

ALFALFA SPROUTS: in salads 49, 52; as salad garnish 53
ALMOND; ALMONDS:
Apricot-Almond Bread 193
Eggplant-Almond Enchiladas 167

butter 117; in desserts 187, 194, 197, 201, 205, 216, 217; in entrées 152, 154, 174; in graham cracker crust 211; in salads 59, 72
ANCHOVIES, 81
ANTIPASTO (*see also* Mezza):
Bell Peppers 65, 119
Cauliflower and Carrots 66
Gingery Marinated Chick Peas 64
Marinated Mushrooms 67, 119
Marinated Small Artichokes 65
Roasted Green Beans 67
Swiss Chard 66, 119

defined 64; in sandwiches 119
APPLE; APPLES:
Chutney 98
Cloud Cake 196
Cottage Cheese and Apple Pancakes 145
Crisp 201
-Custard Pie 202
Strudel 218
Yogurt Dessert 217

in entrées 134, 152, 155, 174; as garnish 93, 181; in salads 48, 54, 72; in sauces 97, 98; in Waldorf salads 58–59
APPLESAUCE, as topping 146
APRICOT; APRICOTS:
-Almond Bread 193
-Cherry Crisp 201

in desserts 194; in entrées 153
ARTICHOKE; ARTICHOKES:
Marinated Small 65
Stuffed 149
canned, discussion xii; in pasta sauces 75; in salad 63

ARUGULA: in salad 70; in sauce 78
ASPARAGUS:
Cream Soup 3
-Mushroom Sauce 77
Rarebit 93
AVOCADO; AVOCADOS:
Guacamole 108, 117

in salad dressings 41, 58; in sandwiches 117

Baked goods. *See* Breads
BANANA; BANANAS:
Bread 193
Bread Pudding 199
-Cream Cheese Pie 211

in desserts 213, 217; in salads 55
BARLEY:
Mushroom-Barley Soup 28
BASIL:
in antipasto 65, 66; in entrées 133, 138, 141, 151, 154, 156, 157, 159, 161, 164, 165, 166, 176, 179, 184; in marinade 182; in pasta sauce 76, 80, 83, 84; in salad 45, 50, 60, 63; in salad dressings 41, 42, 43, 57; in soups 5, 7, 11, 12, 14, 23, 24, 25, 31, 33; as soup garnish 4, 10, 12
BAY LEAF: in entrées 179; in sauces 83; in soups 17
BEANS (*see also* Chick Peas, Lentils, and Soybeans):
Baked 134
Just White Beans Salad 60
Minestrone Soup 7
Multi-Bean Salad 61
Refried 168, 169
Tart and Tangy Baked Beans 134
White Bean and Black Olive Soup 24
Zingy Bean Dip 106
BLACK:
Brazilian Black Bean Soup 26
in salad 61

Kebabs, Vegetable 182
Kiwis, 55

Leeks, in salad 40
Legumes, discussed xii
Lemon:
 Meringues 197
 Mousse 215
 Pound Cake 191

 in dessert 189, 192; as topping 181
Lentil; Lentils:
 -Bulgur Salad 47
 Soup 25
 -Walnut Burgers 147
Lettuce:
 in entrées 169; in salads 39, 50; in soup stock 1;
  in vichyssoise 33
Lima beans:
 Succotash Chowder 11
Lime, as topping 181
Lowfat cooking xvi 10, 17
Lowfat salad dressings 43

Mango; Mangos:
 Salsa 96

 in salads 55, 58
Maple syrup
 Custard 200
 -Peach Custard 200
 -Walnut Pie 204

 in desserts 194, 198, 202, 217; discussed xiii; as entrée
  topping 145; in salad dressing 42
Margarine, discussed xii
Marinade 182
Marjoram:
 in entrées 179; in marinade 182; in salads 45, 63, 65,
  157, 166; in soups 12, 23, 24

Mayonnaise:
 Green 44
 Homemade 44
 Plain Fake 90; in dips and spreads 101, 102; in salads
  52, 53
 Sesame 44
 Tofu 44; in salad 72; in salad dressings 42, 43, 57,
  58, 59
Melons, in salad 55
Meringues 197
Milk (see also Rice milk; Soy milk):
 in breads 111; in desserts 189, 190, 198, 199,
  200; in dips and spreads 101; discussed xii,
  xv, xvi, 1; in entrées 133, 135, 156, 157, 159; in
  sauce 92; in soups 3, 6, 11, 12, 14, 16, 18, 19, 21,
  30, 33
Milk, evaporated 203
Millet 129
Mint:
 in entrées 144, 148; in salads 46, 47, 50, 69; in sauce
  96; in soup 22; as soup garnish 23, 32
Miso 9
Molasses: in desserts 203; in entrée 134, 177
Mousse:
 Lemon Mousse 215
Mushroom; Mushrooms:
 Asparagus-Mushroom Sauce 77
 -Barley Soup 28
 Bisque 19
 Broccoli Mushroom Noodle Casserole 127
 Cauliflower Marranca 129
 Carrot-Mushroom Loaf 184
 Curried Squash and Mushroom Soup 15
 Curry 174
 Hungarian Mushroom Soup 18
 Marinated 67
 Moussaka 130
 Stellar Sauce 77–78
 Strudel 163
 Swiss Cheese and Mushroom Quiche 157
 Tofu Salad 56
 in dips and spreads 104; in entrées 126, 147, 151, 153,
  154, 158, 165, 177, 182; as entrée topping 166; in
  salads 40, 63; in sauces 80, 83; in soups 8, 12, 13,
  33, 34; stir-fried 89
 Chanterelles 79
 chinese black:
  in sauces 79; in soups 8, 13
 Oyster 79
Mustard:
 Chinese 120

 in salad dressings 42, 44, 57
Mustard, dry:
 in entrées 137, 157; in salads 71; in salad dressing 44;
  in sauces 91, 93, 97; in soups 17, 20, 21
Mustard Greens 40

TOMATO; TOMATOES:
  Cavolfiore Sauce 80
  Chutney 98
  Curry 175
  Grilled Eggplant with Fau Aioli and Tomatoes
  Gypsy Soup 5
  Italian Sauce 80
  Marinara Sauce 80
  Mexican Red Sauce 95
  Minestrone 7
  Nachos 94
  Pesto 84
  Raita 99
  Salsa 96
  Sauce Puttanesca 81
  Spicy Tomato Soup 4

  in dips and spreads 106; discussed, canned xii; in
    entrées 83, 134, 138, 141, 176, 179; in salads 39, 46,
    47, 49, 50; in soups 4, 25, 26; in soup stock 1
  CANNED: in entrée 130, 141, 179; in soups 4,7
  CHERRY:
  in entrées 182; as salad garnish 52, 57, 61, 63; in
    sauces 82
  FRESH:
  in dips and spreads 106; in entrées 134, 138, 151, 157,
    165, 169, 174, 175, 176; as entrée topping 166; as
    garnish 53, 93; in salads 45, 46, 47, 49, 50, 56;
    in sandwiches 121; in soups 4, 5, 7, 17, 25, 26
  JUICE:
  in entrées 176; in salad dressings 43; in soups 31, 33,
    34
  PASTE:
  in entrées 130, 141, 176, 177; in sauces 80, 81; in
    soups 24
  PURÉE: in entrées 175; in soups 27
  SAUCE, in entrées 132
  SUN-DRIED 82
Tools cooking xiv-xv
Toppings (garnishes) for soup 4
TORTILLAS:
  Eggplant-Almond Enchiladas 167
  Flour 115

  in tostadas 168
TOSTADAS 169
  defined 168

VEGETABLE PURÉES
  Beet 86
  Carrot 87

Pesto Impersonation 87
  Red Pepper 86
  Spinach 87
VEGETABLES (*see also* indivdual names):
  Chinese Chowder 13
  Chowder 12
  Kebabs 182
  Marinated 63, 182
  Salad 41
  soup stock 1
  Stew 177

  as salad garnish 57
Vegetarian Chili 176
Vichyssoise 33
VINAIGRETTE:
    as a marinade 63; as salad dressing 42
VINEGARS:
  BALSAMIC,
    in antipasto 66, 67
  CIDER:
  in dips and spreads 107; in entrées 134, 147, 181, 183;
    in salad 50, 52, 53, 60, 72; in salad dressings 44,
    56; in sauces 88, 96, 97, 98, 170; in soups 8, 27; in
    vegetable purée 86
  RASPBERRY,
    in salad dressing 70, 71
  WINE:
  in antipasto 64, 65; in marinade 182; in salad 40,
    45, 60, 61, 62, 63; in salad dressing 42, 51, 70; in
    sandwich dressing 180; in soup 17, 31; as soup
    garnish 25

WALDORF SALADS 58–59
WALNUTS:
  Lentil-Walnut Burgers 147
  Maple Walnut Pie 204
  patés 101, 117

  in desserts 187, 192, 195, 199, 204, 213, 214, 218;
    in dips and spreads 101; in entrées 140, 153; as
    garnish 93; in salads 47, 58, 68, 69; in sandwiches
    118; in sauces 78
WATER CHESTNUTS:
    discussed, canned xii; in salads 51; in soups 13
WATERCRESS: as soup garnish 34; in vichyssoise 33
WATERMELON, in salad 55
WINE:
  CHINESE RICE:
    in entrée 183; in soup 8

RED DRY:
    in soup 24; in stew 177
WHITE DRY:
    in dips and spreads 101; in entrée 134; in sauce 77, 78; in soup 20

YEASTED BREADS: *See* Breads, yeasted
YOGURT:
    Carrot Salad 72
    Chilled Berry Soup 34
    Cucumber Soup 32
    Fruited Desserts 217
    Pie 210
    Paita 99

    in bread 114; in desserts 188, 195, 198, 202, 211, 212; as dessert topping 216; in dips and spreads

104; in entrées 126, 136, 137, 140, 163, 174; as entrée topping 144, 145, 146, 152, 158, 177; in pastry 170; in salads 52, 57, 58, 59, 69; in salad dressings 42, 57, 58, 59; in sandwiches 122; in soups 33, 34, 36; as soup garnish 4, 15, 27, 35
YOGURT CHEESE: *See* Cheese, Yogurt

ZUCCHINI:
    Crusted Pizza 166
    -Feta Pancakes 144
    Stuffed 154
    Zuccanoes 154

    in entrées 144, 154, 165, 166, 177, 179, 182; in salads 41, 63; in salad dressing 41; in sauce 80; in soups 7, 10, 24, 33

"A highly-regarded trilogy of cookbooks that . . . give the feeling of visiting in the kitchen with a warm, witty, well-informed friend."

—THE NEW YORK TIMES

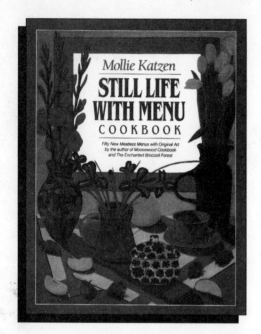

In *Still Life with Menu Cookbook*, Mollie Katzen's third volume of vegetarian cookery, fifty still life pastel illustrations are matched with delicious complete menus. With this work wholesome, satifying meals become more feasible for those whose busy lives admit less time for cooking:

"The purpose of this book is to help reintroduce good eating into our increasingly complex schedules; to provide encouragement and ideas as well as recipes and menus; to make interesting, genuine, and inexpensive food as accesible and convenient as possible."

The recipes for each meal, from appetizers to desserts, are gathered together with useful indications of time for total preparation and tips for making much of the menu ahead of time. An introduction breaks down preparation into tasks that can be done one, two, and three days ahead.

8-1/2 x 11 inches   352 pages   Fully illustrated in color
$24.95 *paper*   ISBN 0-89815-236-4
$34.95 *cloth*   ISBN 0-89815-256-9

The Enchanted Broccoli Forest is the second collection of vegetarian recipes by Mollie Katzen—a wide-ranging sampling of soups (both hot and chilled), salads, breads, main dishes, "light meals for nibblers," dips, and desserts. Cooks will find a spectrum of ethnic cooking styles, as well as a range of complexity from quick and simple to elegant and exotic. Handlettered and illustrated throughout with witty and delightful drawings.

8-1/2 x 11 inches   320 pages   Handlettered/illustrated
$16.95 paper   ISBN 0-89815-078-7
$19.95 cloth   ISBN 0-89815-079-5

Available from your local bookstore, or order direct from the publisher.
Please include $1.25 shipping & handling for the first book, and 50 cents for each additional book.
California residents include local tax.
Write for our free complete catalog of over 400 books and tapes.

TEN SPEED PRESS   P O Box 7123   Berkeley, California 94707